Essex County Virginia

LAND RECORDS

1761–1772

Mary Marshall Brewer

HERITAGE BOOKS
2019

HERITAGE BOOKS

AN IMPRINT OF HERITAGE BOOKS, INC.

Books, CDs, and more—Worldwide

For our listing of thousands of titles see our website
at
www.HeritageBooks.com

Published 2019 by
HERITAGE BOOKS, INC.
Publishing Division
5810 Ruatan Street
Berwyn Heights, Md. 20740

International Standard Book Number
Paperbound: 978-1-68034-925-2

CONTENTS

INTRODUCTION

This book contains abstracts from the deed books, Numbers, 29 and 30, recorded in the period, 1761 to 1772. Our intention was to derive information useful to family historians. The records include not only deeds in the format of leases and releases, but also bonds, mortgages, quit claims, deeds of gift, bills of sale (of slaves), depositions, and assignments of power of attorney. In many of these instruments will be found clues to familial and marital relationships.

At the end of each paragraph is a citation to the original record.

Earlier works

Between 1938 and 1949 Beverley Fleet created 34 volumes of *Virginia Colonial Abstracts* covering the earliest vital records of birth, marriage and death; tax lists; court orders; militia lists; wills; and deeds. In volume 29 (1947) he published data from the first half of Essex County Deeds and Wills No. 12, 1704-1707. He also published abstracts from the first thirty-six pages of Essex County Deeds and Wills No. 15, 1716-1718, in *Virginia Colonial Abstracts*, volume 9 (1940).

To fill the gaps in Fleet's works John Frederick Dorman has abstracted and published abstracts of in a single volume, Deeds and Wills No. 12 at the point Mr. Fleet terminated his work, and abstracts of all records in Deeds and Wills No. 15 (1716-1718). In three additional volumes he covered (1) Deeds and Wills, No. 13 (17017-1711; (2) Deeds, etc. No. 16 (1718-1721), Wills, Inventories and Settlements of Estates, No. 3 (1717-1722); and (3) Wills, Bonds, Inventories, etc. (1722-1730).

F. Edward Wright
2006

ABBREVIATIONS

£ - pounds sterling
a. - acres
ackn - acknowledged
adj - adjoining
adminr - administrator or
administratrix
afsd - aforesaid
attest - attested
atty - attorney
Bk - Book (liber)
br - branch
co - county
cr - creek
c.t.a. – cum testamento
annexo
dau(s) - daughter(s)
d.b.n. – de bonis non
decd - deceased
dep - deputy
e - east

esqr - esquire
ft - feet
gent - gentlemen
Junr - junior
mi - miles
n - north
pg - page
Prob - probated
pt/o - part of
purch - purchased
rd - road
s - south
sd – said
Senr - senior
tr - tract
twp - township
uxor - wife
w - west
w/o - wife of
wit - witness

ESSEX COUNTY, VIRGINIA LAND RECORDS
1761-1772

DEED BOOK VOLUME 29
1761-1765

A poll of the freeholders at an election of burgesses in Essex Co taken by me
Thomas Bowler for William Covington gent sherif of the sd co this 6 May 1761.
(Pgs 1-7)

    Candidate Francis Waring: John Colquit, William Bastin, Thomas
Johnson, James Atkinson, Daniel Stodghill, David Pitts Senr, James Martin,
Rhodes Greenwood, James Daniel, Foster Samuel, James Colquit, Thomas
Sullivan, Nicholas Atkinson, John Edmondson, John Conduit, Charles Tayler,
Joshua Bougton, Henry Woolbanks, William Fretwell, John Garnett, William
Gordon, William Cox, John Harper, Nicholas Faulconer, John Haynes, Reuben
Meador, Samuel Henshaw, Peter Samuel, Ambrose Wright, William
Greenwood, William Webb, John Vass, Abner Cox, Thomas Gaimes, John
Rodden, John Rowzee, Leonard Hill, Richard Hill, Richard Hill Junr, James
Emerson, Benjamin Carighland, Robert James, Rice Noel, John Dunn, Samuel
Smith, John Sadler, John Hill, Heretage Howerton, Richard Covington, Simon
Golding, John Bidlecomb, Thomas Newbell, John Davis, Thomas Howerton,
John Jones, John Ball, James Webb, John Rennold, Benjamin Jones, Richd
Jones, John Crow, Ezekiel Byrom, James Jones, William Gray.

    Candidate John Upshaw: William Boulware, Caleb Lindsey, Owen
Carter, Barthw Clark, James Clark, Peter Dishman, John Clark, James Boulware
Junr, William Clark, James Clark Junr, Marmeduke Thorp, Richard Holt, Mark
Boulware, Richard Johnson, William Boulware Junr, Daniel Stodghill, John
Satterwhite, Martin Willard, Peter Treble, Griffin Johnson, Mark Samuel,
Richard Hodges, Nicholas Smith, Stephen Neal, James Johnson, John Mitchel,
Thomas Tinsley, Foster Samuel, William Mitchell, Nicholas Atkinson, John
Edmondson, John Andrews, Robert Sale, John Garnett Junr, John Fogg, Henry
Wollbanks, George Wright, Josiah Mintor, James Cauthorn, Vincent Cauthorn,
Alexr Sanders, John Blatt, William Montague, John Broocks, Henry Cauthorn,
William Howerton, Samuel Coats, James Noel, Isaac Hans, Bernartt Gaines,
Edward Vawter, Angus Vawter, Benjamin Boulware, Jacob Sharewood,
Nicholas Faulconer, Thomas Henry Broocks, John Gatewood, Samuel Croxton,
Thomas Clark, Charles Mortimer, Richard Hipkins, James Davis Senr, John
Tayler, Edmund Ball, Benjamin Dunn, Abner Ball, Thomas Pamplin, Phillip
Kidd, John Brizendine, Andrew Allen, Henry Kidd, Thomas Dix, John Dix,
John Harper Junr, John Latanee, Thomas Newman, William Dobson, Francis

Graves, Robert Rennolds, Daniel Sullivan, William Watkins, John Sullivan, Leonard Hill, Richard Hill, Richard Hill Junr, Richard Thos Haile, Thomas Croxton, James Emerson, Benjamin Caughland, James Sullivan, Phillip Gatewood, Rice Noel, John Dunn, Samuel Smith, John Sadler, John Castle, John Hill, William Watkins, Harraway Owen, John Williamson, John Davis, Smith Young, Henry Crutcher, John Richards, William Upshaw, John Lee, James Rennolds, Ischar Degraffenreidt, James Webb, Henry Vass, William Roane, Thomas Boulware, William Porter, Greensbey Evans, Threesevilus Minor, James Medley Junr, Edward Davis, John Rennolds, William Young, Benjamin Jones, Richard Jones, John Crow, John Mitchell, Merewether Smith, James Webb Junr, Francis Smith, Samuel Hipkins, Archibald Ritchie, Ambrose Hoard.

Candidate John Lee: William Boulware, Caleb Lindsey, Owen Carter, Bartholw Clark, James Clark, John Colquit, William Bastain, Peter Dishman, Thomas Johnson, John Clark, James Boulware Junr, William Clark, James Clark Junr, Marmeduke Thorp, Richard Holt, Mark Boulware, James Atkinson, Richard Johnson, William Boulware Junr, John Satterwhite, David Pitts Senr, Martin Willard, Peter Treble, Griffin Johnson, James Martin, Mark Samuel, Richard Hodges, Nicholas Smith, Stephen Neal, James Johnson, Rhodes Greenwood, John Mitchell, Thomas Tinsley, James Daniel, William Mitchel, James Colquit, Richard Hipkins, William Hawkins, James Davis Senr, John Tayler, Phillip Kidd, John Brizendine, Andrew Allen, Thomas Dix, John Dix, John Harper Junr, John Latanee, William Bates, Francis Graves, Daniel Sullivan, John Sullivan, Richard Thomas Haile, Thomas Croxton, James Sullivan, Phillip Gatewood, Robert James, John Castle, Richard Covington, Simon Golding, John Biddlecomb, William Watkins, Harraway Owen, John Williamson, Thomas Newbell, Smith Young, Thomas Howerton, Henry Crutcher, John Jones, John Richards, William Upshaw, John Lee, John Rose, James Rennolds, Ischar Degraffenreidt, William Booth, James Webb, Henry Vass, William Roane, Thomas Boulware, William Parter, Greensby Evans, James Webb, Threesivelus Minor, James Medley Junr, Edward Davis, William Young, John Mitchell, Merewether Smith, James Webb Junr, Francis Smith, Samuel Hipkins, Ezekel Bryam, Archibald Ritchie, James Jones, Ambrose Howard, William Gray.

William Booth votes for Charles Mortimer. Alexander Cruden voted for Col Francis Smith. William Loury votes for Col Frans Smith & William Roane. James Campbell votes for Col Francis Smith. John Fauntleroy votes for Col William Daingerfield. Richard Brown, John Ball & John Rose vote for Col Smith.

William Covington gent sherif of Essex Co this day made oath before me James Webb justice of the peace of same co that this is a true copy of the original poll

of the election of burgesses for the sd co on 6th day this instant. Certified 19
May 1761. Truly recorded & exd by John Lee Junr clerk. (Pg 7)

15 Jun 1761. Deed. Henry Brown & Elizabeth his wife of South Farnham
Parish, Essex Co for 65 pd sold to Henry Brown Junr all their estate right & title
to a 75 a. parcel of land bounded by Caty Gatewood, Middle Br & Horse Path or
Road ... . Wit: John Brown, Mordecai Brown, John Pendleton, John Mitchell
Junr. Ackn 15 Jun 1761 by Henry Brown & Elizabeth his wife she being first
privily examined & recorded. Attest: John Lee Junr clerk. (Pg 8)

28 Mar 1761. Deed. Thomas Davis taylor of Notoway Parish, Amelia Co, VA
for 15 pd sold to Francis Graves of South Farnham Parish, Essex Co carpenter a
100 a. parcel of land in St. Anns Parish which John Davis father of the sd
Thomas Davis formerly purch of George Coleman by deeds of lease & release
bounded by John Garnett ... . Wit: Leonard Hill, Jas Evans, Richd Hill Junr,
Martha (Marthy) Beazee. Proved 15 Jun 1761 & recorded. Attest: John Lee
Junr clerk. (Pg 10)

10 Jun 1761. Deed. Richard Johnson of South Farnham Parish, Essex Co
planter & Sarah his wife for 6 pd sold to Francis Brizendine of same place
planter all their estate right & title to a 75 a. tr of land now in the possession of
the sd Francis Brizendine (by virtue of a sale to him made by Thomas Cooper
son of Thomas Cooper late of Essex Co decd & the afsd Sarah widow & relict of
the sd Thomas Cooper) ... . Wit: Nichos Smith, Isaac Brisendine, John
Fouracres. Ackn 15 Jun 1761 by Richard Johnson & Sarah his wife she being
first privily examined & recorded. Attest: John Lee Junr clerk. (Pg 11)

16 Oct 1760. Deed of Lease. Robert Coleman & Sarah his wife of St. Marks
Parish, Culpeper Co & Thomas Coleman & Mille his wife of Drisdel Parish,
King & Queen Co for 5 sl leased to Richard Hill Junr of South Farnham Parish,
Essex Co a 207 a. tr of land in South Farnham Parish whereon Thomas Coleman
late of Essex Co decd lived bounded by William Rennolds, Richard Hill Senr,
John Rennolds, Daniel Sullivan & Gilsons Swamp ... for the term of 1 year
paying the rent of one ear of Indian corn upon the last day of the sd term if
demanded ... . Wit: W. Watkins, James Sullivan, Leonard Hill, Jno Smether,
John Casell, Richd Hill. Proved 15 Jun 1761 & recorded. Attest: John Lee Junr
clerk. (Pg 12)

17 Oct 1760. Deed of Release. Robert Coleman & Sarah his wife of St. Marks
Parish, Culpeper Co & Thomas Coleman & Mille his wife of Drisdel Parish,
King & Queen Co for 172 pd 10 sl released unto Richard Hill Junr of South
Farnham Parish, Essex Co a 207 a. tr of land ... [same as above] ... . Wit: W.
Watkins, James Sullivan, Leonard Hill, Jno Smether, John Casell, Richd Hill.

Proved 15 Jun 1761 & recorded. Attest: John Lee Junr clerk. (Pg 13)

1 Nov 1760. To William Williams & Daniel Brown gent of Culpeper Co greeting, whereas Robert Coleman & Sarah his wife, Thomas Coleman & Mille his wife by their deeds of lease & release [*see above*] have conveyed to Richd Hill Junr a 207 a. tr of land, & whereas the sd Sarah is unable to travel to our co court of Essex to make acknowledgment thereof, therefore we command you to go to the sd Sarah & that you privily & apart from the sd Robert her husband take such acknowledgment as the sd Sarah shall make ... . Wit John Lee clerk. 11 Nov 1760 By virtue of the above commission to us directed we Danl Brown & William Williams have privily examined Sarah w/o the sd Robert Coleman & she declares that she acknowledges the same freely & that she is willings that the sd deeds be recorded. At a court held 15 Jun 1761 this commission & return thereunder written was admitted to record. Attest: John Lee Junr clerk. (Pg 17)

1 Nov 1760. To Robt Brooking, John Pendleton & John Richards gent of King & Queen Co, whereas Robert Coleman & Sarah his wife & Thomas Coleman & Mille his wife by their deeds of lease & release [*see above*] have conveyed to Richard Hill Junr a 207 a. tr of land, & whereas the sd Mille is unable to travel to our co court of Essex to make acknowledgment thereof, therefore we command you to go to the sd Mille & that you privily & apart from the sd Thomas her husband take such acknowledgment as the sd Mille shall make ... . Wit John Lee clerk. By virtue of the above commission to us directed we Robert Brooking & John Richards have privily examined Mille w/o the sd Thomas Coleman & she declares that she acknowledges the same freely & that she is willing that the sd deeds may be recorded ... . At a court held 15 Jun 1761 this commission & return thereunder written was ordered to be recorded. Attest: John Lee Junr clerk. (Pg 17)

11 Mar 1761. Deed. Francis Smith of South Farnham Parish, Essex Co gent for 7 pd 3 sl sold to Vincent Cauthorn of same place planter a 5 ½ a. parcel of land in the sd parish being pt/o 30 a. granted to the sd Francis Smith by pattent dated 26 Jun 1755 bounded by sd Smith's line, Smith Young, James Jones & Thomas Cauthorn ... . Wit: Meriwether Smith, Godfrey Young, Henry Johnson, Francis Smith Junr. Ackn 15 Jun 1761 & recorded. Attest: John Lee Junr clerk. (Pg 18)

15 Jun 1761. Deed. Smith Young & Elizabeth his wife of South Farnham Parish, Essex Co for 5 pd sold to Vincent Cauthorn of same place a 4 a. parcel of land in the sd parish bounded by the afsd Smith Young, James Jones & Col Frs Smith, being pt/o a tr of land of Henry Young (gent) decd which fell to the afsd Smith Young by heirship ... . Wit: John Richards, Henry Kidd. Ackn 15 Jun 1761 & recorded. Attest: John Lee Junr clerk. (Pg 20)

25 Nov 1760. Deed. Richard Coleman of Spotsylvania Co carpenter & Ann his wife for 200 pd sold to Robert Spilsby Coleman of the Town of Tappa four lotts or ½ acres of land in the Town of Tappahannock on the s side of Rappahannock River numbered 39 &41 which four lotts the sd Robert Spilsby Coledman did take up & purch of William Beverly & William Daingerfield gent feoffees of the sd town by deed dated 16 Jun 1747 … . Wit: Vivion Brooking, William Connell, John Johns, Andrew Crawford, Elizabeth Coleman, Robinson Daingerfield. Ackn 15 Jun 1761 & recorded. Attest: John Lee Junr clerk.(Pg 22)

18 Jun 1761. Deed. Henry Purkins Taylor & Sarah his wife of South Farnham Parish, Essex Co for 20 pd sold to Mary Broocke same place a 50 a. tr of land in the sd parish upon the brs of Webbs Mill Swamp bounded by Constant Edmondson, Thomas Edmondson decd, Benjamin Smith & Francis Jones … . Wit: Saml Piles, Vincent Piles, Luke Covington. Wit to receipt: James Webb Junr, Vincent Piles. Ackn 15 Jun 1761 by Henry Purkins Taylor & Sarah his wife (she being first privily examined) & recorded. Attest: John Lee Junr clerk. (Pg 23)

15 Jun 1761. Bond. Henry Purkins Taylor & Jeremh Moody of Essex Co are firmly bound unto Mary Broocke of sd co for 100 pd … the condition of this obligation is such that if the afsd Henry Purkins Taylor shall well & truly perform & keep all & singular the agreements, articles & bargains mentioned & included in an indenture of sale [see above] & defend & maintain the title of & in the land mentioned in the sd indenture then this obligation to be void … . Wit: James Webb Junr, John Burnett, Vincent Piles. Ackn 15 Jun 1761 & recorded. Attest: John Lee Junr clerk. (Pg 25)

15 Jun 1761. Deed. William Degge Junr & Jane (Jean) his wife of King & Queen Co for 37 pd sold to Arthur Tate of Essex Co a 100 a. tr of land bounded by William Dunn, Benjamin Smith, Archibald McCall & the afsd Arthur Tate being the land the sd William Degge purch of James Boughan who purch the same of Jonathan Dunn & the sd Jonathan Dunn purch the same of William Tyler … . Wit: W. Gatewood, Catherine Corrie, Tamzen Gatewood. Ackn 15 Jun 1761 & recorded. Attest: John Lee Junr clerk. (Pg 26)

14 Feb 1761. Deed. John Fauntleroy (Fantleroy) & Elizabeth his wife of Essex Co gent for 120 pd sold to John Rennolds of same co planter a 200 a. tr of land in South Farnham Parish being the land the sd Fauntleroy purch of John Merritt by deeds of lease & release dated 19 & 20 May 1746 & also one other 30 a. tr of land in the sd parish bounded by the afsd 200 a. of land & the land of Robert Brooking which he sold to Robert Gresham … . Wit: W. Rennolds, Wm

Johnson, Leonard Sale, Richd Hill. Ackn 15 Jun 1761 by John Fauntleroy & recorded. Attest: John Lee Junr clerk. (Pg 27)

20 Feb 1759. Bill of Sale. Benjamin Atkins of Luningburg Co have sold unto my brother in law James Hearndon all my right & title to two Negroes formerly belonging to my father William Herndon named Jack & Milley & all the remaining pt/o my father in laws estate due to me which right I do warrant from any person whatsoever laying of any claim right or title thereto. Wit: Joseph Ryland, Joseph Dillon. Proved 20 Jul 1761 & recorded. Attest: John Lee Junr clerk. (Pg 29)

XVIII Jul 1761. Deed. Thos Henry Brooke & Mary his wife & Jonathan Radford & Rebecca his wife of South Farnham Parish, Essex Co for 57 pd sold to John Clements gent of same place an 85 ¾ a. parcel of land in the sd parish being the land whereon the sd Thos Henry Brooke & the sd Jonathan Radford now live bounded by Henry Purkins, Jacob Sheerwood, Capt Thos Roane & the line of Boughan's ... . Wit: Thomas Holt, John Broocke, Sarah Holt. Ackn 20 Jul 1761 by the parties & recorded. Attest: John Lee Junr clerk. (Pg 30)

2 Apr 1761. Deed of Lease. Richard Pemberton of Dinwiddie Co, VA for 16 pd sold & leased to William Ayres of Essex Co a 50 a. parcel of land that Richard Booker formerly gave unto John Pemberton (father of the sd Richard Pemberton) by deed of gift dated 19 Feb 1722 bounded by Scot's line now in possession of Thomas Ayres's widow, Gum Swamp, Ambrose Hord, Thomas Coghill & Edward Murrah ... during the term of 1 year paying the rent of one ear of Indian corn at the feast of Saint Michael the Arch Angel if demanded ... . Wit: James Bowie, James Gouge, Frans Thorp, Bernard Gaines. Proved 17 Aug 1761 & recorded. Attest: John Lee Junr clerk. (Pg 32)

- Apr 1761. Deed of Release. Richard Pemberton of Dinwiddie Co, VA for 16 pd released unto William Ayres of Essex Co a 50 a. tr of land ... [same as above] ... . Wit: James Bowie, Frans Thorp, James Gouge, Bernard Gaines. Proved 17 Aug 1761 & recorded. Attest: John Lee Junr clerk. (Pg 34)

2 Apr 1761. Bond. Richard Pemberton of Dinwiddie Co, VA am firmly bound unto William Ayres of Essex Co for 16 pd ... the condition of this obligation is such that whereas the afsd Richard Pemberton hath sold & conveyed unto the sd William Ayres 50 a. of land [see above] & whereas Amy Pemberton w/o the sd Richard Pemberton was not present at the sealing & delivery of the sd deeds & lives so remote that her relinquishment of her right of dower can't be conveniently taken, now if the sd Richard Pemberton's heirs, executors & adminrs shall keep harmless & indemnify the sd William Ayres his heirs or assigns from the claim of dower the sd Amy Pemberton may chance to have in

& unto the afsd conveyed land then this obligation to be void ... . Wit: James Bowie, Frans Thorp, James Gouge, Bernard Gaines. Proved 17 Aug 1761, 19 Oct 1761 & 16 Nov 1761 & recorded. Attest: John Lee Junr clerk. (Pg 36)

29 Jul 1760. Deed. William Motley planter & Elizabeth his wife of Saint Anns Parish, Essex Co for 50 pd sold to William Thomas Junr planter of same place all their right & title after my mother Elizabeth Thomas' death that part & parcel of land which Wm Motley Senr purch of Henry Berry it being pt/o a pattern granted to William Harper in 1662 it being the last purch in the sd pattern containing 78 a. on the s side of Occupatia Cr bounded by William Thomas Senr ... . Wit: Wm Thomas, Alexander Newman, John Motley. Ackn 17 Aug 1761 by William Motley & Elizabeth his wife (she being first privily examined) & recorded. Attest: John Lee Junr clerk. (Pg 37)

On the request of Thomas Newman surveyed & divided a 154 a. tr of land agreeable to the plan [drawing not included here] 28 Aug 1760 per Edward Vawter. Names in the drawing: Land of Brookes, Newman, Fogg & Waring. (Pg 41)

--- 1761. Articles of Agreement. Whereas the partition made on the lands between Robert Brooke gent & Elias Newman now decd on 29 & 30 Jun 1749 according to an order of Essex Co Court there having since been found out a mistake in the survey & division of the sd lands which made an error to each party mentioned in the sd order, now we the sd Robert Brooke & Thomas Newman son & heir unto the afsd Elias Newman decd being willing to do justice to each other do hereby mutually agree for each of ourselves & each our heirs &c to stand to abide & forever hereafter confirm the measure & division of the sd lands between us as follows, bounded by land of the sd Brooke & Newman, Foggs land & Waring's land, allotting 102 2/3 a. to the sd Brooke on the e side & 51 1/3 a. of land to the afsd Newman on the w side of the afsd division line ... . Wit: None. Ackn by Robert Brooke gent & Thomas Newman 17 Aug 1761 & recorded. Attest: John Lee Junr clerk. (Pg 41)

25 Mar 1761. Deed of Lease. John Boughan & Cary his wife of South Farnham Parish, Essex Co for 40 pd to be paid to them by one payment on 1 Jan 1763 & also the further payment of 20 barrells of Indian corn to be paid annually out of the mill farm let unto James Edmondson of same place a water grist mill together with all the ponds & dams belonging with all the benefit of toll & custom for grinding corn during the further term of 21 years the expiration of the time of the former lease that now is unexpired ... whereas the sd John Boughan by an instrument of writing under his hand & seal dated 5 Jan 1746 did devise unto Ben Johnson for & during the term of 21 years one water grist mill in the sd parrish called Boughans Mill, convey'd by the sd Ben Johnson unto Philip

Edward Jones & by the sd Jones convey'd to Thomas Edmondson gent late of sd
co decd father to the afsd James Edmondson & by the will of the sd Thomas
Edmondson gent decd vested in the sd James Edmondson during the term of
years yet to come & unexpired in the afsd lease ... if the sd John Boughan &
Cary his wife shall faile for their parts to perform all or any pt/o the within
premises which ought to be performed & done that then he or they shall forfeit
& pay to the sd James Edmondson the full sum of 200 pd & also if the sd James
Edmondson shall faile to perform all that is on his part to be pay'd perform'd
fulfilled & done that then the sd James Edmondson shall forfeit & pay to the sd
John Boughan the like sum of 200 pd ... . Wit: Thomas Barker, Hugh Wilson,
Josiah Minter, John Boughan. Proved 21 Sep 1761 on the pt/o John Boughan &
the sd Cary (being first privily examined) ackn the sd indenture which is
admitted to record. Attest: John Lee Junr clerk. (Pg 43)

21 Sep 1761. Deed of Lease. William Kidd & Mary his wife of King & Queen
Co, VA for 5 sl leased & sold to Thomas Faver (son of Theophilus Faver decd)
of Essex Co a 40 ½ a. tr of land ... whereas the afsd Mary Kidd hath equal right
with her sister Sarah Charles to ½ of 162 a. of land in Saint Anns Parish, being
the land & plantation that John Cooke decd the great grandfather of the sd Mary
Kidd lived on & the sd William Kidd for 52 pd 13 sl hath agreed to sell &
convey unto the afsd Theophilus Faver all their right unto the afsd tr of land as
by a bond given by the sd William Kidd unto the sd Theophilus Faver which was
proved 20 Sep 1757, & the sd Theophilus Faver in his will did give & bequeath
all the afsd land unto his sd son Thomas Faver & his heirs forever the sd
William Kidd with Mary his wife is now free & willing to comply with his bond
& fulfill the afsd will ... during the term of 1 year paying the rent of one ear of
Indian corn at the feast of Saint Michael the Arch Angel if demanded ... . Wit:
Waters Dunn, John Bransom, John Thomas. Ackn 21 Sep 1761 by William
Kidd & Mary his wife (she being first privily examined) & admitted to record.
Attest: John Lee Junr clerk. (Pg 45)

21 Sep 1761. Deed of Release. William Kidd & Mary his wife of King &
Queen Co, VA for 52 pd 13 sl released unto Thomas Faver (son of Theophilus
Faver decd) of Essex Co ½ of a 162 a. tr of land ... [same as above] ... . Wit:
Waters Dunn, John Bransom, John Thomas. Ackn 21 Sep 1761 by William
Kidd & Mary his wife (she being first privily examined) & admitted to record.
Attest: John Lee Junr clerk. (Pg 47)

22 Sep 1761. Power of Attorney. John Chamberlain of Essex Co have
appointed my trusty friend Joseph McWilliams of same co gent my atty to ask,
demand, recover & receive of John Edmondson, Andrew Craffard & Richard
Coleman the two last execrs of the estate of the late decd Robert Sp. Coleman &
all other persons that shall concern me or my intrust in the sd co ... . Wit: John

McWilliams, William Connell, Phillip Gatewood. Ackn 22 Sep 1761 & recorded. Attest: John Lee Junr clerk. (Pg 49)

19 Sep 1761. Deed. James Emerson (Emmerson) & Anne his wife for 35 pd sold to Archibald McCall merchant a lot or ½ a. of land No. 2 in the Town of Tappahannock which sd lot formerly belong'd to Patrick Barcley & the same by Edmond Pendleton esqr by virtue of powers recited in a deed from the sd Pendleton to the sd James Emerson was conveyed to the sd James Emerson in fee simple ... . Wit: Al Rose, Chs Mortimer, Elener Armstrong. Ackn 22 Sep 1761 by James Emerson & Ann his wife (she being first privily examined) & admitted to record. Attest: John Lee Junr clerk. (Pg 50)

22 Sep 1761. Deed. Robert Beverley of South Farnham Parish, Essex Co esqr son & heir of the Honorable William Beverley late of sd co esqr decd for 15 pd sold to Archibald McCall of South Farnham Parish, Essex Co a lott or ½ a. of land in the Town of Tappahannock by a plott of the sd town drawn by Robert Beverley gent numbered 1... . Wit: None. Ackn 22 Sep 1761 & recorded. Attest: John Lee Junr clerk. (Pg 52)

12 May 1761. Deed. Edwd Donoho & Betty his wife now of Essex Co for 85 pd sold to Thomas Gouldman of same co a 100 a. tr of land whereon the sd Edward Donoho now lives in St. Ann Parish binding on the land of Daniell Noel, Robert Parker late the land of Benja Landrum & Mark Boulware ... . Wit: Francis Gouldman, Henry Sears, Stephen Johnston. Proved 21 Sep 1761 & 19 Oct 1761 & recorded. Attest: John Lee Junr clerk. (Pg 53)

15 Aug 1761. Deed. William Williamson of Middlesex Co, John Williamson Junr & Alice his wife & John Williamson the younger of Essex Co for 10 pd sold to John O'Neal of Essex Co all their estate right to 50 a. of land being two (sic) parts in 150 a. which William Brizendine decd father of Ann Williamson the late w/o the sd William Williamson & Alice w/o John Williamson Junr afsd died possessed of (which remains undivided) ... . Wit: John Williamson, John Mann, John O'Neal. Proved 19 Oct 1761 on the pt/o William Williamson & John Williamson Junr & ackn by the sd Alice (she being first privily examined & assenting) which are admitted to record. Attest: John Lee Junr clerk. (Pg 54)

31 Oct 1761. Deed. Nathan Breedlove of South Farnham Parish, Essex Co for 5 pd sold to Alliman Breedlove of same place a 25 a. parcel of land in the sd parish bounded by Mary Treble's land formerly John Page's, Trebles Spring Br & sd Nathan Breedlove's other land ... . [Signed] Nathan Breedlove & Mary Breedlove. Wit: Robt Mann, Fras Jones, Peter Trible, John Daly. Ackn 16 Nov 1761 by Nathan Breedlove & recorded. Attest: John Lee Junr clerk. (Pg 56)

14 Nov 1761. Deed of Gift. Samuel Noel & Martha his wife of Essex Co for love, good will & most tender effection have given unto my son in law Samuel Henshaw of same co 38 a. of land being pt/o 138 a. the afsd Samuel Noell had of his father Daniel Noel decd & is bounded by Thomas Andrews & Popoman Swamp ... . Wit: Wm Boulware, William Bates, Thomas Boulware. Proved 16 Nov 1761 & recorded. Attest: John Lee Junr clerk. (Pg 58)

15 Oct 1761. Deed. William Picket of Fauquier Co, VA for 89 pd sold to James Kay of Essex Co a 267 a. tr of land being pt/o 500 a. of land which was sold & conveyed by & from John Amiss & Sarah his wife unto Henry Picket by deed dated 10 Jan 1698, the sd 267 a. of land now lying & being in Essex Co & a smaller part thereof in Caroline Co is bounded by a br of Coikelshell Cr, a patent for land formerly granted to William White now Dishman's line, Capt Robert Rennolds, Thacker's line, Portobacco Swamp & Carter's line ... . Wit: Robt Rennolds, Edward Vawter, Joseph Patterson, Wm Gibson, John Carter Junr. Proved 19 Oct 1761 & recorded. Attest: John Lee Junr clerk. (Pg 60)

21 Dec 1761. Bond. William Covington, Roger Shackleford & William Howerton of Essex Co are firmly bound unto our Sovereign Lord King for 1,000 pd ... the condition of this obligation is such that if the afsd William Covington sherif of Essex Co shall well & truly collect from the inhabitants of the sd co for the year 1762 the taxes imposed on the sd inhabitants by several Acts of Assembly & pay the same according to the directions of the sd several acts, then this obligation to be void ... . Wit: Luke Covington, Thos Jessey. Proved 21 Dec 1761 & recorded. Attest: John Lee Junr clerk. (Pg 63)

21 Dec 1761. Bond. William Covington, Roger Shackleford & William Howerton of Essex Co are firmly bound unto Francis Waring, John Rowzee, William Mountague & Samuel Peachey gent justices of Essex Co for 100,000 lbs of tobacco ... whereas the afsd William Covington is appointed collector of the country & county levy for this present year, now the condition of this obligation is such that if the sd William Covington shall well & truly collect the sd levy & pay to the several claimants their respective claims, then this obligation to be void ... . Wit: Luke Covington, Thos Jessey. Proved 21 Dec 1761 & recorded. Attest: John Lee Junr clerk. (Pg 63)

10 Dec 1761. Commission. Thomas Nelson esqr sendeth greeting, whereas application hath been made to me by John Lee clerk of Essex Co to appoint William Young dep clerk under him in the sd office during his absence or indisposition, know ye therefore that I the sd Thomas Nelson by virtue of the powers & authorities to me granted by the Honourable William Adair esqr secretary of VA do by these presents constitute & appoint the sd William Young dep clerk of the sd court giving & hereby granting unto him full power &

authority to perform & execute the sd office during the absence or indisposition of the sd John Lee ... . At a court held 21 Dec 1761 William Young in the above commission named took the usual oaths & on the motion of John Lee Junr clerk of this court the sd commission is admitted to record. Attest: John Lee Junr clerk. (Pg 64)

21 Oct 1761. Deed. Richard Jeffries of Essex Co planter for 20 sl sold to Henry Cauthorn of same co planter a ½ a. parcel of land adj the lands of sd Jeffries & Cauthorn & bounded by Cool Spring Br & Green Br, it being pt/o the land or swamp which the sd Jeffries purch of John Cauthorn ... . Memorandum: The afsd Henry Cauthorn doth hereby oblidge himself & every other person whatsoever that shall or may hereafter claim under him or any of them that there never shall at any time hereafter be a grist mill erected on the ½ a. of land conveyed by the within indenture to the sd Henry Cauthorn by the sd Richard Jeffries under the penalty of 100 pd to be paid to the sd Jeffries or to those that may hereafter claim under him. Wit: W. Young, Richard Cauthorn, Thomas Dean. Ackn 15 Feb 1762 & recorded. Attest: John Lee Junr clerk. (Pg 65)

5 Jan 1762. Deed of Gift. Hannah Seayres widow of South Farnham Parish, Essex Co for natural love & affection have given to her sister Elizabeth Lason of same place all her right & title to a tr of land which formerly belonged to her father Nicholas Lason & descended to his only son & heir at law Richard Lason & after his death to his three sisters the afsd Hannah & Eliza parties hereto & Mary Lason, being in the parish afsd & also all her right & title to all the estate both real & personal which she has or ought to have from Richard Lason her decd brother ... . Wit: Betty Rennolds, Mary Lason, W. Roane, John Rennolds. Proved 15 Feb 1762 & recorded. Attest: John Lee Junr clerk. (Pg 66)

6 Jan 1762. Indenture Tripartite between James Martin of Chesterfield Co planter of the first part, Hannah Seayres of Essex Co widow & relict of Robert Seayres decd of the second part & John Rennolds of Essex Co planter of the third part, wit that in consideration of a marriage intended (by God's permission) to be had & solemnized between the sd James Martin & Hannah Seayres & of such further advancement & benefit in real & personal estate & otherwise as will arrive to the sd James Martin by the sd intended marriage & for the setting & assuring a competent maintainance for he sd Hannah Searyres during her life, as well as for the securing a good & sufficient maintainance of such issue & children that may probably proceed from the sd marriage as also for 5 sl by the sd John Rennolds to the sd James Martin & Hannah Seayres in hand paid the sd James Martin & Hannah Seayres have sold unto the sd John Rennolds the following Negro slaves (to wit) George, Rose, Winnifred, Judith, Frank, Hannah, Will, Amie, Dick, Peter, Ned, Frank, Pompey & Fanny, a good riding chair with harness & a pair of horses, & also the sd James Martin doth sell &

release unto the sd John Rennolds for the use herein after expressed so much of his personal estate as is of the value of 500 pd, for the several uses intents & purposes declared (that is to say) to the use & behoof of the sd James Martin & Hannah Seayres during their coverture & after the determinates of the sd coverture by the death of the sd James Martin then to the use & behoof of the sd Hannah Seayres during her natural life, & the sd James Martin for himself doth hereby covenant to & with the sd John Rennolds that he will well & faithfully observe, perform, fulfill the afsd conveyance to the true intent & meaning thereof & well & truly pay or deliver up to the sd Hannah Seayres if she should survive him (or if she should not & have issue by him & make a disposition thereof) then to such person or persons as she shall dispose the same to ... . Wit: Betty Rennolds, Mary Lason, W. Roane. Proved 15 Feb 1762 & recorded. Attest: John Lee Junr clerk. (Pg 67)

1 Jan 1762. Deed. Mary Young of South Farnham Parish, Essex Co for 23 pd 10 sl sold to William Mitchell of same place planter a 23 ½ a. parcel of land in the sd parish bounded by the corner of Jeffries & Johnson & Cheyney's line, it being pt/o the tr of land which the sd Mary Young purch of Philip Jones gent decd ... . Wit: John Vass, Vincent Hudson, James Johnson, John Blatt. Proved 15 Feb 1762 & recorded. Attest: John Lee Junr clerk. (Pg 69)

15 Feb 1762. Deed. Robert Beverley esqr of Essex Co for 20 pd sold to James Ritchie of Glasgow, North Britain merchant a lot or ½ a. of land in the Town of Tappahannock which sd lot is now in the possession of Andrew Crawford merchant factor for the sd James Ritchie the same being contiguous to other lotts or ½ acres the property of the sd James Ritchie & being number 46 ... . Wit: John Somple. Ackn 15 Feb 1762 & recorded. Attest: John Lee Junr clerk. (Pg 71)

16 Nov 1761. Deed. John Minter of Christ Church Parish, Middlesex Co & Susanna his wife, William Minter of [blank] Parish, [blank] Co, Richard Cauthorn, Joseph Minter & Anne his wife & Isaac Kidd & Lucy his wife of South Farnham Parish, Essex Co for 62 pd sold to John Patterson of South Farnham Parish, Essex Co a 178 a. tr of land in South Farnham Parish adj Webb's Mill Swamp, lands of Richard Jeffries, James Webb Junr, William Young, Edmund Mitchell & Richard Cauthorn, it being pt/o the tr of land held by John Minter the elder late of Essex Co decd & whereon he lived ... . Wit: William Young, Peter Trible, John Crow, James Webb Junr, James Breedlove, Newman Miskell, S. Smith, Isaac Kidd. Wit to receipt: William Young, Peter Trible, James Atkins Junr, John Crow, James Webb Junr, James Breedlove, Newman Miskell, S. Smith, Isaac Kidd. Ackn 16 Nov 1761 by Richard Cauthorn, Joseph Minter & Isaac Kidd, & Anne & Lucy relinquished their right of dower to the land & premises conveyed & proved 15 Feb 1762 (as to the pt/o

John Minter & William Minter) & recorded. Attest: John Lee Junr clerk. (Pg 72)

20 Nov 1761. Deed of Mortgage. William Dunn Senr & Winifred his wife & Waters Dunn of Essex Co planters for 150 pd sold to William Roane of same co atty at law a 175 a. tr of land whereon the sd William Dunn & his wife now dwell & also a 150 a. tr of land whereon the sd Waters now lives in South Farnham Parish, & also 10 slaves (to wit) Jacob, Landiff, Violet, Atick, Lucy, Lilly, Jacob, Will, Rose & Tom & their future increase & offspring ... provided that if the sd William Dunn & Winifred his wife or Waters Dunn do well & truly pay unto the sd William Roane the afsd 150 pd with interest when demanded by the sd William Roane then these presents shall cease & be void ... . Wit: Wm Dunn Junr, Nathaniel Dunn, Lucy Dunn. Ackn 16 Feb 1762 by William Dunn & Winifred his wife she being first privily examined & recorded. Attest: John Lee Junr clerk. (Pg 73)

28 Jan 1762. To Thomas & John Tabb of Amelia Co gent greeting, whereas Edward Donohoe & Betty his wife late of Essex Co by their deed dated 12 May 1761 have conveyed unto Thomas Gouldman of same co 100 a. of land whereon the sd Donohoe then lived in St. Anns Parish & whereas the sd Betty is unable to travel to our sd co court to make acknowledgment thereof, therefore we command you to repair to the sd Betty & that privily & apart from her sd husband you take such acknowledgment as the sd Betty shall be willing to make ... . Wit John Lee Junr clerk. By virtue of the dedimus hereto annex'd we have examined Betty the w/o Edward Donohoe which the sd Betty doth declare she doth acknowledge the deed freely & willingly & is willing that the sd deed may be recorded. At a court held 15 Feb 1762 this commission with the commissioners return thereon endorsed was returned & recorded. Attest: John Lee Junr clerk. (Pg 75)

13 Feb 1762. Deed. William Watkins of South Farnham Parish, Essex Co for 30 pd sold to John Crow of same place a 60 a. parcel of land in the sd parish bounded by Isaac Kidd, Baker's & Crow's corner, Rudy Swamp & Lewis Watkins' old plantation ... . Wit: Benjamin Dunn, Isom Crow & Thomas Williamson. Ackn 15 Mar 1762 by William Watkins & Mary the w/o the sd William (being first privily examined & assenting) relinquished her right of dower to the land which is admitted to record. Attest: John Lee Junr clerk. (Pg 76)

12 Mar 1762. Deed. James Johnson of South Farnham Parish, Essex Co & Lettes (Letty) his wife for 100 pd sold to John Vass of same place a 140 a. parcel of land whereon the sd James Johnson & his father Richard Richard (sic) Johnson now live in the sd parish adj Capt John Webb's Mill Swamp, lands of

John Cheyney decd, Robert James, the sd Vass & William Bond of Glouster Co
... . Wit: Robt Mann, Ralph Neale, Stephen Neale. Ackn 15 Mar 1762 by
James Johnson & Letty his wife (she being first privily examined & assenting) &
recorded. Attest: John Lee Junr clerk. (Pg 78)

6 Mar 1762. Deed. William Gatewood of South Farnham Parish, Essex Co for
69 pd 17 sl 4 pn 3 farthings sold to John Upshaw of same place a 137 a. tr of
land that the sd William Gatewood lately became possessed of & which he
claims under the will of his decd grandfather John Gatewood & is the part
allotted him by arbitrators for that purpose appointed which sd parcel of land is
pt/o the tr whereon the sd John Gatewood formerly lived on the s side of
Hoskins's Swamp in South Farnham Parish, bounded by Hoskins's Poquoson ...
. Wit: Nicholas Faulconer, Joseph Fogg, Isaac Gatewood, Maxamilian Davis.
Ackn 16 Mar 1762 & recorded. Attest: John Lee Junr clerk. (Pg 79)

18 Feb 1761. Deed. Robert Cole & Frankey his wife (late Frankey Gatewood)
of South Farnham Parish, Essex Co for 51 pd 15 sl sold to John Thomas of Saint
Anns Parish, co afsd 1/3 pt/o that tr of land in St. Anns Parish whereof Richard
Gatewood died seised & which the sd Frankey claims as her right of dower in &
to the land of the sd Gatewood her late husband ... . Wit: John Richards, John
Rouson, W. Young, Richard Jeffries. Proved 20 Jul 1762 & recorded. Attest:
John Lee Junr clerk. (Pg 81)

1 Sep 1761. Bill of Sale. William Lowry of Essex Co for 260 pd hath sold unto
Robert Lowry of King George Co the following Negro slaves, stock &
household furniture (viz) Dick, Frank, Suckey & Hannah with their increase, 42
head of cattle young & old, 50 head of sheep, 50 hoggs, 1 horse & mare, 3 beds
& furniture, 1 disk & book case, 1 doz chairs, 2 tables, 1 fiddle & case & all the
kitchen furniture ... . Wit: Joseph Warrick, Elizabeth Hammontree. Proved 16
Mar 1762 & recorded. Attest: John Lee Junr clerk. (Pg 82)

21 Sep 1761. Pursuant to an order of the worshipful court of Essex Co dated
July Court 1761 we have survey'd that tr of land of Nicholas Pamplin decd he
devised to be divided between his two sons Thomas & James, which is found to
contain 360 a. adj Henry Purkers Taylor, Mill Road & Capt Thomas Roane,
which leaves each 180 a., Thomas Pamplin's the upper or woods lot & James
Pamplin's the lower or that adj the Mill Swamp including the houses ... . John
Upshaw, Thomas Roane, James Upshaw. This division was returned 16 Mar
1762 & recorded. Attest: John Lee Junr clerk. (Pg 82)

27 Feb 1762. Deed. John Garnet Junr & Mary his wife of Essex Co for 20 pd
sold to Francis Graves of same co a 48 a. tr of land in St. Ann Parish which the
sd John Garnett purch of Thomas Dobson & Susanna his wife by deed dated 10

Apr 1746 ... . Wit: Jas Evans, Ambrose Allen, Thos Sanders, Jno Fogg, Josua Garnett. Ackn 19 Apr 1762 & recorded. Attest: John Lee Junr clerk. (Pg 83)

30 Oct 1761. Deed of Mortgage. John Chamberlaine lately of NC at present of Essex Co, VA for 155 pd sold to Joseph McWilliams of Essex Co six slaves, viz, George, Jeanny, Rachel, Young Rachel, Nann & Isaac with their future increase ... provided that if the sd John Chamberlaine do & shall pay unto the sd Joseph McWilliams 155 pd on or before 30 Oct 1762 with interest then these presents to be void ... . Wit: John McWilliams, Reuben Tankersley, Joseph Mann Junr, Benjamin McWilliams. Ackn 19 Apr 1762 & recorded. Attest: John Lee Junr clerk. (Pg 85)

In obedience to an order of the worshipful court of Essex Co dated 22 Jul 1760 I have measured & divided 672 a. of land on Rappahannock River between Mrs. Mary Pamplin & William Porter, adj the river, Col William Daingerfield & the swamp of Tickners Cr, dividing into two equal parts. Given under my hand 29 Jan 1761 Bo Brooke S.E.C. Pursuant to the within mentioned order we in company with the surveyor have seen the tr of land herein plotted [*drawing not included here*] equally divided between Mary Pamplin & William Porter, the upper part allotted to the sd Mary Pamplin & the lower part including the houses to the sd William Porter. Given under our hands 29 Jan 1761 Wm Daingerfield, Archibald Ritchie, John Upshaw. This division of land was returned 19 Apr 1762 & recorded. Attest: John Lee Junr clerk. (Pg 86)

17 Jan 1762. Deed. Andrew Crawford merchant & Richard Coleman planter acting executors of Robert Spilesby Coleman late of Essex Co decd for 95 pd 10 sl sold to John Richards of King & Queen Co gent two lots or ½ acres of land number'd 23 & 24 in the plot of the Town of Tappahannock ... whereas the sd Robert Sp. Coleman in his life time, to wit, -- Dec 1760, made & published his will wherein he devises as follows, to wit, it is my will that all my Negroes that I have not given away with the stocks & all moveables together with the four lots where the Scots Arms Tavern now stands shall be sold by my executors to the highest bidder & the money arising employed in paying my just debts & legacies & the remainder (if any) to be divided amongst all my children (except my dau Susannah Richards) & whereas the sd Robert Sp. Coleman died possessed & seised of two ½ a. or lots of land in the Town of Tappahannock adj the two lots whereon the sd tavern stands & made no alteration or revocation of the afsd clause in his will & whereas it is believed that the two lots whereon the sd tavern stands were intail'd by the ancestor of the sd Robert Sp. Coleman who died seised of such estate tail in the two last mentioned lots & consequently the afsd clause is of no effect with respect to them, the sd executors to comply with the intention of their testator as far as they legally could did advertise the other two mentioned lots to be sold to the highest bidder & whereas on the day of sale the

sd John Richards bid for the two lots number'd 23 & 24 in the plot of the sd town the sum of 95 pd 10 sl & was reported to be the highest bidder for the same ... . Wit: John Lee Junr, Al Rose, Willm Gatewood. Proved 19 Apr 1762 & 21 Apor 1762 & recorded. Attest: John Lee Junr clerk. (Pg 87)

12 May 1762. To John Lee, Paul Micou & Simon Miller gent greeting, whereas Francis Gouldman & Winifred his wife by their deed dated 12 Dec 1761 have sold unto James Garnett gent the several trs of land in the sd deed recited (to wit) a 1122 a. tr of land from the sd Francis Gouldman to the sd James Garnett dated 30 Dec 1729, also 200 a. of land in a deed from the sd Gouldman to the sd Garnett dated 8 Feb 1734, also 1200 a. in a deed from the sd Gouldman to the sd Garnett dated 8 Feb 1734, & 600 a. by one other deed from the sd Gouldman to the sd Garnett dated 8 Feb 1734, & whereas the sd Winifred is unable to travel to our co court to make acknowledgment thereof, therefore we command you to repair to the sd Winifred & her privily & apart from her sd husband examine her whether she willingly relinquishes her right of dower in the several trs of land ... . Wit John Lee Junr clerk. By virtue of this commission we Simon Miller & Paul Micou have privily examined the sd Winifred & she freely & willingly relinquishes her right of dower to the several trs of land & that she is willing her acknowledgment & the sd deed be recorded. Attest: John Lee Junr clerk. (Pg 89)

1 Jan 1762. Deed. John Sale & Agness his wife of Essex Co for 60 pd sold to Meriday Brown of same co a 120 a. tr of land pt/o a greater tr the sd John Sale formerly purch of John Smith bounded by Mosses Swamp, lands of Davice & Fogg, James Bates, Rice Noel & Horse Br ... . Wit: Thos Sale, Thos Newman, Elizabeth Brown. Ackn by John Sale 17 May 1762 & recorded. Attest: John Lee Junr clerk. (Pg 91)

20 Oct 1761. Deed. John Read & Elizabeth his wife & Tabitha Purkins of Cullpepper Co for 40 pd sold to Arthur Tate of Essex Co a 200 a. tr of land bounded by William Greenwood, James Newbil, John Harper, Thomas Howerton & Richard Covington, it being the lands that Griffin Purkins purch of Edmund Covington ... . Wit: John Draper, Richd Covington, Thos Howerton. Ackn 17 May 1762 by Tabitha Perkins & the same were proved as to the pt/o John Read & Elizabeth his wife & admitted to record. Attest: John Lee Junr clerk. (Pg 93)

24 Dec 1761. Power of Attorney. Robert Falcon of Workingtoun, Cumberland Co shipmaster have appointed my trusty & well beloved friend Edward Dickson of Port Royall on Rappahannock VA my atty to ask, levie, demand & by all lawful ways & means soever to uplift, recover & receive of & from all & every person whom it doeth or may concern inhabiting in VA or MD or any other pt/o

his Majestys plantations any way debtors to me or havers of my effects or any part thereof all & sundrey such sums of money, lands, Negroes, goods, wares, merchandize & other effects or estate whatsoever pertaining & belonging or addebted & owing to me ... . Wit: Colin Campbell, John Smith. By John Paton magistrate of Greenock, that the before designed Robert Falcon did in my presence sign & seall the foregoing power of atty & is attested att Greenock 24 Dec 1761. Proved 17 May 1762 & recorded. Attest: John Lee Junr clerk. (Pg 95)

10 Dec 1761. Deed. John Sadler of Essex Co for 8 pd sold to Lewis Mountague of Middlesex Co a 12 a. parcel of land bounded by sd Mountague's Spring Swamp, it being pt/o a tr of land that the sd Sadler purch of John Medcares ... . Wit: Latn Mountague, Henry Street, Richard Street. Ackn 17 May 1762 & recorded. Attest: John Lee Junr clerk. (Pg 96)

17 May 1762. Deed. Arthur Tate of South Farnham Parish, Essex Co & Lucy his wife for 105 pd sold to Doctor John Clement gent of same place a 129 a. tr of land in the sd parish bounded by the maine road, McCall's house, land that was formerly call'd Tyler's which now is Ramsey's, land the afsd Tate purch by deed of James Boughan, Doctor Clements gent, James Banks, land formerly call'd Tyler's which now is Dunn's, a corner of Peaches' which now is the afsd Dunn's, a corner of Smith's, land that was formerly called the afsd Peaches' & Tyler's which now is Smith's & Ramsey's, the e pt/o the land was purch by the sd Arthur Tate of William Degge & the sd Degge purch the same of James Boughan & the sd Boughan purch the same of Jonathan Dunn who purch the same of William Tyler, & the w part was purch by the afsd Tate of the afsd Boughan ... . Wit: None. Ackn by Arthur Tate & Lucy his wife (she being first privily examined & assenting) & admitted to record. Attest: John Lee Junr clerk. (Pg 98)

19 May 1762. Bond. Simon Miller Junr & Edward Gouldman are firmly bound unto our Sovereign Lord George the third for 20 pd ... the condition of this obligation is such that whereas the afsd Simon Miller Junr is by the court of Essex Co licenced to keep the ferry usually called Laytons Ferry, now if the sd Simon Miller shall constantly keep one sufficient ferry boat to carry five horses with two able hands to attend the same & also give passage without delay as in the regulation & settlement of ferrys & for dispatch of publick expresses to be ferry free & do & perform all & whatsoever ye laws enjoyn & require & truly & faithfully perform & comply with ye duty & business of a ferry keeper then this obligation to be void ... . Wit: None. Ordered to be recorded the date afsd. Attest: John Lee clerk. (Pg 100)

Francis Fauquier esqr his Majesty's Lieut Governor of VA, to James Webb esqr, by virtue of the power & authority to me given I do hereby appoint you to be sherif of Essex Co during pleasure ... . Given my hand at Williamsburg 27 May 1762. Truly recorded John Lee Junr clerk. (Pg 101)

21 Jun 1762. Bond. James Webb, John Edmondson & James Edmondson are firmly bound unto our Sovereign Lord the King for 1,000 pd ... the condition of this obligation is such that whereas the afsd James Webb is appointed sherif of Essex Co during pleasure by commission from the governor [see above] ... if the sd James Webb shall well & truly collect & receive all officers fees & dues put into his hands to collect, & duly account for & pay the same to the officers to whom such fees are due & shall well & truly execute & due return make of all process & precepts to him directed & pay & satisfy all sums of money & tobacco by him received by virtue of such process to the persons to whom the same are due & in all other things shall truly & faithfully perform the sd office of sherif during the time of his continuance therein, then this obligation to be void ... . Wit: None. Ordered to be recorded the date above. Attest: John Lee Junr clerk. (Pg 102)

21 Jun 1762. Bond. James Webb, John Edmondson & James Edmondson are firmly bound unto our Sovereign Lord King for 500 pd ... the condition of this obligation is such that whereas the afsd James Webb is appointed sherif of Essex Co during pleasure by commission from the governor [see above] ... if the sd James Webb shall well & truly collect all quitrents, fines, forfeitures & Americiaments accruing or becoming due to his Majesty in the sd co & shall duly account for & pay the same to the officers of his Majesty's revenue for the time being, on or before the second Tuesday in June annually & shall in all other things truly & faithfully execute the sd office of sherif during his continuance therein, then this obligation to be void ... . Wit: None. Ordered to be recorded the date above. Attest: John Lee Junr clerk. (Pg 102)

22 May 1762. Deed. James Davis & Eliza his wife of St. Anns Parish, Essex Co for 80 pd sold to Thomas Sale of same place a 75 a. tr of land in the sd parish bounded by Tillsons Run & Jeane Munday ... . Wit: John Sale, Thos Munday, Merriday Brown. Ackn 21 Jun 1762 by James Davis Junr & Elizabeth his wife (she being first privily examined & assenting thereto) & admitted to record. Attest: John Lee Junr clerk. (Pg 103)

16 Nov 1761. Deed. Francis Smith of South Farnham Parish, Essex Co gent & Anne his wife for 120 pd sold to William Bond of [blank] Parish, Gloster Co planter a 126 a. parcel of land in South Farnham Parish adj on Webbs Mill Swamp, lands of Andrew Allen, Edward Bomer, Henry Crutcher, John Blatt & the sd Francis Smith, whereon Nicholas Smith the younger decd lately dwelt which was given to him by his father Nicholas Smith the elder decd by deed &

the sd Nicholas Smith the younger dieing intestate the sd land descended to the sd Francis Smith as eldest brother & heir at law ... . Wit: Andrew Allen, Henry Walker, John Blatt. Proved 21 Jun 1762 & admitted to record. Attest: John Lee Junr clerk. (Pg 105)

6 Mar 1762. Deed. John Sadler of Essex Co for 15 pd sold to Josiah Mactier (Macktier) of same co a 21 a. tr of land bounded by Thos Clark, Reuben Shelton, John Cornelius & John Sadler, it being pt/o a tr of land that the sd Sadler purch of John Madearis ... . Wit: Henry Street, Richard Street, William Lee. Ackn 21 Jun 1762 & admitted to record. Attest: John Lee Junr clerk. (Pg 106)

22 May 1762. Deed. John Sadler of Essex Co for 13 pd sold to Abraham Mountague of same co an 18 a. parcel of land bounded by the Causway Bridge, Richd Street, Thos Clark & sd Abrm Mountague, it being pt/o a tr of land the sd John Sadler purch of John Meadaras ... . Wit: Henry Street, William Lee, Richard Street. Ackn 19 Jul 1762 & admitted to record. Attest: John Lee Junr clerk. (Pg 108)

12 Dec 1761. Quit Claim. Francis Gouldman & Winefred his wife of Essex Co for 100 pd quit claim unto James Garnett all manner of dower & right & title of dower whatsoever which the sd Winefred now have may might should or of right ought to have or claim in or out of all & every the messuages & lands which the sd Francis Gouldman her husband has conveyed by the several deeds & conveyances (in case the sd Winefred shall survive her sd husband Francis Gouldman) that is to say a deed made by the sd Francis Gouldman to the sd James Garnett for 1122 a. dated 30 Dec 1729, one other deed made by the sd Francis Gouldman to the sd James Garnett for 200 a. of land dated 8 Feb 1734, & in one other tr conveyed by the sd Francis Gouldman to the sd James Garnett by deed for 1200 a. dated 8 Feb 1734 & in one other 600 a. tr of land conveyed by the sd Francis Gouldman to the sd James Garnett by deed dated 8 Feb 1734 & also all manner of actions & writs of dower whatsoever in all or any of the sd lands ... . Wit: William Boulware, Richd Evans, Charles Munday Junr, James Hipkins, Simon Miller, Paul Micou. Proved 17 May 1762 & ordered to be certified. Further proved 19 Jul 1762 & admitted to record. Attest: John Lee Junr clerk. (Pg 110)

19 Jul 1762. Deed. John Upshaw of South Farnham Parish, Essex Co for 21 pd 2 sl 4 pn sold to Thomas Roane of same place a messuage & 40 ½ a. tr of land in the sd parish on the s side of Hoskins's Swamp adj the plantation whereon the sd Thomas Roane now lives bounded by Hoskins's Pocoson, sd Roane's line & Hoskins's Swamp ... . Wit: None. Ackn 20 Jul 1762 & admitted to record. Attest: John Lee Junr clerk. (Pg 111)

A list of prisoners deliver'd up by William Covington late sheriff of Essex Co to James Webb gent present sheriff of sd co with the cause of commitments & their several sums (viz) Robt Cook at the suite of Robt Allenby for debt 39 pd 15 sl 8 pn for want of special bail, April Court; Joseph McWilliams at the suit of Robt Sp. Coleman's exrs debt 375 pd 1 sl for want of special baile, also at the suit of Hannah Edmondson debt 18 pd, also at the suit of William Brooke's exrs debt 82 pd 17 sl 8 pn for want of bail for appearance in May 1762; Thomas Haile at the suit of John Dean's case 60 pd for want of bail for appearance in May 1762; John Cooper at the suit of John Taylar esqr guardian to Robt Tomblin for want of special bail, also at the suit of John Tayler for 15 pd for want of special bail, also by execution for Catron Phil Young 312 ½ lbs of tobacco. L. Covington for Wm Covington SEC. At a court continued & held 20 Jul 1762 Luke Covington late sub sherif for William Covington late high sherif came into court & delivered up to James Webb present high sherif the several prisoners now in custody according to the list afsd which on the motion of the sd Luke is ordered to be recorded. Attest: John Lee Junr clerk. (Pg 113)

25 Mar 1762. Power of Attorney. William Sandford of Liverpoole in the Co of Lancaster & Kingdom of Great Britain merchant & John Oliverson of the same place taylor have appointed Thomas Brereton of Liverpoole afsd mariner captain or commander of the ship Betty now lying in the Port of Liverpoole our atty to settle all & all manner of accounts now depending & unsettled between us the sd constituents with the Reverend Thomas Davies in King George Co on Rappahannock River in VA clerk or elsewhere touching or in any wise concerning all goods merchandize & effects whatsoever returns & produce thereof at any time heretofore sent sold or consigned to the sd Thomas Davies or any person whatsoever for work & labour & materials by us the sd constituents heretofore done & performed found & provided for the sd Thomas Davies & also for us in our names to our use to ask demand sue for recover & receive of & from the sd Thomas Davies all & every such sum of money debts dues duties & demands goods chattels or merchandize commodities & effects whatsoever which now are due owing or belonging unto us or which we now or at any time hereafter have a right to claim … . Wit: John Williamson mayor of Liverpool, Robt Allenby, Robert Swarbrick. Proved 16 Aug 1762 & admitted to record. Attest: John Lee Junr clerk. (Pg 113)

16 Aug 1762. Deed. Vincent Hudson of South Farnham Parish, Essex Co mill wright & Anne (Ann) his wife for 49 pd sold to John Dunn of same place a 79 a. parcel of land in the sd parish bounded by the land of Francis Smith esqr decd, Henry Gardner, John Evans decd, Mary Young, John Cheyney decd & Ralph Neale, which tr of land the sd Vincent Hudson purch of the afsd John Cheyney decd … . Wit: Isaac Williams, John Evans Junr, Willm Dunn. Ackn 16 Aug 1762 by Vincent Hudson & Ann his wife (she being first privily examined &

assenting) & admitted to record. Attest: John Lee Junr clerk. (Pg 115)

17 Nov 1761. Deed. James Dix of Albemarle Co, VA planter for 30 pd sold to John Gatewood Junr of Essex Co planter a 50 a. tr of land in South Farnham Parish which was given to the sd James Dix by his father in law Joseph Reeves bounded by the sd Reeves ... . Wit: Jos Reeves, John Dix, Afryca Stuart, Kerenhappuch Dix. Proved 19 Apr 1762, 17 May 1762 & 16 Aug 1762 & admitted to record. Attest: John Lee Junr clerk. (Pg 116)

1 Jul 1762. Deed. John Carragan of Essex Co planter for 22 pd 12 sl 6 pn sold to Robert Beverley esqr of same co a 45 ½ a. tr of land bounded by the sd Beverley's line, Levingston's line & Carragan's Spring Br ... the sd Robert Beverley doth covenant & agree to & with the sd John Carragan that the sd John shall remain in quiet & peaceable possession of the sd land & premises for & during the term of the sd John's natural life ... . Wit: Robt Runford, Willm Evans, James Mills. Ackn 17 Aug 1762 & admitted to record. Attest: John Lee Junr clerk. (Pg 118)

3 May 1762. Deed. John Clements gent for 100 pd sold to John Boughan a parcel of land in South Farnham Parish it being that tr of land that formerly belonged to Joseph Mann purch of the afsd John Boughan now in the possession & tener of the afsd John Clements gent of same parish ... . Wit: J. Edmondson, Thos Pamplin, L. Covington. Ackn 17 Aug 1762 & admitted to record. Attest: John Lee Junr clerk. (Pg 119)

16 Aug 1762. Robert Beverley esqr of Essex Co for 73 pd 2 sl 6 pn sold to Thomas Boulware of same co a 195 a. tr of land in Saint Anns Parish bounded by a br of Popoman Swamp & Samuel Henshaw, which sd tr of land the sd Robert Beverley claims under the will of his father the late William Beverley esqr decd who purch the same of Nicholas Copeland by deed dated 18 Aug 1740 ... . Wit: John Upshaw, Thomas Roane, W. Roane. Ackn 17 Aug 1762 & admitted to record. Attest: John Lee Junr clerk. (Pg 120)

16 Aug 1762. Deed. Thomas Boulware & Nelley his wife of Essex Co for 53 pd 10 sl sold to Robert Beverley esqr of same co a 107 a. tr of land in Saint Anns Parish bounded by the main road that crosses Brices Run, land late of William Garnett decd, Thomas Fogg & Honr William Beverley decd, which sd tr of land the sd Thomas Boulware claims by a deed of sail from John Davis & Cathrine his wife to the sd Thomas Boulware dated 6 Oct 1760 ... . Wit: John Upshaw, Thomas Roane, W. Roane. Ackn 17 Aug 1762 & admitted to record. Attest: John Lee Junr clerk. (Pg 122)

18 Sep 1762. Deed. Grisel Smith of South Farnham Parish, Essex Co for 32 pd

sold to John & Ozwell Byrom of same place a 50 a. tr of land (being pt/o the same tr of land whereon the sd Grisel Smith now lives) in the sd parish bounded by the road running by Byrom's land, the Glebe or Western Br of Webb's Mill Swamp & land whereon the sd John Byrom now lives ... . Wit: John Williamson, Thos Jessey, Ezekel Byrom, Luke Covington. Proved 20 Sep 1762 & admitted to record. Attest: John Lee Junr clerk. (Pg 123)

20 Sep 1762. Deed of Gift. Samuel Noel of Saint Anns Parish, Essex Co for good will & most tender effection & 5 sl have given to my son Ellison Noel a 138 a. tr of land that the sd Samuel Noel formerly purch of his father Daniel Noel by deeds of lease & release dated 9 & 10 Mar 1736 except 38 a. of the same the sd Samuel Noel hath lately conveyed to Samuel Henshaw ... the sd Samuel Noel doth reserve unto himself the afsd land during his natural life & it is the true intent & meaning of these presents that the afsd Ellison Noel shall have no right title or claim to the sd land during the natural life of his afsd father Samuel Noel .... Wit: David Pitts Junr, Thomas Andrews, William Bates. Proved 20 Sep 1762 & admitted to record. Attest: John Lee Junr clerk. (Pg 126)

21 Jul 1762. Deed. John Patterson of South Farnham Parish, Essex Co planter for 5 pd sold to William Young of same place planter a 6 a. tr of land in the sd parish bounded by land of the sd William Young, Edmund Mitchel, main County Road & James Webb Junr, it being pt/o the tr of land which the sd John Patterson purch of John Minter & others ... . Wit: Samuel Peachey, Mary Webb, Elizabeth Peachey, Thomas Barnes. Ackn 20 Sep 1762 & admitted to record. Attest: John Lee Junr clerk.(Pg 127)

20 Sep 1762. Deed of Gift. John Lee of Essex Co esqr for natural love & affection have given to Susanna the w/o John Lee Junr one Negro girl named Silla the dau of Ruth & her increase ... . Wit: None. Ackn 20 Sep 1762 & recorded. Attest: John Lee Junr clerk.(Pg 129)

20 Sep 1762. Deed of Gift. John Lee of Essex Co esqr for natural love & affection have given to Lettice the dau of John & Susanna Lee one Negro child named Venus the dau of Jembo & her increase ... . Wit: None. Ackn 20 Sep 1762 & recorded. Attest: John Lee Junr clerk.(Pg 129)

20 Sep 1762. Bill of Sale. James Mills of Essex Co merchant for 80 pd sold to Robinson Daingerfield of King & Queen Co a Negro wench called Betty & her child called Planter now in the possession of Susanna Parker ... . Wit: John Lee Junr, John Mills. Proved 20 Sep 1762 & recorded. Attest: John Lee Junr clerk. (Pg 130)

2 Aug 1762. Deed. Daniel Sullivan & Hannah his wife & Katherine Sullivan widow & relict of Daniel Sullivan decd all of Essex Co for 50 pd sold to Benjamin Fisher of South Farnham Parish, Essex Co a messuage & 100 a. tr of land that formerly belong'd to William Arven & by him sold to Joseph Cross decd late of this co & he by his will devis'd the same to his son Samuel Cross who sold & convey'd it to Daniel Sullivan decd father to Daniel Sullivan the now partie to these presents he being his eldest son & heir at law, the sd tr of land is in South Farnham Parish on the s side of the main South Br of Gilsons Cr Swamp & is the plantation whereon the sd William Arven formerly dwell'd bounded by John Rennolds, Richard Hill Junr & the South Swamp of Gilsons Cr ... . Wit: Leonard Sale, James Sullivan, Richard Hill Junr, William Webb. 20 Sep 1762 Daniel Sullivan & Hannah his wife (she being first privily examined & assenting thereto) ackn this deed & proved as to the pt/o Catherine Sullivan. Fully proved 21 Feb 1763 & recorded. Attest: John Lee Junr clerk.(Pg 131)

19 Apr 1762. Deed of Mortgage. Samuel Fawcet of Essex Co planter for 107 pd 3 sl 7 pn now due from the sd Samuel Fawcet to Andrew Crawford for which the sd Samuel some time ago gave bonds hath sold to the sd Andrew Crawford of Essex Co merchant a Negro wench nam'd Jeany, two feather beds & furniture, one mare & one horse ... if the sd Samuel shall pay to the sd Andrew the 107 pd 3 sl 7 pn with interest then this indenture to be void ... . Wit: Alexr Crudon, Necl McCoull. Proved 21 Sep 1762 & admitted to record. Attest: John Lee Junr clerk.(Pg 133)

-- Sep 1762. Deed. William Roane & Betty his wife of Essex Co & John Roane & Susannah his wife of Spotsilvania Co, VA for 514 pd 6 sl 8 pn sold to Thomas Roane of South Farnham Parish, Essex Co a 1243 a. tr of land & water grist mill called Roanes Mill with the land adj thereto on the main run of Hoskins's Swamp in South Farnham Parish on the s side of Hoskins's Swamp afsd being the land lent Mrs. Sarah Roane by the will of her decd husband Wm Roane gent bounded by Hoskins's Pocoson, corner of Pamplin's & Robt Johnston's land, Lowries line, Capt John Lantane's land, Sherewood's line, land of James Upshaw, South Swamp & the Poquoson ... . Wit: James Mills, James Upshaw, Joseph Ryland. Ackn 21 Sep 1762 by William Roane, John Roane & Susanna (she being first privily examined & assenting)& admitted to record. Attest: John Lee Junr clerk.(Pg 134)

18 Oct 1762. Deed. Thomas Howerton & Grissillah his wife of South Farnham Parish, Essex Co for 50 pd sold to Heritage Howerton of same place a 50 a. tr of land on the s side of Covingtons Swamp bounded by the land now in the possession of John Harper & Tate, land now in the possession of Roger Shakleford & land now in the possession of the sd Heritage Howerton ... . Wit: Richd St. John, William Covington, William Ally. Ackn 18 Oct 1762 by

Thomas Howerton & Grissillah his wife (she being first privily examined & assenting) & admitted to record. Attest: John Lee Junr clerk. (Pg 136)

15 Oct 1762. Deed of Lease. Benjamin Dean of King & Queen Co planter & Jane his wife for 5 sl leased to Joseph Minter of Essex Co planter a 50 a. tr of land adj the lands of John Bush, Thomas Watts, Mrs. Parker & Thomas Dean, it being the land devised to the sd Benjamin Dean by the will of his father Thomas Dean decd ... during the term of 1 year paying the rent of one pepper corn at the feast of Saint Michael the Arch Angel if demanded ... . Wit: None. Ackn 18 Oct 1762 by Benjamin Dean & Jane his wife (she being first privily examined assenting) & admitted to record. Attest: John Lee Junr clerk.(Pg 138)

16 Oct 1762. Deed of Release. Benjamin Dean of King & Queen Co & Jane his wife planter for 30 pd released unto Joseph Minter of Essex Co planter a 50 a. tr of land ...[*same as above*]... . Wit: None. Ackn 18 Oct 1762 by Benjamin Dean & Jane his wife (she being first privily examined & assenting)& recorded. Attest: John Lee Junr clerk.(Pg 139)

15 Oct 1762. Deed of Lease. Richard Coleman of St. George Parish, Spotsylvania Co planter & Ann his wife for 5 sl leased to James Gray of Saint Ann Parish, Essex Co gent a 230 a. tr of land in Saint Anns Parish on Rappahannock River which sd tr of land was held by Richard Covington decd father of the afsd Ann to whom the right of the land fell ... for the term of 1 year paying the rent of one ear of Indian corn on Lady Day next if demanded ... . Wit: None. Ackn 18 Oct 1762 by Richard Coleman & Ann his wife (she being first privily examined & assenting thereto) & admitted to record. Attest: John Lee Junr clerk.(Pg 141)

16 Oct 1762. Deed of Release. Richard Coleman of St. George Parish, Spotsylvania Co planter & Ann his wife for 480 pd 5 sl sold to James Gray of Saint Ann Parish, Essex Co gent a 230 a. tr of land ... [*same as above*] ... . Wit: None. Ackn 18 Oct 1762 by Richard Coleman & Ann his wife (she being first privily examined & assenting thereto) & admitted to record. Attest: John Lee Junr clerk. (Pg 142)

A just & true account of the number of hhds of tobacco inspected at Laytons Warehouses in 1762 as also the condition the sd houses are in at present & the No. hhds they will contain. Tobacco inspected at Laytons hhds 441. The scale house is very leeky both the body & the shead, the other two the upper covers is chief of the nayles sterted & draw'd out of the list boards & leaks in several places & the doors out of order, the three houses when conveniently stowed will contain with ridering 320 hhds tobacco with convenient room for the scales & transfer tobacco. Given under our hands this 18 Oct 1762, Jno Rowzee, Simon

Miller. 18 Oct 1762 this report was presented by John Rowzee & Simon Miller gent & ordered to be recorded. Attest: John Lee Junr clerk.(Pg 144)

A just & true account of the number of hhds of tobacco inspected at Occupatia Warehouse in 1762 as also the condition the sd houses are in at present & the No. of hhds they contain. Tobacco inspected at Occupatia 240 hhds. The w sides of the house are entirely rotten & the e siles are loose from the posts, & severall weather boards are off. The scale house is entirely rotten & not fit for receiving tobacco. The two houses will contain about 200 hhds when conveniently stowed. Given under our hands this 18 Oct 1762, Jno Rowzee, Simon Miller. This report was presented 18 Oct 1762 by John Rowzee & Simon Miller gent & ordered to be recorded. Attest: John Lee Junr clerk.(Pg 145)

A just & true account of the number of hhds tobacco inspected at Boulers Warehouses in 1762 as also the condition the sd houses are in & the number they will contain. Tobacco Bowlers 254. The scales house very leakey the main plate & false plate broke in two. The doors out of repair. The locks were out. The sd house when well stow'd well & convenient rider'd hhd 30 with convenient room for the scales & transfer tobacco. The large house will stow about 220 hhd. Piscataway Warehouse 184. The Scale House 22 hhd with room to worke the scales & transfer the other house will stow abought 220 the sd house the gable end beet out the dores much out of repair & leaks very much. Wm Broocke, John Dunn. This report was presented 18 Oct 1762 by William Broocke & John Dunn & ordered to be recorded. Attest: John Lee Junr clerk. (Pg 145)

22 Sep 1762. Bond. Joseph Stevens of Essex Co & Edmund Pendleton of Caroline Co are firmly bound unto our Sovereign Lord King George the third in the penal sum of 200 pd ... the condition of this obligation is such that whereas the sd Joseph Stevens by agreement with the justices of the co court of Essex hath lately built a bridge across Hoskins's Cr near the Town of Tappahannock for the consideration of 10,800 lbs of tobacco & hath undertaken to support such bridge for the term of 10 years from 20 Aug last past, if the sd Joseph Stevens shall well & truly support maintain & keep a good & sufficient bridge for the passage of travelers across the sd cr at the place where the present bridge is for & during the term of 10 years then this obligation to be void ... . Wit: Luke Covington, Vincent Vass, John Ray. Proved 15 Nov 1762 & recorded. Attest: John Lee Junr clerk. (Pg 146)

15 Nov 1762. Deed. William Bates & Elizabeth his wife of Essex Co for 74 pd sold to Griffin Boughan of same co a 74 a. tr of land the sd William Bates purch from William Shortt & Elizabeth his wife by deed dated 18 Mar 1750, adj the lands of William Brooke, Samuel Henshaw, Wm Bowler & Thomas Bowler ... .

Wit: John Edmondson, Jno Henshaw, Daniel Thomas. Proved 15 Nov 1762 by Wm Bates & Eliza his wife (she being first privately examined & consenting) & also relinquished her right of dower in the land & premises which are ordered to be recorded. Attest: John Lee Junr clerk. (Pg 146)

15 Nov 1762. Deed. John Fogg & Anne his wife, Reuben Noel & Sarah his wife all of Essex Co for 170 pd sold to James Rennolds of same co a 297 a. parcel of land that James Fogg father of John Fogg formerly purch of Richard Coleman by deed dated 13 Oct 1741 the sd land now lying in the cos of Essex & Caroline bounded by the sd Rennolds land, John Satterwhite, Capt Robert Rennolds, Thacker land, br of Tuckahoe Swamp & Phillips Sanders ... . Wit: John Sale, Robt Sale, Edward Carter. Ackn 15 Nov 1762 by John Fogg & Anna his wife & Reuben Noell & Sarah his wife (the sd Anna & Sarah being first privately examined & consenting) relinquished their rights of dower to the land & premises & recorded. Attest: John Lee Junr clerk.(Pg 148)

16 Nov 1762. Deed. Susanna Parker of Essex Co widdow for 70 pd sold to William Mountague of sd co gent a 210 a. tr of land purch by the sd Susanna of John Bryant & Frances his wife by indenture of release dated 17 Jul 1722 situate in South Farnham Parish bounded by Jno Croudes & Jones's line ... . Wit: Andrew Baillie, Wm Parker, Thomas Pollard. Ackn 16 Nov 1762 & recorded. Attest: John Lee Junr clerk. (Pg 150)

19 Apr 1762. Bill of Sale. Adam Lynn of Essex Co for 120 pd sold to Joseph Ryland, Henry Perkins & William Gatewood the following goods & chattels (to wit) one sett of chamber organs, one clock, two beds & furniture, two desks, three tables, one horse & cart, one cow, a parcel of books, pewter, iron potts, chests, chairs, one spinnet, one stove, earthen ware, knives & forks & also all other the personal estate of the sd Adam Lynn ... . Wit: James Banks, W. Roane, John Taylar, John Burke, Samll Fawcett, Adam Lynn Junr. Proved 15 Nov 1762 & further proved 16 Nov 1762 & recorded. Attest: John Lee Junr clerk. (Pg 152)

4 Nov 1762. Deed of Mortgage. Edward Meadors of Essex Co for 15 pd 9 pn ½ penny sold to James Ritchie & Company of Glasgow in North Britain merchant sundry household furniture, viz, two beds with furniture, three pewter dishes, 20 plates, one coffee pot & one coffee mill ... if the sd Edward Meadors shall pay to the sd James Ritchie & Company the 15 pd 9 pn ½ penny with interest then this indenture to be void ... . Wit: Jas Emerson, Andrew Crawford. Ackn 16 Nov 1762 & recorded. Attest: John Lee Junr clerk. (Pg 153)

13 Oct 1762. Deed of Mortgage. John Merritt of Essex Co planter for 60 pd now due from the sd John Merritt to James Ritchie & Company for which the sd

John Merritt sometime agoe gave bond hath sold to the sd James Ritchie & Company of Glasgow North Brittain merchants 3 mares, 2 colts, 1 horse, 6 head of cattle, 1 still & 3 beds with furniture ... provided that if the sd John Merritt shall pay to the sd James Ritchie & Company the 60 pd with interest then this indenture to be void ... . Wit: Andrew Crawford, Neil McCoull, Robt Ferguson. Proved 16 Nov 1762 & recorded. Attest: John Lee Junr clerk. (Pg 154)

20 Dec 1762. Bond. James Webb, John Edmondson & James Webb Junr of Essex Co are firmly bound unto Francis Waring, Archibald Ritchie, William Mountague, Paul Micou, John Lee & Meriwether Smith gent justices of Essex Co for 120,000 lbs of tobacco ... whereas the afsd James Webb is appointed collector of the co levy for this present year, now the condition of this obligation is such that if the sd James Webb shall well & truly collect the sd levy & pay to the several claiments their respective claims, then this obligation to be void ... . Wit: W. Young. Ackn 20 Dec 1762 & recorded. Attest: John Lee Junr clerk. (Pg 155)

XX Dec 1762. Bond. James Webb, John Edmondson & James Webb Junr are firmly bound unto our Sovereign Lord the King for 1,000 pd ... the condition of this obligation is such that if the afsd James Webb, sherif of Essex Co, shall well & truly collect from the inhabitants of the sd co for the year 1763 the taxes imposed on the sd inhabitants by several Acts of Assembly & pay the same according to the directions of the sd acts, then this obligation to be void ... . Wit: None. Ackn 20 Dec 1762 & recorded. Attest: John Lee Junr clerk. (Pg 155)

25 Nov 1762. Power of Attorney. I Sarah Samuell of Saint Anns Parish, Essex Co do appoint Foster Samuel to settle and account with my son James Samuell for all money, tobacco & other profits & estate made use of the estate lent me by my decd husband James Samuell which he takes, uses & disposes of without my knowledge or consent & thereby giving unto my sd atty Foster Samuell full & absolute authority to sue for such estate & to cause the sd James Samuell to render & make up a true & just acct thereof so that the sd Foster Samuell may be able to acct for the same as of right ought to be according to the will of the sd decd James Samuell without interrupting the sd Sarah Samuell in her proper right that the proper legatees in the sd decds will may receive their due & proper proportions of the sd estate without fraud or having the same squandered away ... . Wit: John Lee, Thomas Samuell, George Martin, John Martin. Proved 20 Dec 1762 & recorded. Attest: John Lee Junr clerk. (Pg 156)

23 Mar 1762. Deed of Mortgage. Adam Lynn (Lyn) of the Town of Tappahannock, Essex Co for 46 pd 9 sl 5 pn sold to Thomas Brereton marriner & Archibald Ritchie of sd town one 1/2 a. lott in the sd town marked in the plan of the sd town number 7 ... . Memorandum: this conveyance to be void on Adam Lynn's reembursing Thomas Brereton & Archibald Ritchie the afsd sum of 46 pd 9

sl 5 pn with interest ... . Wit: David Cochrane, Samuel Hipkins Junr, Jeremiah Allen. Proved 16 Nov 1762 & ordered to be certified. Further proved 20 Dec 1762 & recorded. Attest: John Lee Junr clerk. (Pg 157)

27 Oct 1762. Deed. Isaac Brizendine (Brisendine) of South Farnham Parish, Essex Co & Anne his wife planter for 50 pd sold to Francis Brizendine of same place a 50 a. parcel of land in the sd parish adj the lands of John Oneale, Thomas Bush, Andrew Allen, Thomas Dobbyns decd & the afsd Francis Brizendine, it being the land whereon the sd Isaac Brizendine & Anne his wife now live & which he lately purch of William Cole ... . Wit: John Vass, Drury Dobbyns, John Brizendine. Proved 20 Dec 1762 & recorded. Attest: John Lee Junr clerk. (Pg 158)

28 Dec 1762. Deed of Gift. Samuel Hipkins of Essex Co for natural love & affection have given unto my son Richard Hipkins of same co these following slaves, viz, Letty, Grace & Butler & their increase which sd slaves that I gave to the sd Richard Hipkins at the time of his marriage ... . Memo: it is agreed by the parties that the afsd Negroes are of the value of 200 pd & the sd Richard Hipkins agrees to have recd them as full satisfaction for any promises made by the sd Samuel Hipkins in respect of Negroes to be given him on his marriage. Wit: John Lee Junr, LeRoy Hipkins. Proved 17 Jan 1763 & recorded. Attest: John Lee Junr clerk. (Pg 159)

1 Jun 1762. Deed of Gift. I Godfrey Young of Essex Co for 200 pd hath sold unto William Young of the afsd co the following Negro slaves (to wit) Dick, Harry, Reuben, Ben, Lue & Winny with their future increase ... . Wit: L. Covington, Grisel Smith. Proved 17 Jan 1763 & recorded. Attest: John Lee Junr clerk. (Pg 160)

20 Dec 1762. Deed of Lease. John Andrews of Essex Co for the consideration hereafter mentioned doth farm let unto Edward Gouldman of same co the land & plantation whereon the sd Andrews now lives together with five Negroes namely Hannah, Sarah, Frank, Sam & Davy during the full term of 21 years from 1 Jan 1763 ... the sd Edward Gouldman doth hereby agree to & with the sd John Andrews to pay to the sd John Andrews 15 pd yearly on 31 Dec during the afsd term & also to give the sd Andrews his boardage during the sd term & to build a shed to the sd Andrews house 20' long & 12' wide within the sd term ... . Wit: William Pitts, Ralph Farmer, Goin Murrow (Gawen Murro), Francis Gouldman & recorded. Attest: John Lee Junr clerk. (Pg 161)

13 Sep 1762. Bill of Sale. I Godfrey Young of Essex Co for & in consideration of Smith Young's becoming security for my appearance to last court to a suit brought by John Humphrys in an action of debt for 12 pd 2 sl 6 pn agt me also for my

appearance to a suit brought by Archibald Ritchie in an action of trespass on the case damage 50 pd do sell to the sd Smith Young two Negroes, to wit, Judy & Nan ... . Wit: W. Young, Elizabeth Young. Proved 21 Feb 1763 & recorded. Attest: John Lee Junr clerk. (Pg 162)

1 Sep 1762. Deed of Mortgage. Reubin Noel of Essex Co planter for 30 pd sold to Francis Waring of same co gent a 190 a. tr of land whereon the sd Reubin now dwells bounded by Thos Andrews, the dower land of Mary Andrews, Popoman Swamp & Samuel Noel ... if the sd Reubin Noel shall truly pay unto the sd Francis Waring 30 pd with interest before the expiration of 5 years together with all costs & charges that the sd Francis Waring shall be put to by means of these presents then this present indenture to cease & be void ... . Wit: Robt Payne Waring, Thomas Waring, William Waring. Ackn 21 Feb 1763 & recorded. Attest: John Lee Junr clerk. (Pg 162)

6 Dec 1762. Deed. John Smith of South Farnham Parish, Essex Co for 100 pd sold to John Smith Junr all his estate right title intrest claim & demand whatsoever to a 150 a. persel of land in the sd parish bounded by John Fargeson, Thos Barker, Blew Spring Br, Main Pocoson, Amerkd Line, Latney's Line & Hugh Wilson ... . Wit: Alexr Miles, John Burnett, Thos Pamplin, Jonathan Radford. Proved 21 Feb 1763 & recorded. Attest: John Lee Junr clerk. (Pg 164)

30 Jul 1762. Deed. William Norvell (Norvel) of Sussex Co, VA for 11 pd sold to Thomas Dix of Essex Co planter a tr of land whereon the sd William Norvell formerly lived on the Main Br of Piscataway Cr adj Latane Allen & the afsd Dix, the sd lands having formerly descended to his late wife Sarah (who was the dau of James Fullerton) from her brother James Fullerton decd ... . Wit: Joseph Gatewood Junr, Nathaniel Garnett, Thomas Wright, Sam Davis. Proved 21 Feb 1763 & recorded. Attest: John Lee Junr clerk. (Pg 166)

13 Dec 1762. Deed of Mortgage. John Chamberlain late of NC at present of Essex Co, VA for 218 pd 7 sl 10 pn sold to Joseph McWilliams of Essex Co six slaves, viz, George, Jenny, Rachel, Young Rachel, Nan & Isack together with their future increase ... provided that if the sd John Chamberlain shall pay unto the sd Joseph McWilliams the sd sum on or before 25 Dec 1764 with interest then these presents shall cease & be void ... . Wit: Joseph Mann Junr, John Emerson, Jacob Houce, William McWilliams. Proved 21 Feb 1762 & recorded. Attest: John Lee Junr clerk. (Pg 167)

20 Jan 1763. Articles of Agreement between John Deans merchant of the Town of Tappa & Robert Brooke of Saint Anne Parish each of Essex Co are in substance & order for following, viz, the sd Robert Brooke doth agree to lett to the sd John Deans for the term of 13 years already commenced from 1st day of this present

month a tr of land & houses near the Town of Tappa together with four slaves
named Cooper, Newman, Will & Jenny now the property of William Brooke an
orphan ward to the sd Robert Brooke ... the slaves are not to be treated with
inhuman or barbarous treatment as might sometime happen from the misguided
fury & conduct of an ill overseer ... if the sd John Deans should at any time leave
this colony and go to Great Britain he may deliver up the sd plantation & slaves to
the sd Robert Brooke for the remainder of the term afsd to any other person
provided it be with the sd Robert's or their approbation ... . Wit: Andrew
Crauford, Andr Baillie, Neele McCoull. Proved 21 Feb 1763 & recorded. Attest:
John Lee Junr clerk. (Pg 169)

8 Feb 1763. Deed. Samuel Cross & Ann his wife of Essex Co for 35 pd sold to
Joseph Noel of same co a 50 a. tr of land whereon the sd Joseph Noel now lives in
Saint Anns Parish on the e side of a br that runneth between the house where I now
live & the sd Noel's house bounded by land of Richard Hill, John Smither,
William Upshaw decd & land whereon Elizabeth Smither now lives ... . Wit:
Reuben Noell, Thomas Farmer, James Hambleton, Richard Hambleton. Ackn 21
Feb 1763 by Samuel Cross & Ann his wife (she being first privily examined &
assenting thereto) & recorded. Attest: John Lee Junr clerk. (Pg 170)

15 Jan 1762. Deed. John Lataone of Essex Co gent for 20 sl sold to William
Roane of same co gent 1 a. of land on the Main Br of Piscataway Cr near Pickets
Bridge ... . Wit: George Wright, Joseph Ryland, Richd Brown, Thomas Wright.
Ackn 21 Feb 1763 & recorded. Attest: John Lee Junr clerk. (Pg 172)

6 Feb 1763. Deed. John Garnett Junr of Essex Co & Mary his wife for 26 pd sold
to James Upshaw of same co a 10 a. 42 1/2 perches tr of land with a water grist
mill thereto adj it being the land & mill purch by the sd John Garnett of John Lee
& Mary his wife which sd land are situate 1 a. on the n side of the sd mill & 9 a. 42
1/2 perches on the s side of Gilsons Run or Swamp adj to the sd mill ... . Wit:
Thos Upshaw, Wm Fogg, Thos Streshly. Ackn by John Garnett Junr & admitted
to record. Attest: John Lee Junr clerk. (Pg 173)

3 Mar 1763. To John Upshaw & John Lee of Essex Co gent greeting, whereas
John Garnett Junr of sd co & Mary his wife have by their deed [see above] sold
unto James Upshaw of same co a water grist mill & 10 a. 42 1/2 perches of land,
and whereas the sd Mary is unable to travel to our co court to make
acknowledgment thereof, therefore we command you to repair to the sd Mary &
her privily & apart from her husband examine touching the premises, & whether
she is willing the sd deed & her acknowledgment may be recorded ... . 16 Mar
1763 By virtue of the within dedimus to us directed, we John Upshaw & John Lee
in obedience thereto did go to the sd Mary & hath examin'd touching & concerning
her right & dower in the premises who sd she did voluntarily & freeley relinquish

all her right to the same. At a court held 21 Mar 1763 this commission & the commissioners return were presented & ordered to be recorded. Attest: John Lee Junr clerk. (Pg 174)

7 Jan 1763. Deed. Mark Boler (Boulware) & Elizabeth his wife now of Essex Co for 30 pd sold to Thomas Gouldman of same co a 35 a. tr of land whereon Susanah Shepard now lives in St. Anns Parish adj John Biddlecom, James Adkinson & sd Thos Gouldman .... Wit: Robt Parker Junr, John Adkinson, Edward Carter, John Tucker. Proved 21 Mar 1763 & recorded. Attest: John Lee Junr clerk. (Pg 175)

17 Feb 1763. Deed. George Clayton of Hanover Co planter & Delphia his wife for 625 pd sold to Nicholas Flood physician of Richmond Co, VA a 300 a. tr of land in South Farnham Parish on the e side of Piscataway Cr bounded by Haraway Owens, Green Spring Br, the road that leads to Lourys Ferry & Jno Robinson esqr .... Wit: R. Tunstall, Geo Brooke, Robert Brooking, William Todd, John Semple. Proved 21 Mar 1763 & recorded. Attest: John Lee Junr clerk. (Pg 176)

16 Feb 1763. To Richard Johnson, John Syme, Saml Gist & John Merriwether of Hanover Co gent greeting, whereas George Clayton of Hanover Co & Delphia his wife have by their deed of sale [see above] a 300 a. parcel of land, & whereas the sd Delphia is unable to travel to our co court to make acknowledgment thereof, therefore we command you to repair to the sd Delphia & that privily & apart from her husband you take such acknowledgment as she shall be willing to make touching the premises .... 9 Mar 1763 In obedience to the within writ we Richard Johnson & John Meriwether gent justices of the peace for Essex Co did repair to the within named Delphia & examined her privily & apart from her sd husband & do certify that she ackn the sd deed freely & willingly .... At a court held 21 Mar 1763 this commission & the commissioners return was presented & recorded. Attest: John Lee Junr clerk. (Pg 179)

21 Dec 1762. Deed of Lease. Frances Thorp of Essex Co for the rents covenants & agreements hereafter mentioned have farm letten unto Thomas Thorp all the late dwelling houses & plantation & land adj of the late Thomas Thorp of Essex Co decd for the life of the sd Frances Thorp paying yearly 25 pd on 21 Dec in every year during the life of the sd Frances Thorp, & if it shall happen that the sd yearly rent of 25 pd be unpaid by the space of 90 days after lawfully demanded that then & thenceforth it shall & may be lawfull to & for the sd Frances Thorp upon the sd demised premises to reenter & the same to have a gain reposess & injoy as her estate & the sd Thomas Thorp & every other occupier of the sd demised premises from thence utterly to expell remove & put out .... Wit: Thos Goode, William Ayres, Thomas Ayres. Proved 21 Mar 1763 & recorded. Attest: John Lee Junr clerk. (Pg 180)

19 Dec 1762. Deed. William Fauntleroy of Richmond Co gent & Peggy his wife for 1100 pd sold to Joseph Stevens of the Town of Tappahannock in Essex Co eight lots or 1/2 acres of land with the several messuages thereon in the Town of Tappahannock numbers 17, 18, 21, 22, 25, 26, 29 & 30, the four first mentioned being the square whereon the sd Joseph now lives & fronting the Main Street of the sd town & the Publick Square and the last mentioned four lots being the square whereon the stables of the sd Joseph now stand, which sd eight lots were purch by the sd William Fauntleroy of James Mills gent late of sd town ... . Wit: Chs Mortimer, Jno Brokenbrough, Jas Crane, Richard Stevens. Proved 23 Feb 1763 & ordered to be certified. Proved 23 Mar 1763 & recorded. Attest: John Lee Junr clerk. (Pg 181)

17 Mar 1763. Deed of Gift. Winifred Gouldman of Essex Co for love good will & tender effection & 5 sl hath given to her son Edward Gouldman of same co that 150 a. tr of land & plantation that James Garnett lately hath given her by deed for it being the land & plantation that she now lives on bounded by Robert Parker Junr, Elizabeth Donoho, Cornelias Noel, Elizabeth Ramsey & the Main Stream of Occupation Swamp ... . Wit: Richard Gouldman, Thomas Harves, John Covington. Proved 18 Apr 1763 & recorded. Attest: John Lee Junr clerk. (Pg 184)

23 Feb 1763. Deed. William Booth & Elizabeth his wife and Anne Washington widow of Westmoreland Co for 70 pd sold to Richard Hodges of Essex Co a 200 a. tr of land in South Farnham Parish, the sd land being pt/o a devidend formerly taken up by Joseph Goodrich, William Ball & John Price & binding on the lands of John Lightfoot & Edward Chilton, called by the name of Mountmaple, the sd land being sold & convey'd to the sd Joseph Goodrich by deed dated 2 Feb 1691 by John Clark then of Rappahannock Co & afterwards became vested in Benjamin Goodrich by Act of Law as heir to the sd Joseph Goodrich who conveyed the same by deed dated 8 Dec 1703 to William Aylett & was by the sd William Aylett devised to his son William Aylett father to the sd Elizabeth & Anne parties to these presents who inherit the same as coheirs to the last mentioned William Aylett ... . Wit: LeRoy Hipkins, Richard Lee, John August. Washington, Thomas Fargeson, John Herndon. Proved 18 Apr 1763 & ordered to be certified. Fully proved 16 May 1763 & recorded. Attest: John Lee Junr clerk. (Pg 185)

24 Mar 1763. Indenture Tripartite made between John Hammond of Essex Co of the first part, Anne Tyler of Amelia Co widow & James Turner of Essex Co of the second part & Grisel Smith of Essex Co widow of the third part, whereas the sd John Hammond was seised of a conveyance from the executors of John Tyler decd of & in three undivided fourth parts of a water grist mill subject to the dower of the afsd Anne Tyler widow of the sd John Tyler & being so seised the sd John Hammond did agree to sell the sd 3/4 parts to Benjamin Smith late husband of the

sd Grisel who died before a conveyance thereof was made to him & devised his interest in the sd mill to his sd wife Grizel Smith, and the sd Anne Tyler having sold her dower in the sd 3/4 parts to the afsd James Turner & received the consideration for the same but executed no conveyance to the sd James Turner had sold his sd interest to the sd Grizel Smith. Now this indenture for 66 pd which the sd John Hammond ackns to have received of the sd Benjamin Smith in his lifetime & 15 pd by the sd Grizel in hand paid to the sd James Turner who had before paid the like sum to the sd Anne Tyler, which the several sums of money the sd partys do hereby respectively ackn they the sd John Hammond, Anne Tyler (by the direction & appointment of the sd James Turner testified by his being party to these presents) and the sd James Turner have sold unto the sd Grisel Smith all their several & respective estate right & interest to the sd three undivided fourth pts/o the sd water grist mill ... . Wit: James Lang, Pitm Clements, Luke Covington, Thos Turner, Wm Howerton. Ackn 18 Apr 1763 by John Hammond & Ann his wife (she being first privily examined & assenting thereto) & ackn by James Turner & admitted to record. Attest: John Lee Junr clerk. (Pg 187)

16 May 1763. Bond. James Webb, James Webb Junr, William Young & John Lee Junr of Essex Co are firmly bound unto Francis Waring, Simon Miller, John Clements, William Mountague & Samuel Peachey gent justices of Essex Co for 40,000 lbs of tobacco ... whereas the afsd James Webb is appointed collector of the co levy for this present year now the condition of this obligation is such that if the sd James Webb shall well & truly collect the sd levy & pay to the several claimants their respective claims then this obligation to be void ... . Wit: None. Ackn 16 May 1763 & recorded. Attest: John Lee Junr clerk. (Pg 188)

16 May 1763. Deed. Ambrose Jeffries of King & Queen Co & Rachel his wife for 123 pd 15 sl sold to Richard Fisher of Essex Co a parcel of land bounded by William Cole, Isaiah Cole, Greenwood's land, Covington's corner & land of John Cole decd, which land the sd Ambrose Jeffries lately purch of Robert Cole & Frankey his wife ... . Wit: Richard Jeffries, Andrew Allen, W. Young. Ackn 16 May 1763 by Ambrose Jeffries & Rachel his wife (she being first privily examined & assenting) & admitted to record. Attest: John Lee Junr clerk. (Pg 189)

4 Oct 1762. Deed. Abraham Mountague of South Farnham Parish, Essex Co & Lewis Mountague of Christ Church Parish, Middlesex Co for 137 pd sold to Thomas Watts of South Farnham Parish, Essex Co a parcel of land the bounds thereof agreeing with the same that was purch by Abraham Mountague gent decd their father except a piece of that sd tr of land on the w side of the Main Road which was sold to James Medley Junr since the death of Abraham Mountague which is bounded on the road containing 370 a. which sd parcel of land was given to Abraham Mountague by his father Abraham Mountague decd in his will & Lewis Mountague eldest son & heir to the sd Abraham Mountague decd claims the

reversion in fee of the sd land after the death of his sd brother & by virtue of this deed the sd Lewis Mountague doth willingly relinquish all manner of right & title to the sd premises ... . Wit: James Medley, Titus Farguson, Betty Watts, Saml Hoskins, Mary Hemingway, Mary Hoskins. Proved 18 Apr 1763 & ordered to be certified. Ackn 16 May 1763 & admitted to record. Attest: John Lee Junr clerk. (Pg 191)

17 May 1763. Deed. Edmund Mitchell of South Farnham Parish, Essex Co & Dorothy his wife for 15 pd sold to Henry Cauthorn of same place a 10 a. parcel of land in the sd parish bounded by William Young, John Richards, sd Henry Cauthorn & the main County Road ... . Wit: John Vass, Alexr Saunders, John Segar, W. Young. Ackn 17 May 1763 by Edmund Mitchell & Dorothy his wife (she being first privily examined & assenting thereto) & recorded. Attest: John Lee Junr clerk. (Pg 194)

17 May 1763. Deed. Richard Fisher & Ann his wife of South Farnham Parish, Essex Co for 40 pd sold to Rhodes Greenwood of same place a 34 a. tr of land bounded by land of William Cole Senr, Isaak Cole & the sd Rhodes Greenwood ... . Wit: Robert Read, William Greenwood, George Newbill. Ackn 20 Jun 1763 by Richard Fisher & Ann his wife (she being first privily examined & assenting thereto) & admitted to record. Attest: John Lee Junr clerk. (Pg 195)

23 Dec 1762. Deed. Richard Hodges & Betty his wife of South Farnham Parish, Essex Co for 400 pd sold to Joseph Burnett of same place all their right in & to a 400 a. parcell of land in the sd parrish bounded by Samuel Fawcett, George Wright, Western Br, Thomas Croxton, Ambrose Wright, Richard Jones & Darbys Br ... . Wit: Thos Barker, John Farguson, Josiah Minter, Leonard Burnett. Ackn 20 Jun 1763 by Richard Hodges & admitted to record. (Pg 197)

14 Jun 1763. Deed. Francis Jones of Soath Farnom (sic) Parish, Essex Co for 27 pd 10 sl sold to William Williamson of same place an 85 a. tr of land in the sd parish bounded by the Mill Dam formerly called Capt Covington's which now is Capt Webb's, Byrom's lands, the Gleabe Swamp, Mary Broock, Tribit's land, Hardy's land & Megg's land, the sd land was purch by the afsd Jones of the afsd Clark (sic) & John Hardy which the lands of Megg's was mortgaged to the Ritchie's ... . Wit: John Williamson Junr, Richd Brown, John Byrom. Memorandum: That on 14 Jun 1763 possession of the land & premises within mentioned was giving & deliver'd by Francis Mary Royal Jones by turf & twigg percel thereof in lieu of the whole to the sd Wm Williamson ... . Ackn 20 Jun 1763 by Francis Jones & recorded. Attest: John Lee Junr clerk. (Pg 199)

XX Jun 1763. Deed. Samuel Fawcett & Isabell his wife of Essex Co house carpenter for 45 pd sold to William Johnson (Johnston) of same place chaise maker

a 50 a. tr of land in South Farnham Parish adj William Roane & James Allen ... .
Wit: None. Ackn 20 Jun 1768 by Samuel Fawcett & Isbel his wife (she being first
privily examined & assenting thereto) & recorded. Attest: John Lee Junr clerk.
(Pg 201)

19 Jan 1763. Deed. James Mills of Essex Co gent for 20 pd sold to Archibald
Ritchie merchant of same co one lot in the Town of Tappahannock numbered 79
according to the plan of sd town together with the houses ... . Wit: Wm
Daingerfield Junr, Samuel Hipkins Junr, Chs Mortimer. Proved 22 Jun 1763 &
ordered to be certified. Fully proved 18 Jul 1763 & recorded. Attest: John Lee
Junr clerk. (Pg 202)

24 Feb 1763. Deed of Mortgage. Godfry Young of Essex Co planter for 400 pd
sold to William Snodgrass of same co merchant a parcel of land bounded by the
estate of Richd Gatewood land, John Webb, John Mitchell & Mrs. Evans ...
provided that if the sd Godfry Young shall well & truly pay unto the sd William
Snodgrass the afsd 400 pd before 1 Mar next ensuing together with interest (this to
be void) ... . Wit: Robert Maxwell, Will Waddrop, Archibald McCall, Rob Reid.
Proved 18 Jul 1768 & recorded. Attest: John Lee Junr clerk. (Pg 205)

13 Mar 1762. To Thomas Roane, John Upshaw & John Lee of Essex Co gent,
whereas John Garnet & Mary his wife of Essex Co by their deed of feofmt dated 4
Feb 1762 have conveyed unto Frans Graves of same co 48 a. of land in St. Anns
Parish, & whereas the sd Mary is unable to travel to our sd co court to make
acknowledgment thereof, therefore we command you to repair to the sd Mary &
that you privily & apart from her sd husband take such acknowledgment as the sd
Mary shall be willing to make. 29 Jan 1763 By virtue of this commission to us
directed we Thomas Roane, John Upshaw & John Lee have examined Mary w/o
the sd John Garnett Junr privily & apart from her sd husband & she acknowledges
the deed & that she is willing that the sd deed be recorded. At a court held 15 Aug
1763 this commission & the commissioners return thereon endorsed were returned
& ordered to be recorded. Attest: John Lee Junr clerk. (Pg 207)

15 Aug 1763. Deed. Elizabeth Sadler of (St. Anns?) Parish, Chesterfield, VA for
60 pd sold to Isaac Haws of St. Anns Parish, Essex Co a 50 a. tr of land in Saint
Anns Parish on the s side of Occupatia Main Swamp ... . Wit: John Lee Junr,
Owen Carter, Caleb Hines, Wm Webb. Ackn 15 Aug 1763 & recorded. Attest:
John Lee Junr clerk. (Pg 208)

18 Feb 1763. Deed. James Garnett of Essex Co for all her right of dower in
sundry trs of land mentioned in a certain deed made by Francis Gouldman &
Winefred his wife sold unto the sd Winefred Gouldman all his right of in or to all
that tr of land whereon the sd Winefred Gouldman now dwells being 150 a.

bounded by Robt Parker, Elisabeth Donoho, Cornelias Noel & the Main Run of
Occupatia, the land being purch by the sd Garnett of Young Hawkins & Augt
Ramsey ... . Wit: Thomas Gouldman, Richard Gouldman, Thos Haws. Proved 18
Jul 1763 & ordered to be certified. Fully proved 15 Aug 1763 & recorded. Attest:
John Lee Junr clerk. (Pg 210)

14 Jan ----. Deed. John Thomas & Keziah his wife of Essex Co for 30 pd sold to
David Pitts of same co a 100 a. tr of land being that land that the sd John Thomas
purch of Chesley French Boulware bounded by James Atkinson, Mark Boulware
decd, the land (of) Norvin (in) the possession of Esther Landram & the afsd David
Pitts ... . Wit: Thomas Pitts, David Sullivan, Thomas Sullivan, Lunsphard Pitts.
Ackn 15 Aug 1763 & recorded. Attest: John Lee Junr clerk. (Pg 211)

4 Aug 1763. To Simon Miller & Paul Micou of Essex Co gent greeting, whereas
John Thomas of Essex Co & Keziah his wife have by their deed [see above]
conveyed unto David Pitts of sd co a 100 a. tr of land, & whereas the sd Keziah is
unable to travel to our co court to make acknowledgment thereof, therefore we
command you to repair to the sd Keziah & that privily & apart from her husband
you take such acknowledgment as she shall be willing to make. 14 Jan 1763 In
obedience to the within order we Simon Miller & Paul Micou have apart from her
husband examined Keziah Thomas who declares that she freely acknowledges her
right of dower of the sd land. At a court held 15 Aug 1763 this commission & the
commissioners return thereon endorsed were returned & ordered to be recorded.
Attest: John Lee Junr clerk. (Pg 213)

30 Dec 1762. Deed. Thomas Pamplin of South Farnham Parish, Essex Co hath
given & granted unto Thomas Roane of same place a messuage & 180 a. tr of land
divised him by his decd father Nicholas Pamplin in the sd parish bounded by
Henry Purkins Taylor, James Pamplin, sd Thos Roane, South Swamp of Hoskins's
Cr & Upshaw's land ... in exchange for 180 a. of that messuage of land divised the
sd Thomas Roane by his father William Roane gent decd in the sd parish on some
of the brs of Piscataway Cr bounded by the sd Roane's land, Mrs. Brown, Jacob
Sherwood, Middle Br, corner of Croxton, Boughan & Brown & Brown's Spring ...
for which consideration the sd Thomas Roane hath given & granted unto the sd
Thomas Pamplin all the sd messuage last above mentioned ... . Wit: LeRoy
Hipkins, Samuel Hipkins Junr, John Hipkins. Ackn by the parties 15 Aug 1763 &
recorded. Attest: John Lee Junr clerk. (Pg 214)

1 Jan 1763. Deed. Thomas Pamplin of South Farnham Parish, Essex Co for 60 pd
sold to Thomas Roane of same place a messuage & plantation tr of land in the afsd
parish containing 180 a. being the tr of land which the sd Thomas Pamplin lately
had in exchange of the sd Thomas Roane for another tr of land of the like quantity
[see above] bounded by sd Roane's land, Mrs. Brown, Jacob Sherewood, br of

Piscataway Cr, Middle Br, corner of Croxton, Boughan & Brown & Brown's
Spring Br ... . Wit: LeRoy Hipkins, Samuel Hipkins Junr, John Hipkins. Ackn 15
Aug 1763 & recorded. Attest: John Lee Junr clerk. (Pg 216)

16 Aug 1763. Deed. William Roane & Betty his wife of South Farnham Parish,
Essex Co for 550 pd sold to John Upshaw of same place a messuage & tr of land
part in King & Queen Co & part in Essex Co & is pt/o Braxton's or Mount Maple
Tract & containes 791 a. bounded by corner to Moody & Baylor, Moody's Path, br
of Piscataway new McCouter's old Quarter, a beach marked "RB", Piscataway
Run, Mare Br, Holt's Br near Broacke's House, Piney Bottom & Poultry Run ... .
Wit: None. Ackn 16 Aug 1763 by William Roane gent & Betty his wife (she
being first privily examined & assenting thereto) & recorded. Attest: John Lee
Junr clerk. (Pg 218)

19 Sep 1763. Deed. Richard Holt Senr & Mary his wife of King & Queen Co for
35 pd 14 sl 4 pn 1/2 penny sold to Francis Graves of Essex Co a 47 1/2 a. tr of land
in South Farnham Parish bounded by John Hill, sd Graves, Wm Watkins & Jetsons
Cr, being the land which the sd Richard Holt purch of Robert Holt & Eliza his wife
by deed dated 20 Jul 1743 ... . Wit: George Cordell, John Bezlee, Jas Evans,
Mary Davis. Ackn 19 Sep 1763 & recorded. Attest: John Lee Junr clerk. (Pg
220)

5 May 1763. Deed of Mortgage. Henry Purkins Taylor of Essex Co planter for 28
pd 17 sl sold to James Ritchie & Company of Glasgow in North Brittain merchants
three feather beds with furniture, two cows & calves, one cow & two yearlings,
one mare, three sows & three barroes ... provided that if the sd Henry Purkins
Taylor shall pay to the sd James Ritchie & Company the sd sum with interest then
this indenture to be void ... . Wit: Robt Fergusson, Andrew Crawford, Neil
McCoull. Proved 19 Sep 1763 & recorded. Attest: John Lee Junr clerk. (Pg 222)

20 May 1763. Deed of Mortgage. John Gatewood Senr of Essex Co planter for 36
pd 1 sl 9 pn sold to James Ritchie & Company of Glasgow in North Briton
merchants one Negro fellow named Isaac also 50 a. of land whereon the sd John
Gatewood now lives ... provided that if the sd John Gatewood shall pay unto the sd
James Ritchie & Company the sd sum with interest then this indenture to be void
... . Wit: Andrew Crauford, Robt Fergusson, Neil McCoull. Proved 19 Sep 1763
& recorded. Attest: John Lee Junr clerk. (Pg 223)

22 Mar 1763. Deed of Mortgage. John Sears of Essex Co planter for 242 pd 6 sl
(now due to James Ritchie & Company) sold to the sd James Ritchie & Company
of Glasgow in North Brittain merchants sundrie Negroes, viz, Kitt, Ben, Adam,
Betty, Milley & Condo ... provided that if the sd John Sears shall pay to the sd
James Ritchie & Company the sd sum with interest then this indenture to be void

... . Wit: Neil McCoull, Andrew Crauford, Robt Ferguson. Proved 19 Sep 1763 & recorded. Attest: John Lee Junr clerk. (Pg 224)

12 Mar 1763. Deed. Jeremiah Moodie of Essex Co planter for 29 pd 5 sl 2 pn sold to James Ritchie & Company of Glasgow in North Brittain merchants one mare, two horses, one colt, five head of cattle, 10 head of hogs & three feather beds ... provided that if the sd Jeremiah Moodie shall pay to the sd James Ritchie & Company the afsd sum with interest then this indenture to be void ... . Wit: Andrew Crauford, Neil McCoull. Proved 19 Sep 1763 & recorded. Attest: John Lee Junr clerk. (Pg 225)

26 Mar 1763. Deed. James Bell of Caroline Co for 45 pd sold to Samuel Fossett of South Farnham Parish, Essex Co all his right of a 50 a. parcel of land in the sd parish bounded by land that was formerly Thomas Gatewood's now in the possession of William Roane & the land of James Allen ... . Wit: John Taylar, Thomas Meador, W. Ramsay, Samuel Hipkins Junr, Pitm Clements. Memo: On 21 Mar 1763 possession & seizin of the land & premises was delivered & given by the within named James Bell & Frances his wife by turff & twig. Proved 20 Sep 1763 & ordered to be certified & fully proved 21 Sep 1763 & recorded. Attest: John Lee Junr clerk. (Pg 226)

20 Jul 1763. To Archibald Ritchie & Charles Mortimer of Richmond Co gent greeting, whereas William Fauntleroy & Peggy his wife of Richmond Co gent have on 13 Dec last past sold & conveyed to Jos Stevens of the Town of Tappahannock, Essex Co the fee simple estate of eight lots or 1/2 acres of land in the sd town, and the sd Peggy being unable to attend our court of Essex Co to make such acknowledgment as is required we have given you power to take the acknowledgment which the sd Peggy shall be willing to make. 12 Sep 1763 Pursuant to the within writt to us directed we have examined Peggy Fauntleroy she voluntarily gives up all right & title she now has or might hereafter have to the within mentioned lotts to Joseph Stevans. At a court held 19 Sep 1763 this commission & the commissioners return thereon endorsed were returned & ordered to be recorded. Attest: John Lee Junr clerk. (Pg 227)

13 Oct 1763. Deed of Gift. I Thomas Coghill of Caroline Co for natural love & affection have given to my son Thomas Coghill Junr of Essex Co all my right & title of a certain 150 a. tr of land it being the same that the sd Thomas Coghill Junr now lives on adj the land of Ambrose Hord & Frederick Coghill ... . Wit: John Penn, William Ayres, James Anderson, Thos Bridgforth. Proved 17 Oct 1763 & recorded. Attest: John Lee Junr clerk. (Pg 228)

17 Oct 1763. Deed. William Ayres of St. Anns Parish, Essex Co for 34 pd sold to Thomas Coghill of same place a 34 a. tr of land being pt/o a tr of land which

William Ayres lately purch of Richard Pemberton in St. Anns Parish bounded by Hord's line, Gum Swamp, Edward Murrah & sd Coghill's land ... . Wit: None. Ackn 17 Oct 1763 & admitted to record. Attest: John Lee Junr clerk. (Pg 229)

8 Oct 1763. Deed. Ambrose Hord & Mary his wife of Caroline Co for 80 pd sold to Thomas Cooper Dickenson of sd co 100 a. of land on Gum Swamp adj the lands of Thomas Coghill, William Ayres & Paul Scott decd which sd 100 a. of land having been escheated by Thomas Hord the elder & patented in the name of John Hord decd ... . Wit: Owen Carter, Thos Ayres, Thos Coghill Junr, John Melear. Proved 17 Oct 1763 & recorded. Attest: John Lee Junr clerk. (Pg 230)

8 Oct 1763. Deed. William Fretwell & Mary his wife of South Farnham Parish, Essex Co for 50 pd sold to Richard Hodges of same place all their estate right to a 100 a. parcel of land in the sd parish it being all that parcel of land as the sd William Fretwell purch of Thomas Younger 19 Sep 1749 bounded by Samuel Croxton, Thomas Miller, Ambrose Wright & place formerly called Reffields Old Field in James Booker's line ... . Wit: Thos Barker, John Croxton, Samll Croxton. Ackn 17 Oct 1763 by William Fretwell & Mary his wife (she being first privily examined & assenting thereto) & recorded. Attest: John Lee Junr clerk. (Pg 232)

11 Oct 1763. Deed. Whereas Thomas Gressom of Amhurst Co not having oppertunity of settling his affairs in VA hath thought fit & by these presents doth appoint his trusty friend John Merritt (Merrett) of South Farnham Parish, Essex Co his atty to sell & dispose of any of his effects in the afsd colony perticular in Essex Co & impower the sd Merritt to use & act all such thing or things as shall be necessary in the law towards the recovering a piece of land in Essex Co & do further impower him to sell, mortgage, rent, lease all other lands & premises in Essex Co & all other estate rite title belonging to the afsd Thomas Gressom to any person whatsoever ... . Wit: Vincent Vass, James Wetherspoon, Thos Herbert. Proved 17 Oct 1763 & recorded. Attest: John Lee Junr clerk. (Pg 233)

18 Apr 1763. Deed. John Clements gent of South Farnham Parish, Essex Co for 35 pd sold to Jonathan Radford planter of same place a 44 a. tr of land in the sd parish being the land the sd Radford lately occupy'd & bounded between Jacob Sheerwood, Capt Thomas Roane & the line of Boughan's ... . Wit: And Baillie, James Lang, Jno Webb. Ackn 17 Oct 1763 & recorded. Attest: John Lee Junr clerk. (Pg 234)

17 Oct 1763. Deed. William Roane & Betty his wife of Essex Co for 76 pd 15 sl sold to Joseph Ryland of same co a messuage & tr of land adj the lands of Morris Broach & is pt/o Braxton's Mount Maple Tract containing 153 1/2 a. bounded by the spring of Morris Broach, the main run of Piscataway & the sd Joseph Ryland ... . Wit: None. Ackn 17 Oct 1763 by William Roane & Betty his wife (she being

first privily examined & assenting thereto) & recorded. Attest: John Lee Junr clerk. (Pg 235)

10 Nov 1763. Deed of Gift. I John Andrews of Essex Co for natural affection give unto my brother Thomas Andrews of same co two Negroes now in the possession of Edward Gouldman, viz, Sarah a Negro woman & Frank a Negro girl & their future increase ... . Wit: John Lee Junr, Richd Hipkins. Proved 21 Nov 1763 & recorded. Attest: John Lee Junr clerk. (Pg 237)

23 Apr 1763. Power of Attorney. William Watson of St. George Parish, Middlesex Co slopseller legatee of the will of Ninion Boog late of VA merchant have appointed Robert Watson master of the Good ship Charming Molley bound to VA my atty for my use & also for my sister Jennet Campbell for her use (I being by her emplower'd so to do being her atty) to ask demand & receive of & from the Reverend Mr. Robert Innys (Inneys) of Drysdale Parish, King & Queen Co, VA executor of the will of Ninion Boog afsd all such effects sums of money as are now due to me by virtue of the will of Ninion Boog afsd & also to ask demand & receive of & from the sd Robert Innys all such effects sums of money as are due to my sd sister by virtue of the sd will ... . Wit: Thomas Dilworth noty publ in Wapping. William Fox, Robert Dickie, Daniel Hawthorn. Proved 21 Nov 1763 & recorded. Attest: John Lee Junr clerk. (Pg 238)

3 Aug 1763. Deed of Gift. Samuel Hipkins gent of St. Anns Parish, Essex Co for natural love & affection have given to my son Leroy Hipkins of South Farnham Parish, co afsd the following slaves, to wit, Jenny & her child Julius, Charles & Sawney ... it's agreed by the parties that the afsd slaves are worth 300 pd ... . Wit: Richd Hipkins, Luke Covington. Proved 21 Nov 1763 & recorded. Attest: John Lee Junr clerk. (Pg 239)

5 Oct 1763. Deed. Whereas there is a marriage already agreed upon by Gods Grace shortly to be had & solemnized between William Sears of Gloucester Co & Sarah Waggoner Sears dau of Elizabeth Waggoner Junr of Essex Co & whereas the sd William Sears on the consummation of the sd marriage will be entitled to the possession of sundry slaves named Gloucester, Sarah, Darrie, Esther, Ange, Pender & Judy, the sole property of the sd Sarah Wagonner Sears & for the great good will love & affection that the sd William hath & beareth to the sd Sarah & to the intent that the sd slaves before mentioned with all their increase shall be & continue on the issue of them the sd William & Sarah in such manner & form as hereafter are expressed & declared, it is fully agreed between the sd parties to these presents that he the sd William Sears for consideration afsd doth promise for himself & his heirs to & with the sd Elizabeth Waggoner Junr that the sd Sarah shall have the free liberty to dispose of 1/2 of the sd slaves & their increase by her will or otherwise as she pleaseth & the other 1/2 of the slaves & all their increase

to the issue of them the sd William & Sarah lawfully begotten of their bodies & if no such issue should proceed by the sd marriage then all the sd slaves to revert & return to the sd Sarah to be disposed of as she pleaseth ... . Wit: Reuben Waggener, Sophi Aggener, Elizabeth Waggener. Proved 21 Nov 1763 & recorded. Attest: John Lee Junr clerk. (Pg 239)

21 Aug 1763. Bill of Sale. Robert Brooke for 152 pd rec'd of the estate of Wm Fauntleroy of Richmond Co gent decd have sold to William Fauntleroy, More Fauntleroy & John Fauntleroy gent exrs of the will of Wm Fauntleroy decd two female slaves named Pender & Dinah together with all their future increase ... to the use & behoof of Robin Brooke son of the afsd Robert Brooke to be & remain to him & his heirs forever, & the consideration is in compliance with & full discharge of 1/7 pt/o the personal estate of the sd William Fauntleroy gent decd that by his will was directed to be laid out in female slaves for the use of the sd Robin Brooke. Ackn 21 Nov 1763 & recorded. Attest: John Lee Junr clerk. (Pg 241)

17 Mar 1763. Bond. I Edward Gouldman of Essex Co am firmly bound unto my mother Winifred Gouldman of sd co in the penal sum of 500 pd ... the condition of this obligation is such whereas the sd Winifred Gouldman hath this day given her afsd son Edward Gouldman deeds of gift for the land & plantation whereon she now lives & it is agreed on by both afsd parties that the sd Edward Gouldman should have no liberty or profet of sd land so long as his mother lives but let her live quietly & peaceably thereon during her life, now if the afsd Edward Gouldman doth quit any claim to the sd land during the life of the afsd Winifred Gouldman then this obligation to be void ... . Wit: Richard Gouldman, Thomas Hawes, John Covington. Proved 21 Nov 1763 & recorded. Attest: John Lee Junr clerk. (Pg 241)

8 Jul 1763. Deed of Mortgage. Henry Gardner of South Farnham Parish, Essex Co for 29 pd 3 sl sold to John Webb, James Campbell & James Edmondson of same place a messuage & 100 a. tr of land the sd Henry Gardner purch of Col Frans Smith late of this co bounded by the land of Evans' & land of Brookes' in the sd parish during the term of 500 years next & immediately ensuing paying yearly during the sd term one peper corn in & upon the 1st of Jan if the same be demanded provided upon condition that if the sd Henry Garner shall well & truly pay unto the afsd John Webb, James Campbell & James Edmondson 29 pd 3 sl with interest upon 10 Jul next ensuing then these presents shall cease & be voide ... . Wit: John Edmondson Junr, Charles Adams, Frances Adams. Ackn 19 Dec 1763 & recorded. Attest: John Lee Junr clerk. (Pg 242)

13 Dec 1763. Bond. James Webb gent sheriff, John Edmondson & Luke Covington are firmly bound unto our Sovereign Lord the King for 1,000 pd ... the

condition of this obligation is such that if the afsd James Webb shall well & truly collect from the inhabitants of Essex Co the taxes imposed on the sd inhabitants by several Acts of Assembly & pay the same according to the directions of the sd Acts then this obligation to be void ... . Wit: Rob Reid, Robert Maxwell. At a court held 19 Dec 1763 this bond was returned & ordered to be recorded. Attest: John Lee Junr clerk. (Pg 244)

13 Dec 1763. Bond. James Webb gent sheriff, John Edmondson & Luke Covington are firmly bound unto the justices of Essex Co for 40,000 lbs of tobacco ... the condition of this obligation is such that whereas the afsd James Webb is appointed collector of the co levy for this present year, now if the sd James Webb shall duly collect the same & pay to the several claimants their respective claims, then this obligation to be void ... . Wit: Rob Reid, Robert Maxwell. At a court held for Essex Co 19 Dec 1763 this bond was returned & ordered to be recorded. Attest: John Lee Junr clerk. (Pg 245)

12 Oct 1763. Deed. James Pamplin & Rachel his wife of South Farnham Parish, Essex Co for 90 pd sold to Thomas Roane of same place a messuage & 180 a. tr of land in the afsd parish being the tr of land divised him by his decd father Nicholas Pamplin by his will bounded by the land the sd Thomas Roane bought of Thomas Pamplin, land the sd Roane has that was his decd father's, the Main Run of Hoskins's Cr, the sd Roane's mill & Henry Purkins Taylor ... . Wit: John Harper, Reubin Smith, Forest Webb. Ackn 16 Jan 1764 by James Pamplin & admitted to record. Attest: John Lee Junr clerk. (Pg 245)

12 Oct 1763. Bond. James Pamplin of South Farnham Parish, Essex Co am firmly bound unto Thomas Roane of same place for 300 pd ... the condition of this obligation is such that if the sd James Pamplin shall from time to time & at all times forever hereafter well & truly observe perform fullfill & accomplish all & singular the covenants grants articles clauses & conditions whatsoever mentioned in a deed of sale [*see above*] in all things according to the intent & meaning of the same then this obligation to be void ... . Wit: John Harper, Reubin Smith, Forest Webb. Ackn 16 Jan 1764 & recorded. Attest: John Lee Junr clerk. (Pg 247)

2 Sep 1763. Deed of Mortgage. Adam Jones of Essex Co to indemnify Richard Hodges from all & every action, suit, cost, charges or troubles whatsoever touching & concerning the goods or merchandizes by them bought whereby they both stand jointly & severally bound have assigned & made over by way of mortgage to the sd Richard Hodges of same co all his rights titles properties claime & demand whatsoever to all & every sort of goods wares & merchandizes as he hath by him as also the store books & all other accts debts duties & all other matters whatsoever concerning their trading or dealing in copartnership ... whereas the sd Adam Jones & Richard Hodges by Articles of Agreement dated 30 Jul 1762

did enter into copartnership as merchant adventurers in the uttering selling or vending all & every such sort of goods wares & merchandizes as they had then in stock or should thereafter be bought or purch as by the sd articles and whereas they by their mutual consents free will & agreement & for divers causes & considerations dissolve & break off the copartnership & from hence forth to become no more copartners together & the sd Richard Hodges for the conditions herein contain'd doth deliver up to the sd Adam Jones all his due share of 1/2 pt/o all such wares goods & merchandizes as is now in stock between them & all his right, title & interest into all the sundry debts duties bills bonds obligations & all other accompts whatsoever due or to become due to them ... & the same to be the sole use property of the sd Adam Jones & whereas the sd Richard Hodges now stands bound together with the sd Adam Jones to sundry persons for sundry goods by them bought to carry on their trade ... provided that & it is hereby agreed between the sd parties that when the sd Richard Hodges & his heirs are absolutely & fully discharged of & from all & every such bills bonds obligations & accompts whereby he stands jointly & severally bound together with the sd Adam Jones that then the sd Richard Hodges shall deliver up to the sd Adam Jones all & every the sd goods, wares merchandizes & all other the books accompts debts whatsoever to the only & proper use & behoof of the sd Adam Jones then this present indenture to be void ... . Wit: Thos Barker, John Herndon, Elisha Alexander. Proved 20 Feb 1764 & recorded. Attest: John Lee Junr clerk. (Pg 248)

29 Jul 1763. Deed of Mortgage. Thomas Bourne (Bourn) of King & Queen Co for 17 pd 15 sl 4 pn now due to James Ritchie & Company sold to the sd James Ritchie & Company of Glasgow in North Briton merchants one Negro woman named Die & her child named Fanny ... if the sd Thomas Bourne shall pay unto the sd James Ritchie & Company the afsd sum with interest then this indenture to be void ... . Wit: Jas Emerson, Thomas Segar, Neil McCoull. Proved 20 Feb 1764 & recorded. Attest: John Lee Junr clerk. (Pg 249)

20 Sep 1763. Deed. Benjamin Coffland of Essex Co for 20 pd 15 sl 5 pn sold to James Ritchie & Company of Glasgow in North Briton one gray horse, four cows & calves, three feather beds, two iron potts & a large pacing horse with a white tail & main branded "HB" ... provided that if the sd Benjamin Coffland shall pay to the sd James Ritchie & Company the afsd sum with interest then this indenture to be void ... . Wit: Andrew Crauford, Neil McCoull. Proved 20 Feb 1764 & recorded. Attest: John Lee Junr clerk. (Pg 250)

30 Dec 1763. Deed of Gift. Samuel Hipkins of St. Anns Parish, Essex Co gent for natural love & affection have given to my son Samuel Hipkins of South Farnham Parish co afsd the following slaves (to wit) Quintos, Cyrus, Hannah & Lucy & their increase ... . Wit: LeRoy Hipkins, Luke Covington, Richd Hipkins. Proved 19 Mar 1764 & recorded. Attest: John Lee Junr clerk. (Pg 251)

30 Nov 1763. Deed. Arthur Tate & Lucy his wife of South Farnham Parish, Essex Co for 72 pd sold to William Howerton of same place a 144 a. tr of land bounded by Covington's Swamp, James Newbill Senr, William Greenwood & Richard Fisher ... . Wit: Robert Read, Richard St. John, William Covington. Proved 19 Mar 1764 & ackn by Lucy w/o the within Arthur Tate (she being first privily examined & assenting thereto) & recorded. Attest: John Lee Junr clerk. (Pg 252)

4 Jan 1764. Deed of Gift. John Garnett Junr & Mary his wife of Essex Co for love good will & most tender effection & 5 sl have given unto their son Leonard Garnett of same co a 92 a. tr of land bounded by Latany's land, Graves's line, Joseph Fogg & the road that leads from Upshaw's mill to Holt's shop ... we the sd John Garnett & Mary his wife do reserve to ourselves during our natural lives timber & firewood out of the sd land to the use of the plantation we do now live on ... . Wit: Edward Vawter, Samuel Cross, Mary Garnett, Susannah Garnett. Ackn 19 Mar 1764 by John Garnett Junr & recorded. Attest: John Lee Junr clerk. (Pg 254)

16 Aug 1763. Deed of Gift. I Mary Jones late w/o Richard Jones of Essex Co decd, whereas my sd decd husband did by his will devise to me his lands during my natural life, & in consideration of a suitable maintainance found & provided for me by my son Benjamin Jones, I do hereby relinquish unto my sd son Benjamin Jones all the right, title or interest that I may might or could claime in and to the lands so bequeathed to me. Wit: Thomas Minor, Richard Hodges, John Herndon, William Young Junr, Thomas Games. Proved 20 Mar 1764 & recorded. Attest: John Lee Junr clerk. (Pg 255)

15 Aug 1763. Bill of Sale. Adam Jones of Essex Co for 177 pd 3 sl 10 pn in hand paid with lawfull interest on the same have sold unto John Corrie of same co my Negro woman Sarah & her child Dinah and a boy mare branded on the near shoulder "D" a natural pacer ... . Wit: Charles Evans, John Fowler. Proved 20 Mar 1764 & recorded. Attest: John Lee Junr clerk. (Pg 256)

30 Aug 1763. Bill of Sale. John Seayres of Essex Co for 30 pd 7 pn have sold unto Corrie Mills & Company of same co my Negro wench Winny ... this bill of sale is void when the above 30 pd 7 pn is discharged with the interest as it is by a bond ... . Wit: Charles Evans, John Fowler. Proved 20 Mar 1764 & recorded. Attest: John Lee Junr clerk. (Pg 256)

20 Mar 1764. Release. I Richd Parker hereby disclaim any right or title that I may have to any slave or slaves in the possession of Mrs. Susanna Parker widow of Alexander Parker gent decd that she had a right to before her marriage with the sd

Alexr as also to the Negro wench Betty & her children. Wit: W. Roane, John Semple. Ackn 20 Mar 1764 & recorded. Attest: John Lee Junr clerk. (Pg 257)

17 Dec 1763. Deed of Mortgage. John Vass of Essex Co for 163 pd 2 sl 10 pn sold to William Snodgrass of same co merchant a 130 a. tr of land bounded by Stephen Neal, Andrew Allen, Robert James & the plantation whereon Richard Johnstone now lives, & also the following Negro slaves, to wit, one Negro wench named Venus & one Negro girl named Milly ... provided that if the sd John Vass shall well & truly pay unto the sd William Snodgrass the afsd sum with interest on or before 18 Dec next ensuing then this deed shall be altogether null & void ... . Wit: James Webb Junr, Will Waddrop, Robert Maxwell. Proved 20 Mar 1764 & recorded. Attest: John Lee Junr clerk. (Pg 357)

24 Dec 1763. Deed of Mortgage. Richard Fisher of Essex Co planter for 60 pd sold to William Snodgrass of same co merchant a 76 a. parcel of land bounded by Rhodes Greenwood, William Greenwood, Wm Coles & Wm Howerton, & also one Negro man slave named Jack ... provided that if the sd Richard Fisher shall well & truly pay unto the sd Wm Snodgrass the afsd sum with interest on or before 1 May next ensuing then this deed to be void ... . Wit: Rob Reid, Robert Maxwell, Will Waddrop. Proved 20 Mar 1764 & recorded. Attest: John Lee Junr clerk. (Pg 259)

3 Nov 1763. Bill of Sale. Samuel Fawcett of Essex Co for 45 pd 12 sl 7 pn sold unto William Snodgrass of sd co my two mares, three beds, one desk, two tables, four iron pots, two dozen pewter plates & gun & two whip saws & 18 chairs ... . Wit: Rob Reid, Robert Maxwell. Proved 20 Mar 1764 & recorded. Attest: John Lee Junr clerk. (Pg 261)

31 Aug 1763. Frances Thorp widdow of St. Anns Parish, Essex Co doe for several good causes & considerations me thereunto moved but more especially to make him full satisfaction for the trouble & charge he has sustained in maintaining two Negro children named Cattenah & Sarah from children to this present day at his cost & charge, I do make over all my right, title & intrest that I have in the two afsd Negroes & their increase to my brother Thomas Hughs for ever, the sd Negroes being now in his possession ... . Memo: That before signing this writing the above reserve was made by Frances Thorp that in case any unforeseen misfortune should befall her such as the death of her slaves so as she is redus'd to poverty & want that then it shall be in her power to call home the two mentioned Negroes for her support & maintainance & in no other case whatsoever. Proved 20 Mar 1764 & recorded. Attest: John Lee Junr clerk. (Pg 262)

20 Mar 1764. Deed of Mortgage. Vincent Vass of Essex Co have for 200 pd sold unto James Emerson of the Town of Tappah six slaves, viz, Bob, Jacob, Lettis,

Patty, Rachel & Toney ... the condition of this bill of sale is that whereas the sd James Emerson hath join'd in a bond with Majr Stevens on acct of the sd Vass payable unto Messrs Upshaw & Roane for 105 pd 4 sl 3 farthings & is the sd Vass's bail in the suit of Wm Snodgrass merchant, Person Groom, Mrs. Dyke & James Snodgrass taylor all which suits are agt the sd Vass in co court of Essex, now if the sd Vass shall indemnifie the sd James Emerson from the afsd ingagements & all other things that the sd Emerson is at stake upon the sd Vass's acct, then this bill of sail to be void ... . Wit: James Webb Junr, William Todd, John Hammond. Ackn 20 Mar 1764 & recorded. Attest: John Lee Junr clerk. (Pg 262)

4 Aug 1763. Deed. Robert Beverley esqr of South Farnham Parish, Essex Co (son & heir of the Honourable William Beverley esqr late of sd co decd) & Maria his wife for 78 pd 10 sl 9 pn sold to Archibald McCall merchant of same place a lot or 1/2 a. of land in the Town of Tappahannock numbered 1 in the plot of the sd town & likewise all that slip of land numbered 73 in the plan made by Robert Brooke gent surveyor lying between the sd lot & Rappahannock River & whatever more land may be hereafter made between the sd lot number 1 & the sd river ... . Wit: Chs Mortimer, John Brokenbrough, Jas Emerson. Proved 20 Mar 1764 & recorded. Attest: John Lee Junr clerk. (Pg 263)

13 Oct 763. Deed. Thomas Fogg of St. Anns Parish, Essex Co for 240 pd sold to Muscoe Garnett of same place a 120 a. prell of land or woodland in the sd parrish bounded by the Main Road, Mosley's line & Warring's line ... . Wit: William Fogg, Benja Harrison, Thos Upshaw. Ackn 21 Mar 1764 & recorded. Attest: John Lee Junr clerk. (Pg 265)

XVI Apr 1764. Deed. William Roane & Betty his wife of Essex Co for 175 pd sold to James Booker of same co a messuage & 333 1/2 a. tr of land it being pt/o Braxton's Mount Maple bounded by John Lumkin, John Ball, Edmund Ball, Balls Spring Br, Balls Swamp, Old Quaker Spring Br & John Upshaw ... . Wit: Henry Vass, Ambrose Wright, Tandy Dix. Ackn 16 Apr 1764 by William Roane & recorded. Attest: John Lee Junr clerk. Ackn 17 Nov 1766 by Betty w/o the sd William Roane (being first privily examined & assenting thereto) & recorded. Attest: John Lee clerk. (Pg 267)

17 Apr 1764. Indenture Quadripartite between John Upshaw & Thomas Roan gent of Essex Co of the first part, Mary Jenkins late widow of Nicholas Pamplin decd of the second part, Robert Pamplin son & heir at law of the sd Nicholas of the third part & Vincent Vass of the sd co of the fourth part, whereas the sd Nicholas Pamplin by his will dated 9 May 1760 did will & devise as follows, to wit, "it is my will & desire that the plantation I now have in King & Queen Co

shall be immediately sold by my executors to the highest bidder in order to discharge my debts," & soon after making such will the sd Nicholas departed this life & the executors named in the sd will having refused to act as such, administration with the will annexed was granted to the sd Mary widow of the sd Nicholas & whereas Archibald Ritchie gent & others creditors of the sd Nicholas Pamplin brought their bill into the sd co court setting forth the premises & also that the sd Nicholas at the time of making his sd will was seised of a tr of land in King & Queen Co of which he died seised & praying a decree of the sd court to sell the sd tr of land for the payment of the sd testator's debts, & it was ordered & decreed by the court afsd that the sd John Upshaw & Thomas Roan gent justices should sell the sd land at publick sale to the highest bidder & that the sd Mary & the sd Robert when he should come of lawfull age who were defs in the sd suit in Chancery should join them in a conveyance to the purchaser & whereas in obedience to the sd decree the sd John & Thomas did sell the land to the sd Vincent Vass the highest bidder who purch the same at the rate of 8 sl 7 pn per a. & the sd land having been since surveyed & found to contain 245 a., now this indenture the sd John Upshaw & Thomas Roan for 105 pd 5 sl subject to the decree of the sd court for payment of the debts due sold & released unto the sd Vincent Vass that parcell of land whereof the sd Nicholas Pamplin was seised in his lifetime & died seised containing 245 a. in King & Queen Co bounded by Davis's corner & Sadlars Swamp ... . Wit: Frans Waring, LeRoy Hipkins, Thomas Segar. Ackn 17 Apr 1764 & recorded. Attest: John Lee Junr clerk. (Pg 269)

17 Apr 1764. Indenture. John Chattin son of Cornelius Chattin by & with consent & appration (sic) of the co court of Essex Co doth put himself apprentice to Thomas Wood of King & Queen Co carpenter to learn his art & with him after the manner of an apprentice to serve until the sd John Chattin shall attain the full age of 21 years he being 16 years old ... . Wit: None. Ackn by the parties 17 Apr 1764 & recorded. Attest: John Lee Junr clerk. (Pg 271)

9 Feb 1764. Power of Attorney. John Morton Jordan of London merchant do hereby revoke & make void all other & former letters of atty by me made and in the place & stead thereof I have appointed Thomas Jett of VA merchant my atty to sell & dispose of the whole or pt/o all & singular the lands & messuages belonging to me in Richmond Co & Culpepper Co in VA together with all & every the stock Negroes, effects & things whatsoever belonging to the same either together or separate ... . Wit: Muscoe Livingston, James Walker, Henry Milbourn. Proved 21 May 1764 & recorded. Attest: John Lee Junr clerk. (Pg 272)

19 Oct 1763. Bill of Sale. Godfrey Young of Essex Co for 11 pd 4 sl 4 pn with interest on the same from the date of my bond formerly given have sold unto

John Corrie of same co my bay gelding called Buck which sd horse I bought of
Archibald McCall also my white gelding called Fox which sd gelding I bought
of John Harwood ... . Wit: Charles Evans, John Mills. Proved 24 May 1764 &
recorded. Attest: John Lee Junr clerk. (Pg 274)

25 Jan 1764. Deed. Lewis Mountague of Middlesex Co gent for 100 pd sold to
Abraham Mountague of Essex Co all his right & tytle to a 100 a. parcel of land
... whereas Abraham Mountague in his will dated 3 May 1740 did give to his son
Abraham Mountague a 100 a. tr of land lying in the lower end of Essex Co on
Dragon Swamp & the afsd Lewis Mountague being elder son & heir to the afsd
Abraham Mountague doth claime a reversion in the sd land ... . Wit: Thos
Shelton, Richard Street, John Sadler. Ackn 21 May 1764 & recorded. Attest:
John Lee Junr clerk. (Pg 275)

27 Jan 1764. Deed. Edmund Mitchell & Dorothy his wife of South Farnham
Parish, Essex Co bricklayer for 90 pd sold to Vincent Cauthorn of same place
planter a 100 a. parcel of land in the sd parish bounded by the Main County
Road which leads to Piscattaway Ferry, lands of John Patterson, James Webb
Junr, Richard Jeffries & Henry Cauthorn, it being the tr of land whereon the sd
Edmund Mitchel & Dorothy his wife now live ... . Wit: James Webb Junr,
Richard Jeffries, Ralph Neale. Ackn 21 May 1764 by Edmund Mitchell &
Dorothy his wife (she being first privily examined & assenting thereto) &
recorded. Attest: John Lee Junr clerk. (Pg 276)

16 Mar 1764. Deed. Thomas Johnson of South Farnham Parish, Essex Co for
80 pd sold to Richard Jeffries of same place a 106 a. parcel of land in the sd
parish adj to the Dragon Swamp, Hog Neck Br & the lands of Thomas Allen &
Joseph Mann, it being the land which the sd Thomas Johnson purch of James
McCall merchant ... . Wit: W. Young, Thomas Bowden, Elizabeth Johnson.
Ackn 21 May 1764 & recorded. Attest: John Lee Junr clerk. (Pg 278)

16 Apr ----. Deed. Samuel Davice (Davis) & Ann his wife of Essex Co for 27
pd 10 sl sold to Thomas Sale of same co a 55 a. tr of land pt/o a tr of 96 a. of
land the sd Davice have lately purch of James Munday bounded by sd Munday's
old line now a corner between sd Davice & Sale, Sarys Br of Jillsons Run,
Woolbanks's Br & land the sd Sale lately purch of James Davice ... . Wit: John
Sale, James Munday, Nicholas Faulconer Junr. Ackn 21 May 1764 by Samuel
Davis & Ann his wife (she being first privily examined & assenting thereto) &
recorded. Attest: John Lee Junr clerk. (Pg 280)

30 Apr 1764. Deed. James Davice (Davis) & Elizabeth his wife of Essex Co for
20 pd sold to Samuel Davice of same co a 20 a. tr of land pt/o 131 a. of land the
sd James Davice holds on Jillsons Run bounded by the sd Samuel Davice &

Jillsons Swamp ... . Wit: James Falconer, Nicholas Fisher, James Munday. Ackn 21 May 1764 by Elizabeth Davis (she being first privily examined & assenting thereto) & admitted to record. Proved 17 Sep 1764 as to the pt/o James Davies & admitted to record. Attest: John Lee Junr clerk. (Pg 282)

7 Apr 1764. Deed. George Newbill of South Farnham Parish, Essex Co & Mary his wife for 115 pd sold to Humphrey Davis of Lunenburg Parish, Richmond Co a 150 a. parcel of land in South Farnham Parish adj the lands of Francis Smith, William Broocke, Peter Broocke decd, Joshua Boughton & Isaac Williams, it being the parcel of land which the sd George Newbill purch of Vincent Hudson & Anne his wife ... . Wit: Thos Newbill, Henry Crutcher, Rhodes Greenwood, Abner Dobbins. Ackn 21 May 1764 by George Newbill & Mary his wife (she being first privily examined & assenting thereto) & recorded. Attest: John Lee Junr clerk. (Pg 284)

11 May 1764. Deed. John Goode & Anne his wife of South Farnham Parish, Essex Co & Ruth Sale of Drisdal Parish, Caroline Co for 18 pd 15 sl sold to William Fletcher of South Farnham Parish, Essex Co a tr of land (being pt/o the 25 a. tr of land whereon the sd John Goode now lives) in South Farnham Parish bounded by the main road that leads to Webb's Ordinary, a road that leads to Snodgrass's store & the other lands of John Goode ... . Wit: Phillip Kidd, William Gordon, John Mann. Ackn 21 May 1764 by John Goode & Ann his wife (she being first privily examined & assenting thereto) & proved as to the pt/o Ruth Sale & recorded. Attest: John Lee Junr clerk. (Pg 286)

31 Jan 1764. Deed. John Dix of King & Queen Co & Kerenhappuck his wife for 75 pd sold to Ambrose Gatewood of Essex Co planter two trs of land in South Farnham Parish, the one of which is the land whereon the sd Ambrose Gatewood now lives bounded by Thomas Dix, Compton's line, William Roane & John Allen decd, containing 141 a., the other tr is bounded by land of George Coleman decd, Jonathan Sheerwood, George Moody & John Allen decd, containing 39 1/2 a. ... . Wit: John Semple, Martha Dismukes, Geo Brooke, John Pendleton, Smith Young, James Booker. Ackn 21 May 1764 by John Dix & recorded. Attest: John Lee Junr clerk. (Pg 287)

17 Apr 1764. To George Brooke & John Ware gent greeting, whereas John Dix & Kerenhappuck his wife have by their deed of sale [see above] conveyed a tr of land to Ambrose Gatewood & whereas the sd Kerenhappuck is unable to travel to our sd co court to make acknowledgment thereof, therefore we command you that you repair to the sd Kerenhappuck & her privily & apart from her sd husband examine whether she freely & willingly relinquishes her right of dower in the lands. Wit John Lee Junr clerk. By virtue of this writ to us directed we Geo Brooke & John Ware have examined Kerenhappuck privily and apart from

her husband who declares that she freely & willingly acknowledges her right of dower in the lands ... . At a court held 21 May 1764 this commission & the commissioners return thereon endorsed were returned & recorded. Attest: John Lee Junr clerk. (Pg 289)

22 Dec 1763. Deed of Mortgage. Morris Brocke (Broocke) of Essex Co for 70 pd sold to William Snodgrass of Essex Co merchant a 100 a. tr of land bounded by Richard Hodges, Joseph Reyland, Richard Holt & Henry Purkins ... provided that if the sd Morris Brocke shall well & truly pay unto the sd Wm Snodgrass the afsd sum with interest on or before 1 May next ensuing then this deed shall be null & void ... . Wit: Robert Maxwell, James Banks, Will Waddrop. Ackn 21 May 1764 & recorded. Attest: John Lee Junr clerk. (Pg 290)

14 Apr 1764. Deed. John Deans merchant & Thomas Haile & Elizabeth his wife all of South Farnham Parish, Essex Co 84 pd sold to Richard Hodges of same place a 60 a. tr of land ... whereas the sd Thomas Haile by one indenture dated 18 Apr 1761 did give to his son Benjamin Haile the rest residue & remainder of his land that he had purch of Elizabeth Allen containing 60 a. and the sd Benjamin Haile on 21 Mar 1763 for 60 pd did convey the sd land to the sd John Deans ... . Wit: W. Mountague, Lewis Mountague, John Bush Junr. Ackn 21 May 1764 by Thomas Haile & Elizabeth his wife (she being first privily examined & assenting thereto) & recorded. Attest: John Lee Junr clerk. (Pg 292)

16 May 1764. Power of Attorney. I Elizabeth Smether of Saint Anns Parish, Essex Co appoint Joseph Noell to settle & account with my son John Smether for all money, tobacco & other profits & estates made use of the estate lent me by my decd husband William Smether which he takes uses & disposes of without my knowledge or consent & hereby giving unto my sd atty Joseph Noell full & absolute authority to sue for such estate & to cause the sd John Smether to render & make up a true & just acct thereof so that the sd Joseph Noell may be able to acct for the same as of right ought to be according to the will of the sd decd William Smether without interupting of her in her proper right & the proper legatees in the sd decd's will may receive their due & proper proportions of the sd estate without fraud or having the same squandered away ... . Wit: Nicho Faulconer, Richard Hambleton, Richard Hutson. Proved 22 May 1764 & recorded. Attest: John Lee Junr clerk. (Pg 294)

23 May 1764. Deed of Lease. John Richards & Susanna his wife of Drysdall Parish, King & Queen Co for the rents & covenants hereafter mentioned & reserved hath farm let unto John Deans of the Town of Tappahannock pt/o a lott in the slipe annexed to the Town of Tappahannock number'd 75 adj Duke Street & lot number'd 12 now in the possession of James Emmerson ... during the term

of 11 years 6 months from 28 Jun last past, the sd John Deans doth bind himself & his heirs to build a good sound & well built warehouse at least 50' long & 20' wyde with a good brick cellar underneath the same upon the sd parcel of land ... . Wit: None. Ackn 23 May 1764 by John Richards gent & Susanna his wife (she being first privily examined & assenting thereto) & recorded. Attest: John Lee Junr clerk. (Pg 294)

6 Apr 1764. Deed of Mortgage. Keziah Brown of Essex Co for 60 pd sold to James Ritchie & Company of Glasgow in North Britain merchant two Negroes, viz, Daphney & Jack, six cows & calves & my young horse ... provided that if the sd Keziah Brown shall pay to the sd James Ritchie & Company 60 pd with interest this indenture to be void ... . Wit: Neil McCoull, Amose Jones, Andrew Crawford. Proved 24 May 1764 & recorded. Attest: John Lee Junr clerk. (Pg 295)

17 Feb 1764. To Archibald Ritchie, John Upshaw & Charles Mortimer gent greeting, whereas James Pamplin & Rachel his wife have by their deed dated 12 Oct 1763 conveyed unto Thomas Roane gent of Essex Co a 180 a. tr of land in South Farnham Parish & whereas the sd Rachel is unable to travel to our co court to make acknowledgment thereof, therefore we command you to repair to the sd Rachel & that privily and apart from her husband you take such acknowledgment as she shall be willing to make ... . Wit John Lee Junr clerk. 20 Apr 1764 By virtue of this dedimus to us directed & in obedience to the same we John Upshaw & Chs Mortimer did repair to the sd Rachel & her privily & apart from James her husband hath examin'd touching the premises afsd who said she did freely & voluntarily relinquish all her right & dower in the premises. At a court held 18 Jun 1764 this commission & the commissioners return thereon endorsed were returned & ordered to be recorded. Attest: John Lee Junr clerk. (Pg 296)

24 Feb 1764. Power of Attorney. Robert Bogle & William Scott of London merchants & partners have each of us appointed John Bogle now of London merchant but shortly intending to sail to & settle at VA in North America, James Robb of Urbanna in VA merchant & William Fox now of London marriner but intending shortly to sail to VA & each of them jointly & severally our attys to ask demand sue for recover & receive of & from all & every person whatsoever in VA or any other place on the Continent of America all sums of money goods effects debts dividends dues accounts claimes & demands whatsoever which now are or at any time hereafter shall be due owing payable or belonging to us ... . Wit: Robt Watson, Willm Cuzzins, Thos Woodford. Proved 18 Jun 1764 & recorded. Attest: John Lee Junr clerk. (Pg 297)

14 Apr 1764. Deed. James Samuell & Peter Samuell of St. Anns Parish, Essex Co for 50 pd 5 sl 6 pn sold to Foster Samuell of Drysdale Parish, Caroline Co all the lands whereof Mark Samuell died seised bounded by Col John Lee, John Bastin, James Martin, John Colquit, John Samuell & Peter Samuell (subject to the widow's dower) ... whereas Mark Samuell late of Essex Co decd did by his will dated 13 Aug 1763 devise as follows, viz, "I give & devise unto my executors hereafter mentioned all my lands in trust to & for the uses herein after mentioned & to no other uses whatsoever, that is to say, to be sold to the highest bidder by my sd executors & the money arising by such sale to be applied to the education & maintainance of all my children after deducting a childs part which I give to my wife in lieu of her dower in the sd lands," & appointed the sd James Samuell & Peter Samuell executors, & whereas the sd James Samuell & Peter Samuell have pursuant to the trust reposed in them by the sd will exposed the lands afsd (subject the widows dower who renounced the will of her husband) to public auction & the sd Foster Samuell became the highest bidder for the same offering 50 pd 5 sl 6 pn ... . Wit: None. Ackn 18 Jun 1764 & recorded. Attest: John Lee Junr clerk. (Pg 299)

14 Jul 1764. Deed. Samuel Cross of St. Anns Parish, Essex Co & Ann his wife for 45 pd sold to Cornelius Sale of same parish a 100 a. tr of land whereon the sd Samuel Cross now lives in the sd parish ... . Wit: Jno Garnett, Jno Casell, Leod Garnett. Ackn 16 Jul 1764 & recorded. Attest: John Lee Junr clerk. (Pg 300)

16 Jul 1764. Deed of Mortgage. Richard Hodges of Essex Co planter for 250 pd sold to William Snodgrass of same co merchant a 200 a. tr of land also a 100 a. tr of land which he purch lately of Wm Fretwell, also four Negro slaves, viz, Jack, Duffee, Tony men slaves & Nan a woman slave ... provided that if the sd Richard Hodges shall well & truely pay unto the sd William Snodgrass the afsd 250 pd with interest on or before 1 Sep next ensuing then this deed shall be altogether null & void ... . Wit: Boswell Richards, Will Waddrop, John Semple. Ackn 16 Jul 1764 & recorded. Attest: John Lee Junr clerk. (Pg 301)

16 Jul 1764. Deed of Gift. Catharine Gatewood of Essex Co widow in pursuance of her promise & agreement with Thomas Wood upon his intermarriage with Catharine the dau of the sd Catharine Gatewood & for love & affection which she hath & doth bear to the sd Thomas Wood & Catharine his wife & for their better support & advancement hath given unto the sd Thomas Wood of same co carpenter a Negro wench named Kate & a Negro child named Happy dau of the sd wench Kate as also the following goods & chattles, to wit, two feather beds & furniture, a bright bay mare branded on the near buttock "AC" with her sorrill coalt, one woman's side sadle & a black walnut oval table together with all the future increase of the sd Negroes & mares & the use profit benefit & labour of the sd Negroes goods & chattles ... . Wit: William Flitcher,

Richd Brown. Proved 16 Jul 1764 & recorded. Attest: John Lee Junr clerk. (Pg 303)

1 Apr 1764. Deed of Lease. Stark Boulware of Essex Co planter lease & farm let unto Francis Thorp of sd co a 100 a. tr of land in Saint Anns Parish ... during the term of 6 years paying 10 pd yearly to the sd Stark Boulware during the sd term ... . Wit: Thomas Cavanaugh, John Price, Edward Hudson. Proved 16 Jul 1764 & recorded. Attest: John Lee Junr clerk. (Pg 304)

17 Mar 1764. Deed of Lease. John Andrews of Essex Co farm let unto Edward Gouldman the land & plantation whereon the sd Edward Gouldman now lives during the term of 20 years paying to the sd John Andrews 4 pd yearly on 17 Mar during the sd term ... . Wit: Mark Davis, John Tucker. (Pg 305)

16 Jul 1764. Deed. John Thomas & Keziah his wife of Essex Co for 30 pd sold to William Hawkins of same co a 49 a. tr of land bounded by sd Hawkins' line, Short's land, a patent formerly granted to Thomas Page now in possession of Thomas Butler, Rappahannock River, Landrums Cr & Western Br ... . Wit: Thos Newman, Benja Harrison & Richd Thos Haile. Ackn 16 Jul 1765 by John Thomas & Keziah his wife (she being first privily examined & assenting thereto) & recorded. Attest: John Lee Junr clerk. (Pg 306)

21 Jun 1764. Deed of Mortgage. Vincent Vass of King & Queen Co for 120 pd 10 sl sold to William Lyne of sd co & Archibald Ritchie of Essex Co a 245 a. tr of land in King & Queen Co which I purch of the exrs of Nicholas Pamplin & nine slaves, viz, Patt, Jacob, Bob, Toney, Rachell, Jeny, James & Lett with her youngest child Anthony, four feather bedds & all the rest & residue of my household goods also all my stock of cattle, hoggs & one roan horse ... provided that if the sd Vincent Vass shall & do well & truly pay unto the sd William Lyne & Archibald Ritchie the full sum of 120 pd 10 sl at or upon 1 Dec next ensuing then these presents & the estate hereby granted shall cease & be utterly void ... . Wit: John Penn, Jos Stevens, Henry Lyne Junr. Proved 16 Jul 1764 by John Penn & Henry Lyne & ordered to be certified. Attest: John Lee Junr clerk. Memo: this deed being not fully proved is recorded here thro mistake & the original sent to Mr. Lyne to be proved in King & Queen Co where it ought to be recorded. (Pg 308)

15 Jan 1764. Bill of Sale. Grace Johns of Tappahannock, Essex Co for 30 pd sold to John Corrie of town afsd my gray mare, 1 cow & calf, 2 beds & furniture, 3 iron pots, 4 chests, 1 spinning wheel, 1 copper coffee pot, 4 pewter dishes, 1 doz pewter plates, 3 tables, 1 womens side sadle, 2 mens sadles, 1 grid iron, ladle, flesh fork, 7 doz quart bottles, 1 fire lock, 6 flag chairs, a copper saucepan & every other article whatsoever as my property & every debt due to

me ... . Wit: Charles Evans, Sarah Low. Proved 21 Aug 1764 & recorded. Attest: John Lee Junr clerk. (Pg 309)

17 Apr 1764. Bill of Sale. Joseph Warrick of Essex Co for 20 pd sold unto John Corrie of same co my schooner boat called Ripley with all her utensils & my white mare called Polly, also my gray mare colt call'd Fanny ... . Wit: John Fowler, Charles Evans. Proved 21 Aug 1764 & recorded. Attest: John Lee Junr clerk. (Pg 310)

27 Jun 1764. Deed. Meriwether Smith of South Farnham Parish, Essex Co gent for 12 pd sold to Doctor Nicholas Flood of North Farnham Parish, Richmond Co all those points of land & marshes which lieth betwixt the sd Flood's land & that pt/o Piscataway Cr which is called the Thoroughfare & which divides the point of land & marsh afsd from an island of sd Smith's upon Piscataway Cr, containing 12 a. in the sd parish bounded by Green Spring Br, the patent granted to John Boboy 4 Oct 1653, Piscataway Cr & the sd Thoroughfare ... . Wit: James Lang, W. Smith, Archd McCall. Ackn 22 Aug 1764 & recorded. Attest: John Lee Junr clerk. (Pg 310)

22 Aug 1764. Deed of Mortgage. Richard Hodges of Essex Co planter for 216 pd with a condition for the payment of 108 pd with interest according to a bond to Hugh Blackburn & Company in the sum of 208 pd with a condition for the payment of 104 pd with interest sold to David Loudon of sd co merchant & Messrs Hugh Blackburn & Company merchants as by the sd last mentioned bond & whereas the sd David Loudon & Messrs Hugh Blackburn & Company prosecuted different suits upon the sd bonds & obtained judgments respectively & moreover the sd David Loudon & Hugh Blackburn & Company sue out & had exns served on the persons of Adam Jones & the sd Richard to oblige them to satisfy the sd judgments & costs respectively whereupon the sd Adam & Richard were committed to close prison & the sd Adam escaped by the neglect or connivance of the goaler (as is supposed) and the sd Richard was left incarcerated alone to discharge the sd judgments & costs for which in fact he was only security, now that the sd Richd Hodges may have it in his power to persue & oblige the sd Jones to do him justice, the parties first above written have come to an agreement as follows, to wit, whereas the sd Richard Hodges has heretofore mortgaged to William Snodgrass a considerable pt/o his estate for payment of a considerable sum of money mentioned in the sd mortgage (but whither the sd Snodgrass or his constituents McCall & Company is uncertain) and whereas the parties to these presents are desirous to reserve to themselves a right to prosecute the sd Adam Jones, the sheriff or goaler for the more effectually securing their respective debts, and for the ease & benefit of the sd Richard Hodges, especially as it is uncertain whither the estate of the sd Richard hereby intended to be mortgaged will be sufficient to satisfy the sd judgments &

costs ... now this indenture in consideration of the debts due by the sd judgments & costs the sd Richard Hodges hath & hereby doth sell unto the sd David Loudon & Messrs Hugh Blackburn & Company his estate heretofore mortgaged to the sd Messrs McCall or the sd Snodgrass their agent to wit 500 a. of land in South Farnham Parish, four Negroes named Jack, Toney, Coffe & Nan together with their increase, 23 head of cattle, one yoke of oxen, three breeding sows, nine pigs, 19 showets, 14 sheep, four feather beds & furniture, 13 flag bottom chears, two horses, one mare, one ovel table, one pair hand irons together with all my other furniture & personal estate & also what corn I may have left after serving my family & crops of tobacco &c ... if the sd Richard Hodges shall well & truly pay to the sd David Loudon & Messrs Hugh Blackburn & Company the sd judgments & all costs then this indenture shall be void ... . Wit: Vincent Vass, Jas Emmerson, Joseph Noell, Nicholas Fisher, Andrew Baillie. Ackn 22 Aug 1764 & recorded. Attest: John Lee Junr clerk. (Pg 311)

12 Apr 1764. Deed. Mary Young gent of South Farnham Parish, Essex Co for 25 pd sold to Samuel Johnson of same parish a 40 a. parcel of land & premises in the sd parish bounded by Mitchel's & Johnson's corner & Cheney's orphans lands ... . Wit: Griffen Johnson, Sarey Mitchel (Mitch), Richard Jeffries. Proved 17 Sep 1764 & recorded. Attest: John Lee Junr clerk. (Pg 313)

2 Feb 1764. Deed. Henry Cauthorn of South Farnham Parish, Essex Co & Mary his wife for 40 sl sold to William Young of same parish a 1 a. parcel of land in the sd parish bounded by land which the sd William Young purch of John Patterson, the Main County Road, land which the sd Henry Cauthorn purch of Edmond Mitchell & Dorothy his wife & land which the sd William Young purch of Ritchard Gatewood & Frankey his wife, it being pt/o the tr of land which the sd Edmund Mitchell & Dorothy his wife lately sold to the sd Henry Cauthorn ... . Wit: John Richards, James Townley, Millicene Richards. Ackn 17 Sep 1764 & recorded. Attest: John Lee Junr clerk. (Pg 314)

18 Aug 1764. Deed. John Williamson the younger of Middlesex Co & Sarah his wife for 10 pd sold to John Oneale of Essex Co a parcel of land it being pt/o the tr of land formerly held by William Brizendine decd containing 25 a. ... . Wit: Josiah McTyer, James Oneall, Wm Collins. Proved 17 Sep 1764 & recorded. Attest: John Lee Junr clerk. (Pg 316)

10 Sep 1764. Deed of Gift. Richard Shackleford of King & Queen Co gent & Frances his wife for natural love & affection & 5 sl have given to their son Roger Shackleford of Essex Co a 700 a. tr of land in South Farnham Parish on the Best Land Swamp ... whereas the sd Richard Shackleford hath by an instrument of writing by him executed as & for his will bequeathed to the sd Roger Shackleford 300 pd to purch lands & whereas since the executing the sd

will the sd Richard Shackleford hath come to a resolution to give unto the sd Roger Shackleford a tr of land in lieu of the sd 300 pd ... . Wit: Archibald Ritchie, John Corrie, Robinson Daingerfield, Wm Snodgrass. Proved 17 Sep 1764 & recorded. Attest: John Lee Junr clerk. (Pg 317)

20 Jul 1764. To Thos Reede Rootes & Armistead Bird gent greeting, whereas Richard Shackleford of King & Queen Co & Francies his wife have by their deed [*see above*] have conveyed unto Roger Shackleford a 700 a. tr of land, & whereas the sd Francies is unable to travel to our co court to make acknowledgment thereof, therefore we command you to repair to the sd Francies & that privily & apart from her husband you take such acknowledgment as she shall be willing to make ... . Wit John Lee Junr clerk. King & Queen to wit, Francies Shackleford this day came before us & voluntarily assented to making the deed mentioned in the above writ, certified under our hands & seals 10 Sep 1764 Thos R. Rootes, Armistd Bird. At a court held for Essex Co 17 Sep 1764 this commission & the commissioners return thereon endorsed were this day returned & ordered to be recorded. Attest: John Lee Junr clerk. (Pg 318)

24 May 1764. Power of Attorney. James Gildart of Liverpoole in the Co Palatine of Lancaster & Kingdom of Great Britain merchant have revoked, disannulled & made void all former & other letters of atty by me any time heretofore made & I in consideration of the trust & confidence which I have in John Gawith of Liverpoole afsd master & mariner have appointed the sd John Gawith master of the ship Rogers belonging to Liverpoole my atty to ask demand sue for levy recover & receive of & from all & every person whatsoever in VA who have stood indebted to me in any sum of money or otherwise all sums of money goods chattels or merchandize commodities or effects whatsoever which are now due owing & belonging to me ... . Wit: James Wignet, Thomas Shaw, John Wren. Proved 17 Sep 1764 & recorded. Attest: John Lee Junr clerk. (Pg 319)

18 Sep 1764. Power of Attorney. John Chamberlain of Essex Co have constituted my trusty friends Archd Ritchie & Richard Parker gent to be my atty to ask sue for levy require recover & receive of all & every person whatsoever all & every such debts & sums of money as are now due unto me or which any day hereafter shall be due owing belonging unto me ... particularly to carry on my suite in Chancery which I have brought agt Coleman for the recover of land I have sued for ... . Wit: None. Ackn 19 Sep 1764 & recorded. Attest: John Lee Junr clerk. (Pg 320)

17 Jan 1764. Bill of Sale. I William St. John of Essex Co for & in consideration of a Negro woman slave named Hannah by me received of William Gatewood of same co have sold unto the sd William Gatewood two Negro slaves, to wit,

Jenny a Negro girl & Tom a boy and the future offspring & increase of the sd girl ... . Wit: Elizabeth Lyal, Henry Allen. Ackn 17 Sep 1764 & recorded. Attest: John Lee Junr clerk. (Pg 321)

17 Jan 1764. Bill of Sale. I William Gatewood of Essex Co for & in consideration of two Negro slaves named Jenny & Tom by me received of William St. John of same co have sold unto the sd William St. John one Negro woman slave named Hannah & her future offspring & increase ... . Wit: Elizabeth Lyal, Henry Allen. Ackn 17 Sep 1764 & recorded. Attest: John Lee clerk. (Pg 322)

Observations & Dimensions of 240 1/2 a. of land lying in South Farnham Parish and on both sides of the road leading from Wm Snodgrass' store to the ordinary formerly called Sanders' now Joseph Mann's & survey'd at the request of James Banks of the parish afsd & Edwards Phil Jones of Kingston Parish, Gloucester Co which the afsd Jones being grgn? for the orphan's estate of Martin Conner decd to which the afsd Banks & Jones being minded to have an equal division have made choice of James Booker & John Edmondson both of South Farnham Parish to see the same done. Surveyed 7 Feb 1764 by me Richard Brown. (Pg 322)

The Explanation of the drawing [*drawing not included here*], names mentioned in the drawing: Doctor John Clements gent, Thos St. John, Mundays Spring Br, Lucreashe Munday, William Dunn, road that leads from Piscataway Old Mill Bridge to Mathews ditto, James Banks & the orphan of Martin Conner decd. This division of land was returned 17 Sep 1764 & ordered to be recorded. Attest: John Lee Junr clerk. (Pg 323)

12 Oct 1764 at Williamsburg. To Archibald Ritchie esqr, by virtue of the power & authority to me given as Commander in Chief of this Colony I hereby appoint you to be sheriff of Essex Co during pleasure ... . Given under my hand & seal Francis Fauquier esqr. Truly recorded. Attest: John Lee Junr clerk. (Pg 324)

15 Oct 1764. Bond. Archibald Ritchie, John Upshaw, John Lee Junr & William Young are firmly bound unto our Sovereign Lord the King for 500 pd ... the condition of this obligation is such that whereas the afsd Archibald Ritchie is appointed sheriff of Essex Co during pleasure by commission from the Governor [*see above*] if therefore the sd Archibald Ritchie shall well & truly collect all quitrents, fines, forfeitures & Americiaments accruing or becoming due to his Majesty in the sd co & shall duly account for & pay the same to the officers of his Majesty's Revenue then this obligation to be void ... . Sealed & delivered in presence of Essex Co court & ordered to be recorded. Attest: John Lee Junr clerk. (Pg 324)

12 Oct 1764. Bond. Archibald Ritchie, John Upshaw, John Lee Junr & William Young are firmly bound unto our Sovereign Lord the King for 1,000 pd ... the condition of this obligation is such that whereas the afsd Archibald Ritchie is appointed sheriff of Essex Co during pleasure by commission from the Governor [*see above*] if the sd Archibald Ritchie shall well & truly collect & receive all officers fees & dues put into his hand to collect & duly acct for & pay the same to the officers to whom such fees are due respectively & shall well & truly execute & due return make of all process & precepts to him directed & pay & satisfy all sums of money & tobacco & shall faithfully perform the sd office of sheriff during the time of his continuance therein then this obligation to be void ... . Sealed & delivered in presence of Essex Co court & ordered to be recorded. Attest: John Lee Junr clerk. (Pg 325)

18 Aug 1764 at Antigua. Power of Attorney. I Alexander Willock of sd Island merchant send greeting, whereas Francis Moore late of the Island & John Pyne of the Island of Antigua merchants partners in trade are jointly & severally indebted to me in severall large sums of money, & whereas the sd Francis Moore & John Pyne are jointly & severally possess'd of severall goods & valuable effects in VA & NC (and other provinces in North America) & have also severall large sums of money due to them from severall persons in North America, now know ye that I Alexander Willock have appointed Robert Tucker the elder & Robert Tucker Junr of the City of Norfolk, VA merchants, Robert Jones & John Hodgson of Edowton, NC merchants my attys to ask, demand, sue for, recover & receive of all & every person whatsoever in VA & NC or any other part of North America all such sums of money, goods & effects, debts & demands whatsoever which now are due & owing or in any wise belong to the sd Francis Moore & John Pyne ... . Wit: John Taylor, Arthur Morson. Proved 15 Oct 1764 by the oath of John Taylor a wit hereto & on the motion of David Loudon ordered to be recorded. Attest: John Lee Junr clerk. (Pg 326)

9 Oct 1764. Deed. John Andrews of Essex Co for 25 pd sold to Edward Gouldman of same co a 100 a. tr of land being pt/o the tr of land the sd Andrews rented to the sd Gouldman & all that land the sd Andrews have rented to Robert Farmer bounded by Mrs. Ann Barbee, Capt James Garnett, lands of Shaddock & Beverley's lines ... . Wit: Francis Barbee, John Sutton, Frances Davis, Edward Carter, Thomas Gouldman, Robert Gouldman, Christopher Barbee. Proved 15 Oct 1764 & recorded. Attest: John Lee Junr clerk. (Pg 327)

13 Oct 1764. Deed. Francis Jones of South Farnham Parish, Essex Co for 71 pd 10 sl sold to Meriwether Smith of same place a 143 a. tr of land in the sd parish bounded by Webbs Mill & the Bever Dam ... . Wit: John Daly, Willm Dunn Junr, W. Smith, P. Smith. Ackn 15 Oct 1764 & recorded. Attest: John Lee Junr clerk. (Pg 328)

12 Sep 1764. Deed. Meriwether Smith of South Farnham Parish, Essex Co gent & Alice Corbin Smith his wife for 241 pd sold to Harway Owen of same place planter a 253 a. tr of land in South Farnham Parish bounded by sd Smith & John Fauntleroy, Roan's Mill Swamp & the main road ... . Wit: Frans Jones, John Daly, Erasmus Jones. Ackn 15 Oct 1764 by Meriwether Smith & Alice his wife (she being first privily examined & assenting thereto) & recorded. Attest: John Lee Junr clerk. (Pg 329)

12 Oct 1764. Deed. Meriwether Smith of South Farnham Parish, Essex Co & Alice Corbin Smith his wife for 211 pd 10 sl sold to Francis Jones, John Daly & Erasmus Jones of same parish a 471 a. tr of land in the sd parish bounded by Hawkins's Pocoson, Brooken's corner, Harway Owen, Roane's mill & the Mill Swamp ... . Wit: Wm Dunn Junr, Will Smith, P. Smith. Ackn 15 Oct 1764 by Meriwether Smith gent & Alice his wife (she being first privily examined & assenting thereto) & recorded. Attest: John Lee Junr clerk. (Pg 330)

19 Jul 1764. Deed. Henry Purkins of St. Stephens Parish, King & Queen Co merchant & Mary his wife for 150 pd sold to George Newbill of South Farnham Parish, Essex Co planter a 113 a. parcel of land in South Farnham Parish bounded by the Mill Dam, Major John Boughan, Spring Br, br called the Harry Laine, Doctor John Clements gent & the Main Pocoson, it being the tr of land whereon the sd Henry Purkins formerly lived ... . Wit: Ben Johnson, William Dunn B, John Johnson. Ackn 15 Oct 1764 by Henry Purkins & recorded. Attest: John Lee Junr clerk. (Pg 331)

3 Oct 1764. Deed of Gift. Francis Ramsey (Ramsay) Senr of St. Anns Parish, Essex Co for love good will & affection hath given to his son Francis Ramsey the younger of same parish 100 a. of land it being pt/o that dividend whereon the sd Francis Ramsey Senr now lives bounded by Thomas Ramsey, br of Popoman, Robt Parker & Cornelius Noell ... . Wit: Robt Parker, Edward Carter, Benja Boulware. Proved 10 Oct 1764 & recorded. Attest: John Lee Junr clerk. (Pg 333)

12 May 1764. Deed. John Clark of South Farnham Parish, Essex Co & Elizabeth his wife for 26 pd sold to Thomas Bridgforth of St. Anns Parish, Essex Co 50 a. of land in South Farnham Parish being the sd plantation & tr of land whereon the sd John Clark did formerly reside bounded by Pickets Road & Old Mill Br ... . Wit: Lewis Mountague, Titus Farguson, Charles Medearis (Meadearis), Ann Medearis (Meadearis), Phil Mountague, Robt Clark, Wm Owen. Ackn 15 Oct 1764 by John Clark & Elizabeth his wife (she being first privily examined & assenting thereto) & recorded. Attest: John Lee Junr clerk. (Pg 335)

21 Jun 1764. Deed. Richard Hill Junr & Mary his wife of South Farnham Parish, Essex Co planter for 30 pd sold to John Cassell of St. Anns Parish, co afsd a 40 a. tr of land in South Farnham Parish being all the land the sd Richard Hill purch of John Garnett binding on the lands of Francis Graves, John Hill, John Rennolds & Lick Swamp ... . Wit: Leonard Hill, Leonard Hill Junr, Alexander Roane. Wit to receipt: Leonard Hill, Joseph Patterson, Alexander Roane. Proved 15 Oct 1764 & recorded. Attest: John Lee Junr clerk. (Pg 336)

9 May 1764. Bill of Sale. Whereas Samuel Shaw has become jointly bound with Jeremiah Moody to Andrew Crawford for the payment of 29 pd 5 sl 6 pn & cost, and a sum of money that I the sd Moody was oweing to the sd Shaw before amounting to 30 pd 10 sl 3 pn, now know ye that I the sd Jeremiah Moody of Essex Co in consideration of the sd Samuel Shaw having become bound as afsd & for the sd debt I was owing to him before & in order to endamnify the sd Shaw on account of the securityship afsd & the other debt, do by these presents grant & make over to the sd Shaw one mare, one horse, eight head of cattle, nine head of hogs, three beds & furniture, one trunk, two chists, two pots, one frying pan, one gun, nine plates, two dishes, two basons, five flag chears, one spinning wheel, a weavers lume, three axes, three hoes & 1/2 doz gees ... . Wit: John Taylor, Thomas Moody. Ackn 15 Oct 1764 & recorded. Attest: John Lee Junr clerk. (Pg 338)

21 Jul 1762. Bond. James Emmerson & William Roane gent of Essex Co are firmly bound unto James Webb sheriff of sd co for 1,000 pd ... the condition of this obligation is such that whereas the afsd James Webb hath appointed the sd James Emmerson keeper of the goal of the sd co during pleasure, if the sd James Emmerson shall well & truly keep & perform the business of goaler & save harmless & indemnify the sd James Webb from all troubles costs & damages that shall or may accrue or arise as well by his not performing the duty of goaler according to law as for all escapes of prisoners out of his custody & also from all manner of suits which shall be prosecuted agt the sd James Webb as sheriff for any thing concerning the office of goaler then this obligation to be void ... . Wit: John Penn, Simon Miller Junr, Luke Covington. Ackn 15 Oct 1764 & recorded. Attest: John Lee Junr clerk. (Pg 339)

24 Jun 1764. Deed of Mortgage. Henry (Hendry) Purkins Taylor of Essex Co for 34 pd 15 sl 7 pn 1/2 penny sold to James Ritchie & Company of Glasgow in North Britain merchants 50 a. of land where he now lives, six head of cattle, a young colt, six head of hoggs, three beds with the whole of his household furniture ... provided that if the sd Henry Purkins Taylor shall pay to the sd James Ritchie & Company the afsd sum with interest then this indenture to be void ... . Wit: Andrew Crawford, Thos Montgomerie, Robt Ferguson, Neile

McCoull. Proved 19 Nov 1764 & recorded. Attest: John Lee Junr clerk. (Pg 339)

16 Jul 1764. Deed of Mortgage. William Porter of Essex Co for 341 pd 3 sl 6 pn sold to James Ritchie & Company of Glasgow sundrie Negroes, viz, Tom, Jamie, Rolling, Harry & Aggie & all my stock of cattle &c ... provided that if the sd William Porter shall pay to the sd James Ritchie & Company the afsd sum with interest then this indenture to be void ... . Wit: Neile McCoull, Andrew Crawford. Proved 19 Nov 1764 & recorded. Attest: John Lee Junr clerk. (Pg 340)

15 Oct 1764. Deed of Mortgage. James Dycke of Essex Co for 190 pd 11 sl 6 pn sold to James Ritchie & Company of Glasgow in North Britain merchants a 480 a. tr of land on Hoskins Cr & one Negro wench named Rose & child ... provided that if the sd James Dycke shall pay unto the sd James Ritchie & Company the afsd sum with interest then this indenture to be void ... . Wit: Andrew Crawford, Thomas Montgomerie, Robt Farguson. Proved 19 Nov 1764 & recorded. Attest: John Lee Junr clerk. (Pg 341)

29 Sep 1764. Deed of Mortgage. Ambrose Cox of Essex Co for 33 pd sold to James Ritchie & Company of Glasgow in North Briton merchants one Negro man Simon & 100 a. of land whereon William Yarrington now lives ... provided that if the sd Ambrose Cox shall pay to the sd James Ritchie & Company the afsd sum with interest then this indenture to be void ... . Wit: Andrew Crawford, Robt Ferguson, Neil McCoull, Willm Gatewood. Proved 19 Nov 1764 & recorded. Attest: John Lee Junr clerk. (Pg 342)

17 Nov 1764. Deed of Lease. Samuel Henshaw of Essex Co let to farm unto Daniel Thomas & Frances his wife a 50 a. parcell of land in St. Anns Parish during the term of 9 years & the sd term to commence 25 Dec next ... the sd land is land formerly belonging to Ownby now adj the lands of Thomas Bridgforth decd, land whereon Jeremiah Bizwell now lives & the sd Samuel Henshaw's land ... on consideration whereof the sd Daniel Thomas & Frances his wife to pay unto the sd Samuel Henshaw 2 pd 10 sl upon 25 Dec annually untill the afsd term of 9 years is expired ... . Wit: Wm Boulware, Thomas Boulware, John O. Mohundro Junr. Proved 19 Nov 1764 & recorded. Attest: John Lee Junr clerk. (Pg 343)

11 Oct 1764. Deed. Francis Smith Junr of South Farnham Parish, Essex Co for 24 pd 11 sl 3 pn sold to Henry Crutcher Senr of same place a 32 3/4 a. parcel of land in the sd parish bounded by William Brooke Senr, sd Henry Crutcher, Thomas Newbill Senr, Thomas Newbill & sd Francis Smith ... . Wit: Robt

Read, Richard Broocke, Susannah Broocke, Ruben Crutcher. Proved 17 Dec 1764 & recorded. Attest: John Lee Junr clerk. (Pg 344)

XVII Dec 1764. Deed. William Lyne & Lucy his wife of Drysdale Parish, King & Queen Co, VA for 124 pd 10 sl sold to Thomas Roane of South Farnham Parish, Essex Co a 200 a. tr of land on the brs of Hoskins's Cr in South Farnham Parish being the land which he purch of Robert Johnson & Mary his wife 20 Aug 1764 bounded by the sd Thomas Roane, Nicholas Pamplin's orphans, sd Roane's land & Prewet's line ... . Wit: None. Ackn by William Lyne 17 Dec 1764 & recorded. Attest: John Lee Junr clerk. (Pg 345)

1 Sep 1764. Bond. John Daniel & James Daniel of Caroline Co, Priscillia Daniel, Harison Daniel, Nathaniel Conduitt & Ann Daniel of Essex Co are firmly bound unto either to other in the penal sum of 1,000 pd ... the condition of this obligation is such that if the afsd John Daniel, James Daniel, Priscillia Daniel, Harison Daniel for himself & for Mary Daniel an infant, Nathaniel Conduitt for himself & for Thomas Farmer & Ann Daniel do for themselves & each of their heirs &c stand to abide and for ever hereafter fulfill & keep to the division & settlement of James Rennolds, David Dishman & Edward Vauter settlers elected named & chosen by the parties afsd to divide & settle the estate of James Daniel decd equally amongst the afsd parties after their mother's part is assigned her out of the same & she the sd Priscilla Daniel doth hereby oblige herself to take no more than the two old Negroes George & Phillis for her part of the slaves, also to let the afsd John Daniel have the first choice of the ballance of the slaves after the two afsd are assigned to his mother & that the sd settlers (or either two of them) do give up their schedule of such division under their hands & seals at the next Nov court for this co after such division, then this bond to be void ... . Wit: James Rennolds, David Dishman, Edward Vauter, James Conduitt. Proved 17 Dec 1764 by James Rennolds a wit hereto & on the motion of the parties is admitted to record. Attest: John Lee Junr clerk. (Pg 346)

The subscribers being named elected & chosen by Priscillia Daniel, John Daniel, James Daniel, Harrison Daniel for himself & for Mary Daniel an infant, Nathaniel Conduitt for himself & for Thomas Farmer an infant & Ann Daniel to divide equally the estate of James Daniel decd according to bonds [see above] after duely considering the matter do judge & determine as follows, that is to say, we allot to Mrs. Priscillia Daniel the two old Negroes George & Phillis which she has already taken as her choise during her natural life & them afterwards to fall & descend to the heir at law of the sd James Daniel decd as also all the personal estate of sd decd that is now in her possession during her natural life & after her decease that it should be divided amongst her children, next we judge & determine that John Daniel have two Negroes named Hannah & Esther & their increase & that he should return back to the estate of the sd decd

25 pd, also we do award judge & determine that James Daniel have one Negro named Will as also to be paid out of the afsd estate 2 pd 19 sl 6 pn as an acct as also 7 pd 17 sl 6 pn for his pt/o Negro money, we also adjudge that Harrison Daniel have one Negro named Sam as also 6 pd 11 sl 5 pn out of the afsd estate being his pt/o Negro money, also we allot to Nathaniel Conduitt one Negro named Davy as also Bob whom he have purch & 19 pd 3 sl 9 pn out of the sd estate, we also award that Ann Daniel have one Negro named Bett and her increase also 6 pd 11 sl 5 pn out of sd estate, also we allot to Harrison Daniel for an on the acct of Mary Daniel an infant for whom he is guardian one Negro named George as also 6 pd 11 sl 5 pn, also we do allot to Nathaniel Conduit for an on the behalf of Thomas Farmer an infant one Negro named Ben as also 3 pd 11 sl 5 pn out of the afsd estate, we also judge that Harrison Daniel be paid 14 sl out of the sd estate, we do also adjudge that John Daniel have 6 pd 11 sl 5 pn out of the sd estate & further we allot that Mrs. Priscillia Daniel receive & pay the above accts by us here set forth ... . In wit whereof we have hereunto set out hands & seals 16 Nov 1764 James Rennolds, David Dishman, Edward Vawter. This settlement & award was presented to the court 17 Dec 1764 & on the motion of the parties is admitted to record. Attest: John Lee Junr clerk. (Pg 347)

21 Oct 1764. Deed. John Read Junr & Elizabeth his wife of Culpepper Co for 20 pd sold to William Howerton of South Farnham Parish, Essex Co all the tr of land that belonged to Griffing Purkins decd which the afsd Elizabeth Read w/o the sd John Read Junr being a lawfull coheir of the sd Griffing Purkins decd's body to the 1/2 of the sd tr of land the other 1/2 being now in the lawfull possession of the sd William Howerton, the sd tr of land being in South Farnham Parish on Covingtons Swamp bounded by James Newbill Senr, William Greenwood, Richard Fisher, William Covington Junr, Heritage Howerton & John Harper containing 72 a. ... . Wit: Luke Covington, LeRoy Hipkins, James Pendleton, W. Brown, Lucy Tate. Proved 17 Dec 1764 & recorded. Attest: John Lee Junr clerk. (Pg 348)

8 Oct ----. To William Williams & Henry Pendleton of Culpepper Co gent greeting, whereas John Read (Readd) Junr & Elizabeth his wife of co afsd have by a deed [see above] sold to William Howerton of Essex co a 72 a. parcel of land, & whereas the sd Elizabeth living at a great distance from the court cannot conveniently travel thereto to make such acknowledgment as in that case is required, as we have received information, we therefore in this case have given you power to take the acknowledgment which the sd Elizabeth shall be willing to make ... . Wit John Lee Junr clerk. 25 Oct 1764 By virtue of this writ to us directed William Williams & Henry Pendleton did personally go to the sd Elizabeth Read & examined her privily & apart from the sd John Read Junr her husband & she freely & voluntarily ackn the deed & is willing the same should

be recorded. At a court for Essex Co 17 Dec 1764 this commission & the commissioners return were presented & ordered to be recorded. Attest: John Lee Junr clerk. (Pg 350)

17 Dec 1764. Bond. Archibald Ritchie, William Roane & William Young of Essex Co are firmly bound unto Francis Waring, John Clements, Samuel Peachey, Robert Beverly, Meriwether Smith, Simon Miller & James Roy gent justices of Essex Co for 35,000 lbs of tobacco ... whereas the afsd Archibald Ritchie is appointed collector of the co levy for the ensuing year, now the condition of this obligation is such that if the sd Archibald Ritchie shall well & truly collect the sd levy & pay to the severall claimants their respective claims then this obligation to be void ... . Wit: None. Ackn 17 Dec 1764 & recorded. Attest: John Lee Junr clerk. (Pg 350)

17 Dec 1764. Bond. Archibald Ritchie, William Roane & William Young are firmly bound unto our Sovereign Lord the King for 1,000 pd ... the condition of this obligation is such that if the afsd Archibald Ritchie sheriff of Essex Co shall well & truly collect from the inhabitants of sd co for the year 1765 the taxes imposed on the sd inhabitants by several Acts of Assembly & pay the same according to the directions of the several Acts then this obligation to be void ... . Wit: None. Ackn 17 Dec 1764 & recorded. Attest: John Lee Junr clerk. (Pg 351)

13 Jul 1764. Deed of Mortgage. John Garnett Junr of St. Anns Parish, Essex Co for the considerations set forth sold to Richard Noell of same parish & Mark Andrews of Cumberland Co the following Negroes, viz, Dick a Negro man slave, Frank a Negro woman slave & the increase of the sd Frank ... whereas the sd Noell & Andrews became securities for the sd John Garnett for his due & faithfull administration of the estate of Thomas Garnett decd, & whereas the sd Noell & Andrews being apprehensive of suffering by the securityship afsd have petitioned the sd co court & obtained an order agt the sd Garnett for counter security & on failure of giving such security to deliver up the estate of the sd Thomas Garnett to the sd Noell & Andrews for their indemnification, & the sd John Garnett being unable to give security agreeable to the order afsd it is proposed by the sd Garnett to make over to the sd Noell & Andrews the Negroes named to secure them to the sd Noell & Andrews from any damages or costs that they or either of them may sustain by means of the sd securityship afsd ... provided that if the sd John Garnett shall pay all & every claim agt the estate of the sd Thomas Garnett & shall produce to the sd Richard Noell & Mark Andrews sufficient discharges & acquittances from under the hands of the several claimants in order to satisfy them of the sd John Garnett's having fully administred the sd estate then this indenture shall be void ... . Wit: John Lee

Junr, William Webb. Proved 18 Feb 1765 & recorded. Attest: John Lee Junr clerk. (Pg 351)

13 Jul 1764. Deed. Thomas Roane of South Farnham Parish, Essex Co for 75 pd sold to Robert Johnson of same parish a 100 a. tr of land & premises in the sd parish being the land the sd Robert Johnson sold to Phillip Gatewood 10 Jul 1754 ... . Wit: John Upshaw, James Webb Junr, James Upshaw, Henry Kidd. Ackn 18 Feb 1765 & recorded. Attest: John Lee Junr clerk. (Pg 352)

7 Dec 1764. Deed of Gift. Henry Motley of Essex Co for love & affection have given to my son Edwin Motley of sd co the following Negro slaves, viz, Mot, Tommy, Sue & Hanner & their future increase ... . Wit: Wm Thomas Senr, Wm Thomas Junr, James Samuell. Proved 18 Feb 1765 & recorded. Attest: John Lee Junr clerk. (Pg 354)

7 Dec 1764. Deed of Gift. Henry Motley of Essex Co for love & affection have given to Benjamin Harrison of sd co the following Negro slaves (viz) Stephen, Tabb, Harry & Sary & their future increase ... . Wit: Wm Thomas Senr, Wm Thomas Junr, James Samuell. Proved 18 Feb 1765 & recorded. Attest: John Lee Junr clerk. (Pg 354)

15 Feb 1765. Deed. Walter Stallard & Hannah his wife of Essex Co for 200 pd sold to James Garnett of same co a 250 a. tr of land bounded by Lucuses Line nigh John Price's old field, James Landram, Forrest Road, Parker's old field & Lucuses pattent ... . Wit: Harry Garnett, David Pitts, William Cavenaugh. Ackn 18 Feb 1765 by Walter Stallard & Hannah his wife (she being first privily examined & thereto consenting) & recorded. Attest: John Lee Junr clerk. (Pg 355)

18 Feb 1765. Bond. Archibald Ritchie, John Upshaw & Alexander Rose of Essex Co are firmly bound unto Simon Miller, William Mountague, Samuel Peachey, Paul Micou, Robert Beverley & Meriwether Smith for 200,000 lbs of tobacco ... the condition of this obligation is such that whereas the sd Archibald Ritchie sheriff of sd co is appointed collector of the public levy for this present year, now if the sd Archibald Ritchie shall well & truly collect the sd levy & pay the several claimants their respective claims, then this obligation to be void ... . Wit: None. Ackn 18 Feb 1765 & recorded. Attest: John Lee Junr clerk. (Pg 356)

DEED BOOK VOLUME 30
1765-1772

[Pages 1-6 are missing]

... [First part missing] ... parcel of land & premises &c unto the sd McCall ....
the sd Garnett give security to sd McCall's liking this to be of [?] effect &c but
void. Wit: John Deans, John Steven, James Lang. Ackn & delivered for the
uses within mentioned before us 28 Feb 1765 John Lee Junr, Jos Gillon. In a
court continued & held 19 Feb 1765 this deed of mortgage from Leonard Garnett
to Archibald McCall proved by the oaths of James Lang a wit hereto who also
made oath that he was John Stephens decd sign the same as a wit & on -- Mar
1765 was fully proved by the oaths of John Lee Junr & John Deans wits hereto
& recorded. Attest: John Lee Junr clerk. (Pg 7)

27 Aug 1764. Deed of Mortgage. John Seayres of South Farnham Parish, Essex
Co for 200 pd sold to John Orr, David Chives (Cheves) & Alexander Smith all
my right & title to a piece of land in Lancaster Co, quantity unknown, a Negro
man slave named Lewis & the ballances due me from Thomas Herbert &
securitys Thomas Loyd & John Thomas ... provided that if the sd John Seayres
will truely pay unto the sd John Orr, David Chevis & Alexander Smith the sd
sums that they have obtained judgments & executions agt me together with costs
before 5 Dec next ensuing the sale hereby made to be void ... . Wit: Archibald
Ritchie, William Muir, Pitman Clements. Proved 18 Mar 1765 & recorded.
Attest: John Lee Junr clerk. (Pg 8)

7 Aug 1764. Deed. William Churchill & John Robinson & Mary his wife
which sd William & Mary are exors of the will of John Armistead gent decd for
130 pd paid to Ralph Wormley, Christopher Robinson, John Page & Edmund
Barkley gent surviving trustees in the sd Act named sold to John Corrie of Essex
Co merchant two lots of land in the Town of Tappahannock numbered in the
plan of sd town 27 & 28 being pt/o eight lots ... whereas by an Act of Assembly
his late Majesty George the second initiated an act to impower John Armistead
gent to sell & dispose of certain intailed lands to raise money for the
performance of his father's will the sd John Armistead, and in case of his death
his executors & adminrs are severally impowered to sell eight lots of land in the
Town of Tappahannock ... . Wit: Wm Snodgrass, James Campbell, John
Powers, William Mountage (Mountague), George Davis. Proved 18 Mar 1765
& recorded. Attest: John Lee Junr clerk. (Pg 10)

10 Aug 1764. To John Page & Thomas Smith of Gloster Co gent greeting,
whereas William Churchill & John Robinson & Mary his wife have by their
deed [see above] conveyed unto John Corrie of Essex Co two lots or 1/2 acres of

land in the Town of Tappahannock, & whereas the sd Mary is unable to travel to our co court to make acknowledgment thereof, therefore we command you to repair to the sd Mary & privily & apart from her sd husband examine whether she is willing her acknowledgment of the same may be recorded ... . Wit John Lee clerk. 8 Mar 1765 We John Page & Thomas Smith certify that we examined Mary w/o John Robinson privily & apart from her husband & she freely relinquished her right of dower in the two lotts of land. Truly recorded Mar Court 1765. Attest: John Lee Junr clerk. (Pg 11)

7 Aug 1764. Receipt. Whereas by an Act of Assembly John Armistead & in case of his death his executors & adminrs were severally impower'd to sell 1710 a. of land in Essex Co & also eight lotts of land in the Town of Tappahannock, but the consideration money is by the sd Act directed to be paid to us the subscribers for the purposes therein mentioned, & whereas William Churchill & John Robinson & Mary his wife executors of the sd John Armistead decd have by indenture this date sold unto John Corrie of sd co merchant two lotts of land in the sd town being pt/o the eight lots in the sd Act mentioned, we do hereby ackn to have received of the sd John Corrie 130 pd being the consideration by him to be paid for the sd lots of land. Signed by Ralph Wormely, Christopher Robinson, John Page. Wit to Ralph Wormely & Christopher Robinson esqr: James Mills, Archd Ritchie, William Mountague. Wit to John Page esqr: James Lang, John Lewis. Proved 18 Mar 1765 & recorded. Attest: John Lee Junr clerk. (Pg 12)

15 Apr 1765. Deed of Gift. Thomas Barker & Ann his wife being possessed of a parcel of land in South Farnham Parish whereon they now live containing 50 a., 37 a. part thereof was given to the sd Ann by her father Henry Boughan decd by his deed dated 20 Nov 1733 the other part thereof purch of James Boughan decd by his deed dated 16 Nov 1747, bounded by John Smith, Broom Br, John Croxton, Josiah Minter, Western Br & Hugh Willson ... now this indenture the sd Thomas Barker & Ann his wife for natural love & affection have given to their granddau Milly Mason dau of James Mason & Betty his wife decd all their right & title in the sd land reserving to themselves the sole right & property in the sd land for & during both their lives ... under the reservations that in case the sd Milley Mason should die & leave no issue that then the sd land to go to John Minter son of Josiah Minter & Mary his wife decd ... . Wit: Hugh Wilson, Catharine Wilson, James Wilson. Ackn 15 Apr 1765 & recorded. Attest: John Lee Junr clerk. (Pg 12)

1 Dec 1764. Indenture Tripartite between John Vass of Essex Co bricklayer & Ann his wife of the first part James Webb gent late high sheriff of sd co of the second part & Philip Cheyney of same co of the third part, whereas the sd John Vass being indebted to James Johnson & being taken in execution for the sd debt

did deliver in a schedule of his estate in the co court in which schedule was
included a tr of land formerly purch by the sd Vass of the sd Johnson & by the
sd Vass mortgaged to William Snodgrass, & the sd John Vass having complied
with the law for relief of insolvent debtors & been discharged out of executions
for the debt afsd his whole estate became vested in the sd James Webb as high
sherif, now this indenture the sd John Vass & Ann his wife for & in
consideration of the premises & also for 5 sl have sold the sd Philip Cheyney all
that tr of land afsd containing 130 a. bounded by the lands of William Bond, sd
John Vass, Robert James & by Webbs Mill swamp ... & the sd James Webb as
high sherif of sd co also for & in consideration of the premises & 100 pd paid by
the sd Philip Cheyeny hath sold & release unto the sd Philip Cheyney the tr of
land afsd ... . Wit: Andrew Allen, Frans Brizendine, Thos Bush. Proved 15 Apr
1765 & the sd Ann being first privily examined relinquished her right of dower
to the land & premises & recorded. Attest: John Lee Junr clerk. (Pg 14)

12 Dec 1764. Power of Attorney. James Ritchie & Henry Ritchie both
merchants in Glasgow commonly known & in our mercantile transactions
designed by the name and form of James Ritchie & Company have appointed
our trusty friends Andrew Crawford, James Anderson & Neil McCoul all
merchants upon Rappahannock River in Essex Co to be our attys to manage
negotiate & transact our whole business & affairs of every kind in VA & MD &
to account with demand levy recover & receive of & from the heirs executors
adminrs or other representatives of Andrew Anderson decd merchant upon
Rappahannock River in Essex Co & lately one of our factors there, & also from
all & sundry persons our debtors & havers of our effects in MD & VA & all
other concerned & liable all & sundry debts & sums of money due & owing or
that may fall due & be indebted to us by the sd Andrew Anderson decd & other
persons afsd ... . Wit: Matthew Bogle, Alexr Veitch. I John Gray one of the
present baillies of the City of Glasgow do hereby certify that personally
appeared before me Mathew Bogle & Alexander Veitch both merchants in
Glasgow being persons well know & worthy of good credit & did solemnly &
sincerely declare that they did see James Ritchie & Henry Ritchie sign, seal & as
their act & deed in due form of law execute & deliver the power of atty within
written ... . Proved in a court for Essex Co 16 Apr 1765 & recorded. Attest:
John Lee Junr clerk. (Pg 15)

20 May 1765. Deed. John Webb of Essex Co & Lilly (Lily) Ann his wife for 42
pd 7 sl 6 pn sold to John Young of co afsd a 32 1/4 a. parcel of land & marsh
bounded by William Gatewood & Rappahannock River ... . Wit: John
Richards, John Mills, Isaac Webb. Ackn 20 May 1765 by John Webb & Lilly
Ann his wife (she being first privily examined & thereto consenting) & recorded.
Attest: John Lee Junr clerk. (Pg 18)

14 Dec 1764. Power of Attorney. Margaret (Margrat) & Mary Conner (Conners) indwellors in Greenock in Renfrew Co, North Britain & sisters german to the decd Edward Conner merchant in Alexandria in Pottomack River, VA & as such heirs at law to our decd brother have appointed our trusty & well beloved friends Robert & Cumberland Wilsons merchants in Alexandria afsd to administer in all & sundry the goods chattels rights credits lands & other effects whatsoever & estate which belonged to the sd decd Edward Conner our brother within VA or any other pt/o America as also to ask levy demand & by all lawfull ways & means whatsoever to uplift recover & receive of & from all & every person whom it doeth or may concern all such sums of money debts & demands whatsoever that were pertaining & belonging or indebted & owing to our sd decd brother at the time of his decease .... . Wit: Pattrick Robertson, George Forbes. Att Port Glasgow 14 Dec 1764 these are certifying that the before designed Margaret & Mary Conner's did in my presence sign & seal the forgoing power of atty. John Martine J.P. for co afsd. Proved 20 May 1765 at Essex Co & recorded. Attest: John Lee Junr clerk. (Pg 19)

22 Dec 1764. Deed. Joseph Noell & Mary his wife of Essex Co for 22 pd sold to Cornelius Sale of same co a tr of land whereon the sd Joseph Noell now lives in St. Anns Parish & on the w side of a br that runeth between the house where I now live & the sd Sale's house bounded by land of Richard Hill, John Smither, William Upshaw decd & Elizabeth Smither, it being all the land I hold upon the e side of the sd br containing 50 a. .... . Wit: Reubin Noell, Richd Noell, Merriday Brown. Ackn 20 May 1765 by Joseph Noell & recorded. Ackn 18 Nov 1765 by Mary w/o the sd Joseph Noell (being first privily examined & assenting thereto) & recorded. Attest: John Lee Junr clerk. (Pg 21)

In obedience to an order of the Worshipful Court of Essex Co dated 18 Sep 1764 in the presence of James Garnett, James Roy & Muscoe Garnett gent, I have laid off the lands which was showed me whereof George Green decd died seised in fee tail & divided the same into three parts, the first part adj Meadows Cr, Col John Lee, Stark Boulware, Capt Paul Micou, Old Mill Pond, Blackborns Cr, Capt Garnett, Long's line, Mr. Thorp, Major Simon Miller, Capt Micou & land the sd George Green decd formerly escheated from Meador's containing 402 a., for the division I crossed the Old Mill Pond, adj Major Miller, Capt Micou, containing 129 a. This survey I finished 1 Dec 1764, Thomas Goodrich, Berryman Brown & George Green chain carriers. Edward Vawter surveyor. [Drawing not included here] (Pg 22)

23 Apr 1765. Pursuant to an order of Essex Co Court dated 18 Sep 1764 we Jas Garnett, Ja(mes) Roy & Muscoe Garnett in company with the co surveyor have layd off & divided the lands whereof George Green decd died seised in fee taill between the parties George Gaines & Betty his wife & Sarah & Hannah Hipkins

Green ... we have also allotted each person 9 pd as the profits arising from the afsd lands. This division & report were returned & ordered to be recorded. Attest: John Lee Junr clerk. (Pg 24)

20 Feb 1765. Deed of Gift. John Pickett & Mary his wife of Caroline Co, VA for love good will & most tender effection & also 5 sl have given unto their son Mace Pickett of same co a 125 a. parcel of land that the sd John & Mary Pickett holds in South Farnham Parish bounded by William Cox, Henry Cox & Piscattaway Cr ... . Wit: Edward Vauter, William Picket Junr, Mace Pickett Junr. Proved 17 Jun 1765 & recorded. Attest: John Lee Junr clerk. (Pg 24)

29 Dec 1764. Deed of Mortgage. Thomas Johnson of Essex Co for 20 pd sold to Thomas Parron & John Draper of King & Queen Co one small black mare & her horse colt, one large white mare branded on the near buttock "R", one boat, all my stock of hogs, my crop of tobacco now on the plantation where I now dwell & all the profitts due to me for this present year for teaching school ... provided that if the sd Thomas Johnson shall well & truly pay unto the sd Thomas Parron & John Draper 20 pd at or upon 1 Mar next ensuing then this bill of sale to be void ... . Wit: James Upshaw, Wm Coats, James Parron. Proved 17 Jun 1765 & recorded. Attest: John Lee Junr clerk. (Pg 25)

9 Apr 1765. Deed of Mortgage. Benjamin Waggoner (Waggener) of Essex Co for 204 pd 10 pn now due from sd Waggoner to James Ritchie & Company hath sold to the sd James Ritchie & Company of Glasgow in North Britain merchants 200 a. of land whereon the sd Waggoner now lives & one Negro fellow named Essex ... provided that if the sd Waggoner shall pay to the sd James Ritchie & Company the sd 204 pd with interest then this indenture to be void ... . Wit: Andrew Crawford, J. Porter, Robt Ferguson. Proved 17 Jun 1765 & recorded. Attest: John Lee Junr clerk. (Pg 26)

22 Feb 1765. Deed of Mortgage. Jonathan Shearwood of Essex Co planter for 29 pd 18 sl 7 pn 1/2 penny sold to James Ritchie & Company of Glasgow in North Britain merchants one bay horse, one gray mare & colt, nine cows & three yearlings ... provided that if the sd Jonathan Shearwood shall pay to the sd James Ritchie & Company the sd sum with interest then this indenture to be void ... . Wit: W. Ramsay, Robt Fergusson. Proved 17 Jun 1765 & recorded. Attest: John Lee Junr clerk. (Pg 27)

23 Mar 1765. Deed of Mortgage. William Ramsay of Essex Co for 182 pd 4 sl sold to James Ritchie & Company of Glasgow merchants the lots & houses whereon I now live in the Town of Tappahannock ... provided that if the sd William Ramsay shall pay to the sd James Ritchie & Company the sd sum with interest then this indenture to be void ... . Wit: Andrew Crawford, Robt

Ferguson, Wm Snodgrass. Ackn 17 Jun 1765 & recorded. Attest: John Lee Junr clerk. (Pg 28)

13 Nov 1764. Deed. Thomas Williamson younger & Jane Acre his mother of South Farnham Parish, Essex Co for 18 pd 8 sl 3 pn sold to John Hodges of same parish a messuage & 30 1/4 a. tr of land on the n end of the land the afsd Thomas Williamson & Jane Acre now live on in the sd parrish on the brs of Captain James Webb Senr's mill run bounded by Cooper's corner, the Maine Road & Thomas Cox ... . Wit: Richd Brown, Richard Cooper, John Cooper. Ackn 17 Jun 1765 by Thomas Williamson & recorded. Attest: John Lee Junr clerk. (Pg 29)

5 Mar 1765. Deed. Cornelius Sale & Martha his wife of Essex Co for 18 pd 10 sl sold to Thomas Sale of same co a parcel of land which Cornelius Sale decd purch of Daniel Tucker & all the land & plantation on which the sd last mentioned Cornelius Sale lived that lies on the lower side of the Main Road that leads from Capt Garnett's mill to King & Queen Co ... . Wit: John Sale, Elisabeth Jones, Elisabeth Heely. Ackn 17 Jun 1765 by Cornelius Sale & recorded. Attest: John Lee Junr clerk. (Pg 31)

26 Feb 1765. Deed. Thomas Sale & Moly his wife of Essex Co for 6 pd 10 sl sold to Cornelius Sale of Essex Co a 50 a. tr of land which Cornelius Sale decd purch of Francis Pagett (reference to the will of the sd Cornelius Sale recorded in the court of the sd co) ... . Wit: Thomas Heely, John Gray, Katharine Davis, John Sale, Elisabeth Jones, Elisabeth Heely. Ackn 17 Jun 1765 & recorded. Attest: John Lee Junr clerk. (Pg 32)

9 Mar 1765. Bond. Griffen Johnson of Essex Co am firmly bound unto Richard Johnson, Ann Johnson & Elizabeth Johnson of sd co for 500 pd ... the condition of this obligation is such that if the afsd Griffen Johnson shall stand to & abide by a division of the Negroes & other estate of his decd father Isaac Johnson this day made by James Jones, Smith Young & Richard Jefries persons appointed by the court to perform the same that then this obligation to be void ... . Wit: James Jones, Smith Young, Richard Jeffries. Proved 20 May 1765 & recorded. Attest: John Lee Junr clerk. (Pg 33)

27 Nov 1764. Bond. Mildred Parker of St. Anns Parish, Essex Co am firmly bound unto Alexander Ferguson, Samuel Hawes & Francis Ramsay Junr of sd co for 1,000 pd ... the condition of this obligation is such that if the sd Mildred do agree to deliver up there proportionable pts/o the Negroes belonging to the estate of Daniel Farguson decd namely, I agree to take Frank & Hanner & agree Alexr Farguson have Phillis & Bob, Francis Ramsay to have George & Phebe & Samuel Hawes to have Will & Easter & the sd Mildred Parker agrees to deliver

up the land whereon she now lives on to Alexr Farguson & Frans Ramsay for a term of years till a debt is satisfyed due to Andrew Anderson decd & then to return to the sd Mildred Parker if she for her part do agree & stand to the above agreement then this obligation to be void ... . Wit: Edward Carter, Robt Parker, Richard Gouldman, Richard Domagin. Proved 15 Jul 1765 & recorded. Attest: John Lee Junr clerk. (Pg 34)

27 Jun 1765. Deed of Gift. William Daingerfield of Essex Co esqr for love & affection have given to William Meredith who intermarried with Ann Bushead the dau of the sd William Daingerfield the following Negro slaves, viz, Casar, Ned, Moll & her children Patty, Mary, Dide, Winney, Lewis & Bell, which sd slaves are now in the possession of the sd William Meredith ... . Wit: Pitman Clements. Proved 15 Jul 1765 & recorded. Attest: John Lee Junr clerk. (Pg 35)

3 Jan 1765. Deed of Mortgage. Thomas Loyd of Essex Co planter for 46 pd 12 sl 1 penny sold to Archibald McCall of Essex Co a 200 a. tr of land in St. Anns Parish bounded by William Dobson, Nicholas Faulconer, John Garnett & Willm Jones as also my gray mare colt & 16 head of cattle after satisfying John Sale 8 pd out of the sd cattle & my four beds & furniture ... provided that if the sd Thomas Loyd shall well & truely pay unto the sd Archibald McCall the afsd sum with interest on or before 1 Mar next ensuing & all the charges which may accrue by recording this deed that then this deed shall be null & void ... . Wit: Isaac Williamson, John Williamson, James Lang, James Acres. Ackn 17 Jul 1765 & recorded. Attest: John Lee Junr clerk. (Pg 36)

17 Aug 1765. Deed. John Garnett Junr of St. Anns Parish, Essex Co & Mary his wife for 125 pd sold to Augustine Garnett of same parish a 156 a. tr of land on which the sd John Garnett now lives in the sd parish bounded by Joseph Fogg, John Cassell, Leonard Garnett, Francis Graves & John Latane ... . Wit: John Casell, Henry Martin, Susannah Garnett. Ackn 19 Aug 1765 by John Garnett Junr & recorded. Attest: John Lee Junr clerk. (Pg 38)

2 Jul 1765. Deed. John Garnett & Esther his wife of Essex Co for 52 pd 13 sl 9 pn sold to their son Achillis Garnett of same co a 100 a. tr of land bounded by Occupatia Run, Achillis Garnett, Warners Spring Br & Jones's line ... . Wit: Leonard Garnett, Nicholas Faulconer Junr, William Dobson Junr. Proved 19 Aug 1765 & recorded. Attest: John Lee Junr clerk. (Pg 40)

21 Jan 1765. Deed of Mortgage. John Wild (Wyld) sadler of Essex Co for 120 pd sold to Archibald McCall of same co all his right to a trustee estate given by sundrie gent to Edmond Pendleton, James Taylor & Thomas Johnstone in trust for the use of Thomas Wild & family & afterwards to his children John, Thomas & Rebecca Wild, & likewise all his right to 1/6 pt/o 56 Negroes left by my

grandfather James Taylor by will to Tabathy Taylor his dau now in the possession of Edmond Pendleton or Erasmus Taylor recourse being had to the sd will in Caroline Office & division of sd Negroes recorded in Orange Co ... provided that if the sd John Wild shall well & truely pay unto the sd Archibald McCall the afsd sum with interest & all charges which may accrue by this deed that then this deed shall be null & void ... . Wit: Pitman Clements, John Atkinson, James Lang. Ackn 20 Aug 1765 & recorded. Attest: John Lee Junr clerk. (Pg 41)

20 Dec 1763. Deed of Lease. Lyonell Lyde of London merchant for 5 sl leased to Chauncy Poole of Islington in Middlesex Co gent a messuage & 965 a. tr of land whereon Andrew Monroe gent now lives or formerly did live called Kinsale in Washington Parish, Westmoreland Co, VA which the sd Andrew Monroe purch of Daniel Ford, George Gray, Lovel Harrison & John Shelton, & all that messuage & 1,375 a. tr of land in Fairfax Co which the sd Andrew Monroe purch of John Elliot, & also all that undivided 1/2 pt/o a 1,900 a. tr of land in Frederick Co which the sd Andrew Monroe purch together with Colonel Benjamin Grayson of Prince William Co, & also a 109 a. tr of land in Westmoreland Co adj to the land of Spence Monroe, & also a messuage & 75 a. tr of land whereon John Monroe gent son of the sd Andrew Monroe now lives or formerly did live in Washington Parish, Westmoreland Co, & also all other messuages & trs of land of the sd Andrew Monroe in the sd cos ... for the term of 1 year paying the yearly rent of one pepper corn at the expiration of the sd term if demanded ... . Wit: Abram Ogier, John Clement, John Burnham. Reexecuted by Lyonel Lyde 26 Feb 1765. Wit: William Robinson, Alexander Steven, John Forrester, Hugh Wylie. (Pg 43)

21 Dec 1763. Deed of Release. Lyonel Lyde of London merchant for 1,000 pd released unto Chancy Poole of Islington, Middlesex Co gent several messuages & trs of land ... [same as above] ... & slaves, goods & chattles ... whereas by indenture of lease & release or mortgage dated 2 & 3 Jun 1755 & made between Andrew Monroe of Westmoreland Co, VA gent & Lyonell Lyde, the sd Andrew Monroe for 1,730 pd did sell unto the sd Lyonel Lyde several trs of land [same as above] ... & also all those several slaves, goods & chattels, that is to say, Tombo, Peter, Sharper, Devonshire, Kate, Sarah, Pegg, Milly, Sam, Will, Winny, Judy, Nan, Moll, Amos, Little Kate, James, Bob, Isaac, Dinah, Hannah, Williams, Amos the younger, Patience, Jacob, Nancy, Abraham, Keziah, Mimay, Dick, Lucy, Ben, Scipia, Lettice, Dancy, Tim, Charity, Sue, Rachel & Beck together with their future issue, 60 head of cattle, 50 sheep, 8 horses, 8 beds & furniture, 2 doz of chairs, 6 tables, 1 desk, 1 escustore?, 1 spring cloak (clock?), 150 lbs of pewter, 6 iron potts & 2 copper kettles, to the sd Lyonel Lyde subject to the proviso for redemption of the premises therein mentioned in which sd indenture of release is contained a condition for making void the same

indenture & the estate & interest of sd Lyonel Lyde of the sd sum of 1,730 pd with interest, & whereas the sd Lyonel Lyde hath since received of the sd Andrew Monroe pt/o the sd sum but there still remains due to him on the sd mortgage 1,000 pd & upwards & the sd Lyonel Lyde being desirous to get his sd money hath offered to assign over the sd mortgage & security & the whole benefit thereof to the sd Chauncy Poole for 1,000 pd which offer the sd Chauncy Poole hath accepted ... . Wit: Abram Ogier, John Clement, John Burnham. Reexecuted by Lyonel Lyde 26 Feb 1765. Wit: William Robinson, Alexander Steven, John Forrester, Hugh Wylie. (Pg 45)

I William Bridgon esqr Lord Major of the City of London do hereby certify that personally came & appeared before me John Clement the deponent named in the affidavit hereunto annexed being a person well known & worthy of good credit & by solemn oath did declare, testify & depose to be true the several matters & things mentioned & contained in the sd annexed affidavit. In London 18 Aug 17 1764. (Pg 50)

[The name Hodges is either at the end of the above deed or the beginning of the deed below.]

John Clement clerk to Abraham Ogier of London notary publick maketh oath that he was present & did see Lyonel Lyde of London merchant sign seal & as his act & deed execute & deliver the original indenture hereunto annexed dated 20 Dec 1763 purporting to be a lease from the sd Lyonel Lyde to Chauncy Poole of Islington in Middlesex Co gent of the several messuage & lands therein mentioned & further this deponent saith that he was also present & did see the se Lyonel Lyde sign seal & as his act & deed execute & deliver the original indenture hereunto also annexed dated 21 Dec 1763 made between the parties afsd & purporting to be a release of the sd messuage & lands so leased & that thereupon he this deponent together with the sd Abraham Ogier & John Burnham did set & subscribe their names as wits. Sworn 18 Aug 1764 before Wm Bridgen mayor. At a court held for Essex Co 21 Aug 1765 these deeds of lease & release were prov'd to the reexecution & on the motion of James Hunter were recorded. Attest: John Lee Junr clerk. (Pg 51)

16 Sep 1765. Deed. Isaac Scandrett gent of Essex Co & Sarah his wife for neighbourly friendship & love & 5 sl doth discharge William Daingerfield of sd co 1 a. of land adj to the sd William Daingerfield's mill dam adj the mill pond ... . Wit: George Stone, Thomas Ley, John Jones. Proved 16 Sep 1765 & ordered to be recorded. Ackn 17 Sep 1765 by Sarah Scandrett w/o sd Isaac (she being first privily examined & consenting) & recorded. Attest: John Lee Junr clerk. (Pg 52)

14 May 1765. Deed of Mortgage. James Martin of St. Ann Parish, Essex Co for 5 pd 18 sl 6 pn sold to John Broaddus of Drysdale Parish, Caroline Co a 100 a. tr of land in St. Ann Parish bounded by Foster Samuels, William Bastin, James Samuels & James Colquit, the same being that land whereon the sd Martin & his mother Mary Martin now live & is the same which was given to him by the will of his father John Martin decd ... provided that if the sd James Martin shall well & truly pay unto the sd John Broaddus the afsd debt on 10 Jun next ensuing then these presents to be void .... Wit: James Shaddock, Thomas Samuel, Francis Barbee. Attest: John Lee Junr clerk. (Pg 53)

17 Aug 1765. Deed of Gift. William Daingerfield of Essex Co esqr for love & affection have given to William Daingerfield of Spotsylvania Co gent the following Negro slaves, viz, Nell, Kate, Tom, Cheviy, Paint, Jack, Dinah, Rocksie, Andrew, Esther, Adam, Patty & all her children except Sarah now with Ann Bushrod, Meredith, Carpenter & Jamey & their increase .... Wit: Robinson Daingerfield. Proved 16 Sep 1765 & recorded. Attest: John Lee Junr clerk. (Pg 54)

16 Sep 1765. Deed. John Goode & Ann (Anne) his wife of South Farnham Parish, Essex Co for 12 pd sold to LeRoy Hipkins of same parish all their estate right in or to a water grist mill called Fishers Mill & 1 a. of land adjacent to the sd mill & lying on the s side of the pond & dam & also the land covered by the water of the pond of the sd mill .... Wit: John Richards, James Booker, John Madison. Ackn 16 Sep 1765 & John Goode & Ann his wife (she being first privily exam'd & assenting hereto) & recorded. Attest: John Lee Junr clerk. (Pg 55)

19 Sep 1765. To James Jameson & Thomas Lowry of Caroline Co gent greeting, whereas John Picket & Mary his wife have by their deed of gift dated 20 Feb 1765 convey'd unto their son Mace Pickett a tr of land in Essex Co & whereas the sd Mary is unable to travel to our co court to make acknowledgment thereof, therefore we command you to repair to the sd Mary & that privily & apart from her sd husband you take such acknowledgment as she shall be willing to make .... Wit John Lee Junr clerk. 25 Sep 1765 Pursuant to the within commission we James Jameson & Thomas Lowry gent went to the within named Mary Pickett w/o John Pickett who executed & acknowledged the same in our presence privately & apart from her sd husband. This commission & return were returned 21 Oct 1765 & recorded. Attest: John Lee clerk. (Pg 57)

11 Oct 1765. Deed. Thomas Callaway & Mary his wife of Halifax Co, VA for 40 pd sold to Waters Dunn of same co a 97 a. tr of land in Essex Co bounded by the land formerly belonging to Silvanus Tandy & land of Henry Crittendine, being the plantation & land whereon Joseph Callaway formerly lived .... Wit:

Wm Dunn, Richard Dunn, Winifred Jones, Aristips Boughan. Proved 21 Oct 1765 & ordered to be certified & fully proved 22nd instant & recorded. Attest: John Lee clerk. (Pg 58)

16 Mar 1765. Bond. I Henry Griggs of South Farnham Parish, Essex Co am firmly bound unto John Boughan planter of sd co for 15 pd ... the condition of this obligation is such that if the afsd Henry Griggs do well & truly pay unto John Boughan 30 pd by or upon 16 Aug next ensuing then this obligation to be void ... . Wit: John Kerchwall, Major Boughan. Proved 21 Oct 1765 & recorded. Attest: John Lee clerk. (Pg 59)

19 Oct 1765. Deed. Elizabeth Marsters & Sarah Marsters of Essex Co for 46 pd sold to John Henshaw of sd co a 70 a. tr of land being the land which was left unto them by the will of their father James Masters (sic) decd bounded by Boulware's line, Landrum's land, sd Henshaw's land & Popoman Swamp ... . Wit: Edward Gouldman, David Sullivan, Frances Donoho, Cornelius Sale. (Pg 60)

17 Sep 1765. Deed. Carter Braxton acting executor of the late George Braxton decd of King & Queen Co for 19 pd 14 sl being the balance due from Maurice Broche to the sd George Braxton decd for the purch of 129 a. of land in South Farnham Parish (recourse being had to a decree of King & Queen Co Court obtained 14 May 1764 by the sd Maurce Broche agt the sd Carter Braxton & George Braxton an infant & son & heir of the sd George Braxton decd) sold to the sd Maurice Broche of Essex Co the afsd 129 a. of land adj the lands of Joseph Ryland, Richard Hodges, William Roane, John Upshaw & Richard Holt Junr ... . Wit: Jack Power, David Cochran, Geo Brooke, Tandy Dix, Robinson Daingerfield. Proved 23 Oct 1765 & recorded. Attest: John Lee clerk. (Pg 62)

28 Aug 1765. Deed. Mildred Parker of Cumberland Co, VA for 10 pd sold to Francis Ramsey Junr of Essex Co all her right to 50 a. of land which was left unto her by the will of her father Patrick Donoho ... . Wit: Jeremiah Mitchell (Mitcell), John Henshaw, Ann Ramsey, Easter Ramsey. Ackn 21 Oct 1765 & recorded. Attest: John Lee clerk. (Pg 63)

26 Aug 1765. Deed of Mortgage. Thomas & Mary Haden (Haddon) of Essex Co for 60 pd sold to James Ritchie & Company of Glasgow in North Briton merchants one Negro man named Jaccob with the Forest Plantation ... provided that if the sd Thomas & Mary Haden shall pay to the sd James Ritchie & Company 60 pd with interest then this indenture to be void ... . Wit: Alexr Cruden, James Shaw, Andrew Crawford. Proved 21 Oct 1765 & recorded. Attest: John Lee clerk. (Pg 64)

14 Sep 1765. Deed of Mortgage. Henry Purkins of Essex Co for 400 pd sold to William Snodgrass of Essex Co merchant a 300 a. tr of land on the head of Piscataway Cr & also the following Negro slaves, viz, Nan, Rose, Anthony & Hannah & their future increase ... provided that if the sd Henry Purkins shall well & truly pay unto the sd William Snodgrass the afsd sum with interest on or before 1 Jan next ensuing then this deed shall be null & void .... Wit: Will Woddrop, Robt McCandlish, Jno Clements, Robinson Daingerfield. Ackn 21 Oct 1765 & recorded. Attest: John Lee clerk. (Pg 65)

21 Oct 1765. Deed. Samuel Croxton & Elizabeth his wife of [blank] Parish, Bute Co, NC for 21 pd 10 sl sold to Thomas Roane of South Farnham Parish, Essex Co a messuage & 32 a. parcel of land on some of the brs of Piscataway Cr being the land John Croxton bought of Joseph Man & gave his son Thos Croxton who sold it to the sd Samuel Croxton bounded by the Middle Br, Francis Boughan, sd Thomas Roane & John Farguson .... Wit: Richd Holt Junr, John Brooke, John Samuell. Ackn 21 Oct 1765 by Samuel Croxton & Elizabeth his wife (she being first privily exam'd & assenting thereto) & recorded. Attest: John Lee clerk. (Pg 67)

3 Sep 1765. Deed of Mortgage. Reubin Noell & Joseph Noell of Essex Co for 59 pd 9 sl 2 pn sold to James Ritchie & Company merchants in Glasgow five feather beds with furniture, one horse, one mare, 30 head of hogs, nine heads of cattle, one desk, two iron potts, one pan, two pewter dishes, two basons, six plates, two chests & two Negroes Hannah & Isaac ... provided that if the sd Reubin Noell & Joseph Noell shall well & truly pay to the sd James Ritchie & Company the afsd sum with interest on or upon 1 May next ensuing then these presents to be void .... Wit: Thos Montgomerie, James Anderson, John Taliaffero. Ackn 21 Oct 1765 & recorded. Attest: John Lee clerk. (Pg 69)

16 Aug 1765. Deed of Mortgage. John Bidlecomb of Essex Co planter for 37 pd 7 sl 10 pn sold to James Ritchie & Company merchants in Glasgow a 42 a. tr of land formerly the property of Joseph Boulware & one Negro wench named Pallas & Harry her son ... provided that if the sd John Bidlecomb shall well & truely pay to the sd James Ritchie & Company the afsd sum with interest at or upon 1 May next ensuing then these (presents) to be void .... Wit: James Anderson, Thos Montgomerie, Thomas Casson. Proved 21 Oct 1765 & recorded. Attest: John Lee clerk. (Pg 70)

18 Oct 1765. Bill of Sale. Thomas Miller of Essex Co joiner for 20 pd 16 sl 9 3/4 pn sold to James Ritchie & Company merchants in Glasgow 2 feather beds with furniture, 5 pewter dishes, 14 pewter plates, 1 flaggon, 1 tankard, 1 gill, 1/2 gill, 1 quart one pint pot, 1 1/2 doz pewter spoons, 3 iron pots with hooks, 1 iron 1 coppar skillit, 2 smoothing 1 box iron, 3 brass candlesticks, 1 pistle & mortar,

1 frying pan, 2 hoes, 1 large iron baker?, 1 shovel, 1 pocker, 1 pot rack, 4 chairs, 3 pales, 1 washing tub, 2 chests, 1 table, 12 wooden plates, 5 stone jars, 2 doz quart bottles, 1 sett of joiners tools, 1 pair tongs & all the rest of my household furniture ... . Wit: Thos Montgomerie, James Anderson. Proved 21 Oct 1765 & recorded. Attest: John Lee clerk. (Pg 70)

21 Oct 1765. Deed. Richard Fisher of South Farnham Parish, Essex Co carpenter & Ann his wife for 65 pd sold to John Cheaney of same parish planter a 76 a. parcel of land in the sd parish adj the lands of William Greenwood, William Howerton, William Cole Junr & Rhodes Greenwood, it being the tr of land whereon the sd Richard Fisher now lives ... . Wit: Robt Read, Wm Cheaney, James Greenwood. Ackn 22 Oct 1765 by Richard Fisher & Ann his wife (she being first privily examined & assenting hereto) & recorded. Attest: John Lee clerk. (Pg 71)

16 Mar 1765. Deed of Mortgage. Edmond Mitchell of South Farnham Parish, Essex Co for 26 pd 1 sl 2 pn sold to John Williams of same parish two Negro boys named Patrick & Titus ... whereas the afsd Edmond Mitchell is indebted to his two brothers William & Reubin Mitchel the sum afsd who has chose the sd Williams for their guardian & for the more better securing the sd money hath made the above sale, it is therefore agreed between the parties that if the sd Edmond Mitchell shall when required by the sd John Williams make immediate payment of the afsd sum with interest the same is to be void ... . Wit: Richard Cauthorn, Cautharine (sic) Cauthorn. Proved 23 Oct 1765 & recorded. Attest: John Lee clerk. (Pg 73)

14 Oct 1765. Deed. Richard Jeffries of South Farnham Parish, Essex Co for 8 pd sold to Meriwether Smith of sd parish a 4 a. parcel of land in the sd parish bounded by the main run of Webb's Mill Swamp, Smith's corner of the land he purch of Francis Jones, sd Jeffries & Samuel Piles including the swamp only debarring the sd Smith of the privilege of building a mill at that place ... . Wit: Richard Cauthorn, Abraham Campbell. Ackn 21 Oct 1765 & recorded. Attest: John Lee clerk. (Pg 73)

24 Oct 1765. Indenture Tripartite between William Snodgrass of Essex Co merchant of the first part, Meriweather Smith & Samuel Peachey of the same co gent of the second part & Henry Young of the sd co of the third part, whereas one Godfrey Young of sd co being seised in a tr of land in South Farnham Parish by his deed dated 24 Feb 1763 conveyed the same to the sd William Snodgrass with a provisio that if the sd Godfrey should pay unto the sd William Snodgrass 400 pd being the consideration mentioned in the sd deed with interest on the same on or before 1 Mar next ensuing that then the sd deed & conveyance to be null & void, and whereas the sd Godfrey Young failed in making payment

agreeable to the conditions & provisio afsd the sd William Snodgrass brought a suit in the co Court in Chancery to foreclose the equity of redemption of the sd Godfrey Young in the sd land & the sd Godfrey being willing that the sd land should be sold it was decreed & ordered by the court with the consent of the sd parties that the afsd Meriwether Smith & Samuel Peachey should sell the afsd land to the highest bidder, & they sold the sd land to the sd Henry Young the highest bidder for 85 pd, now this indenture wit that the sd William Snodgrass for 85 pd & the sd Samuel Peachey & Meriwether Smith by virtue of the power & authority vested in them by the decree afsd & in obedience to the subsequent decree of the sd court have sold unto the sd Henry Young the afsd tr of land according to the ancient known & reputed bounds of the same ... . Wit: John Semple, Robinson Daingerfield, Wm Elliott. Ackn 24 Oct 1765 & recorded. Attest: John Lee clerk. (Pg 74)

15 Oct 1765. Power of Attorney. Lawrence McDuff of St. Clements Dane Parish in the Strand & City of Middlesex London French plate maker have named & do appoint Charles Mortimer of Tappahannock in Essex Co, VA gent my atty to rent or lease a parcel of land in South Farnham Parish called Mohockney for any term not exceeding 2 years to demand sue for recover & receive all such sums of money as may become due & owing by & from any tenants during the sd term ... . Wit: Charles Tod (Todd), Wm Ramsay, Edmond Shield. Proved 23 Oct 1765 & recorded. Attest: John Lee Junr clerk. (Pg 76)

24 Oct 1765. Bill of Sale. Thomas Fogg (Fog) of Essex Co have for 99 pd 8 sl 4 pn sold unto Archd McCall of Essex Co my Negro fellow Jack, my Negro wench Frank, my Negro girl Aniky? & my Negro boy Aron, my whole stock of cattle, all my hogs, all my horses & household furniture ... . Wit: John Bateman, James Lang, William Sheddon. Proved 24 Oct 1765 & recorded. Attest: John Lee clerk. (Pg 77)

XXIV Oct 1765. Indenture. Henry Miner an infant orphan of Solomon Miner of Essex Co hath with the consent & approbation of the court of Essex Co put himself an apprentice & servant to Richard Holt Junr of same co blacksmith until he shall arrive to the full age of 21 ... the sd Richard Holt will cause the sd apprentice to be learnt & taught the trade of a blacksmith & also cause him to learn to read write & cypher ... . Wit: None. Approved by the court & ackn by the parties 24 Oct 1765 & recorded. Attest: John Lee clerk. (Pg 78)

16 May 1765. Deed. Micajah Evans of South Farnham Parish, Essex Co for 4 pd 9 sl 9 pn & costs of a suite depending in Essex Court sold to Archd McCall of same place 12 a. of land in the sd parish bound by Greensby Evans, Capt John Webb & Philip Gatewood, being had to the deeds I had of Godfrey for it ... .

Wit: Andrew Baillie, James Lang, William Shodden (Shedden), Gosnal Murdock. Proved 24 Oct 1765 & recorded. Attest: John Lee clerk. (Pg 78)

24 Oct 1765. Deed. Henry Young of South Farnham Parish, Essex Co for 100 pd sold to William Young Junr of same place a 168 a. parcel of land adj the lands of Greensbe Evans, John Mitchell, Mary Young, Griffen Johnson, Willm Gatewood, Philemon Gatewood & Micajah Evans, it being the land which the sd Henry Young lately purch of Samuel Peachey, Meriwether Smith & William Snodgrass late the property of Godfrey Young & whereon Mary Young now lives in which she has a property during her natural life ... . Wit: None. Ackn 24 Oct 1765 & recorded. Attest: John Lee clerk. (Pg 79)

[Pages 81 & 82 are blank]

31 Oct 1765. Deed of Gift. William Boulware of Essex Co for divers good causes & considerations have given unto my dau Sarah & son in law Ralph Rowzee a 100 a. tr of land whereon they now live, it being the plantation that my father James Boulware bequeathed to me by his will ... during their natural lives provided they do yearly pay ye quitrents or whatsoever taxes & impositions that shall for the future be laid upon the sd land & after the decease of my dau Sarah & son in law Ralph Rowzee I do give to my grandson Phillip Isaac Boulware son of Thomas Boulware the afsd plantation or tr of land ... . Wit: Edward Rowzee, Thos Bradburn, William Rowzee. Ackn 18 Nov 1765 & recorded. Attest: John Lee clerk. (Pg 83)

28 Oct 1765. Indenture Tripartite between Susanna Parker of the Town of Tappahannock, Essex Co of the first part, Richard Parker of Westmoreland Co gent of the second part & Robinson Daingerfield & John Fauntleroy an infant the son of Moore Fauntleroy late of Richmond Co gent decd of the third part, wit that the sd Susanna Parker in consideration of the natural love & affection she bears to the sd Robinson Daingerfield her grandson & the sd John Fauntleroy her great grandson & for 5 sl in hand paid by the sd Richard Parker she hath given unto the sd Richard Parker in trust all the lands the sd Susanna holds in fee in Essex Co & all her Negro slaves & other estate both real & personal of what nature kind or quality soever with their increase, in trust for the several uses intents & purposes hereafter mentioned & to no other, & first to & for the use of the sd Susanna for & during her natural life for the payment of her debts support & maintenance & after her decease the lands afsd & the two Negroes she purch lately named Jack & Matt & as much money as will purch one young breeding wench to the use of the sd John Fauntleroy, but in case the sd John Fauntleroy shall die under age without issue or shall ever become possessed of the estate in Richmond by death of his brother Moore Fauntleroy then to the use of Henry Armistead an infant the son of William Armistead late of [blank] Co decd the

grandson of the sd Susanna Parker & his heirs forever & all the other slaves & their increase with all the other estate of the sd Susanna both real & personal in trust to & for the use of the sd Robinson Daingerfield forever ... . Wit: Chs Mortimer, Winifred Thomas, Robert Clark, Andrew Bailie. Proved 18 Nov 1765 & recorded. Attest: John Lee clerk. (Pg 83)

27 Sep 1765. Deed. Hannah Edmondson of Essex Co for 20 pd annually for the term of 3 years & after that 14 pd annually during her natural life hath sold unto John Edmondson Junr of same co all her right & title to all the lands that she holds in Essex Co & also all the Negroes (Phillis only excepted) which sd lands & Negroes the sd Hannah Edmondson holds by virtue of certain marriage articles made between her & Thos Edmondson decd in the year 1749, & the sd Hannah Edmondson doth further sell unto the sd John Edmondson Junr all her right to all the lands Negroes & stock lent her by the will of Thomas Edmondson decd the afsd John Edmondson being subject only to the payment of the consideration above mentioned, & the sd Hannah Edmondson is to put the sd John Edmondson Junr in full possession of all the afsd lands, Negroes & stocks on or by 1 Jan next ensuing ... . Wit: None. Ackn 18 Nov 1765 & recorded. Attest: John Lee clerk. (Pg 84)

26 Aug 1765. To Thomas Roane & John Upshaw gent greeting, whereas John Garnett Junr of Essex Co & Mary his wife have by their deed of feoffment dated 17 Aug instant conveyed unto Augustine Garnett of sd co a tr of land, & whereas the sd Mary is unable to travel to our co court to make acknowledgment thereof, therefore we command you to repair to the sd Mary & that privily & apart from her husband you take such acknowledgment as she shall be willing to make ... . Wit John Lee Junr clerk. By virtue of this commission to us directed we Thomas Roane & John Upshaw did go to the afsd Mary & her privily & apart from John her husband hath examined her who said she did freely & voluntarily relinquish her dower in the sd land & was willing & desirous the same should be recorded. This commission & the commissioners return were returned 19 May 1766 & recorded. Attest: John Lee clerk. (Pg 85)

2 Jun 1766. Deed. John Daniel of St Anns Parish, Essex Co for 5 pd sold to Job Spearman of same parish a 10 a. parcel of land in St. Anns Parish bounded by sd Spearman ... . Wit: John Spearman, Charles Taylor, James Spearman, Edward Vawter, Nathanl Conduit. Ackn 16 Jun 1766 by John Daniel & Sarah his wife (she being first privily examined & assenting thereto) & recorded. Attest: John Lee clerk. (Pg 85)

15 Jun 1766. Deed. John Daniel & Sarah his wife of Essex Co for 10 pd 10 sl sold to Charles Taylor of same co 21 a. of land bounded by a road that leads from the plantation of Col Samuel Hipkins decd to the upper church, Robert

Waring, John Conduit, Spearmans Swamp, sd Taylor's land & William Daniel ...
. Wit: Job Spearman, Myse? Taylor, James Spearman. Ackn 16 Jun 1766 by
John Daniel & Sarah his wife (she being first privily examined & assenting
thereto) & recorded. Attest: John Lee clerk. (Pg 87)

31 May 1766. Deed. Leonard Harrison & Margaret his wife of Essex Co for 18
pd sold to Elias Harrison of same co the 50 a. tr of land & plantation the sd
Leonard Harrison now lives on being the land that John Harrison (father to the
sd Leonard Harrison) formerly purch of Richard Long bounded by the lands of
David Pitts, David Pitts Junr, John Spearman & the land of Sullivan ... . Wit:
John Henshaw, Robert Parker, Bereman Brown, Thomas Gouldman. Proved 16
Jun 1766 as to Leonard Harrison & Margaret w/o Leonard (being first privily
examined & assenting thereto) ackn the same which on the motion of sd Elias
are admitted to record. Attest: John Lee clerk. (Pg 89)

16 Jun 1766. Indenture Tripartite between Henry Williamson & Mary his wife
of the first part, Ambrose Jones & Betty his wife of the second part & Doctor
John Clements of Essex Co gent of the third part, wit that the sd Henry Williams
& Mary his wife for 137 pd have sold unto the sd John Clements a 133 a. tr of
land in South Farnham Parish whereof Argyle Blaxton father of the sd Mary
died seised & which by the death of James Blaxton only son & heir of the sd
Argyle Blaxton descended to & became vested in the sd Mary now w/o the sd
Henry, and is contiguous to & bounded by the lands of the sd John Clements
whereon he now lives, Man Page esqr, James Edmondson, another tr of land
belonging to the sd John Clements & the land of John Edmondson Junr ... and
they the sd Ambrose Jones & Betty his wife for 18 pd sold unto the sd John
Clements forever the dower of her the sd Betty of & in the tr of land afsd being
28 1/2 a. laid off & allotted by Robert Brooke surveyor of sd co as & for the
dower of the sd Betty as widow of the sd Argyle Blaxton ... . Wit: None. Ackn
16 Jun 1766 & Henry Williamson & Mary his wife (she being first privily
examined & assenting thereto) & recorded. Attest: John Lee clerk. (Pg 90)

13 Dec 1765. Deed of Gift. John Lee the elder of Essex Co for love good will
& natural affection have given to my cousin John Lee Junr & Susanna his wife
& Hancock Lee their son for & during their natural lives & the longest liver of
them remainder to the sd Hancock Lee & his heirs the 906 a. tr of land on which
I the sd John Lee the elder now lives bounded by James Gray, John Lantane,
John Bastin, Foster Samuel, Peter Samuel, John Samuel & the sd John Lee Junr
... . Wit: Reverend John Matthews, Robt Grier, Frances Smith, Jos Gillon,
Francis Graves. Proved 16 Jun 1766 & recorded. Attest: John Lee clerk. (Pg
92)

31 Oct 1765. Deed. James Newbill & James Newbill Junr of South Farnham Parish, Essex Co for 25 pd sold to Luke Covington of same place a 43 a. tr of land in the sd parish & upon the s side of Rankatank River bounded by Covington's line, corner of Thomas Parron, George Newbill & br of Poankatank River ... . Wit: Richd Brown, Wm Howerton, Richd St. John, Heritage Howerton. Proved 16 Jun 1766 & recorded. Attest: John Lee clerk. (Pg 93)

7 Jan 1766. Deed of Mortgage. Richard Conquest of Essex Co for a debt of 100 pd due & owing with interest from Feb last past & the cost of a suit doth sell unto Edward Gouldman of sd co a 100 a. tr of land purch by the sd Conquest of sd Gouldman & one sorrel mare & also all his right to a 75 a. tr of land in Gloster Co ... provided that if the sd Richard Conquest shall pay unto the sd Edward Gouldman the afsd sum with interest on 7 Feb next then these presents to be void ... . Wit: John Upshaw, James Emerson, James Snodgrass. Proved 16 Jun 1766 & recorded. Attest: John Lee clerk. (Pg 95)

18 Jun 1766. Deed. Henry Purkins Taylor & Sarah his wife of South Farnham Parish, Essex Co for 25 pd sold to Thomas Roane of same place a messuage & 50 a. tr of land in the sd parish on the s side of Hoskins's Swamp which sd tr is pt/o that parcel of land which formerly belonged to Daniel Roberts & was sold by Joseph Reeves (who was atty for the sd Daniel Roberts) at publick auction to John Harper the younger & by the sd Harper conveyed to John Dicks & by the sd Dicks sold to John Ford & by the sd Ford sold to the afsd Henry Purkins Taylor, & is bounded by the old bridge below the mill that is now the sd Roane's & Pamplin's fence ... . Wit: None. Ackn 16 Jun 1766 by Henry Purkins Taylor & Sarah his wife (she being first privily examined & assenting thereto) & recorded. Attest: John Lee clerk. (Pg 96)

21 Jul 1766. Deed. Edward Davis of Essex Co for 50 pd sold to Mary Gatewood of same co a tr of land which the sd Davis purch of William Ferryman? (as by a deed dated 27 Apr 1749), the sd land on the brs of Hoskins's Cr in Essex Co & part in King & Queen Co on the brs of Sadle Swamp bounded by Edward Davis's other land, Gouldman's line, Col Goodrich, Mr. Aubrey & Mrs. Pamplin's now Charles Hutcheson's land ... . Wit: Thomas Roane, Jos Gatewood, Chaney Gatewood, Charles Hutchason. Proved 21 Jul 1766 & recorded. Attest: John Lee clerk. (Pg 97)

17 Mar 1766. Power of Attorney. John Bell of Lowdon, VA merchant did impower Charles Yates of VA merchant to collect & receive the debts due to him in VA & to manage his business there, now know ye that the sd John Bell doth revoke & make void all & every & each of the Letters of Atty by him given to the sd Charles Yates or any other person residing in or near VA ... & the sd John Bell doth hereby make & appoint William Porter now living & residing

with the sd John Bell as his clerk or bookkeeper in the City of London & who shortly intends to go to VA to act as his agent or manager there, to ask demand & receive of & from the sd Charles Yates & all & any other person whom soever living in or near VA all & every & each of the debts sums of money goods & effects whatsoever due owing payable or belonging to him ... . Wit: Jno Carnaby, John Ticknor. Proved 21 Jul 1766 & recorded. Attest: John Lee Junr clerk. (Pg 99)

22 Mar 1766. Power of Attorney. Thos Shenson of London in Middlesex Co mariner constitute my good friend William Porter merchant of London in sd co my atty to ask claim demand recover & receive of & from the officers & commissioners of his Majesty's Navy all such sallary wages bounty money pensions & all other sums of recovery whatsoever as now is or at any time hereafter shall be due payable or belonging unto me ... . Wit: Jno Cannaby. Proved 21 Jul 1766 & recorded. Attest: John Lee Junr clerk. (Pg 100)

Jul Court 1764 James Webb gent is appointed to lay off the prison bounds as they were established before the last alterations made thereon & report the same to the court. Pursuant to the within order I have laid off & renewed the marks of the bounds within mentioned adj Henry Ritchie, Poplar Spring, Robert Beverley, Doctor Jones estate's lotts & William Ramsay ... . James Webb made this return of the prison bounds 18 Aug 1766 which is ordered to be recorded. Attest: John Lee clerk. (Pg 101)

31 Jul 1766. Dead of Lease. Thomas Bradburn of Essex Co leased unto Jessee French Boulware 40 a. of land being pt/o the land the sd Bradburn lives upon lying on both sides of Popoman Run bounded by Thomas Andrews & Samuel Noell during the term of 12 years to commence upon 25 Dec next paying 6 pd upon demand for the first 5 years & 3 pd for each year afterwards upon 25 Dec annually until the sd term of years is expired ... . Wit: William Boulware, Thomas Boulware. Proved 18 Aug 1766 & recorded. Attest: John Lee clerk. (Pg 101)

13 Mar 1766. Power of Attorney. James Ritchie & Henry Ritchie merchants in Glasgow in Company & partnership under the name of James Ritchie & Company in the pt/o Britain called Scotland are seised of lands in VA & whereas certain mortgages have been taken for us & in our name of lands in VA as securities for the payment of certain sums of money or tobacco due & owing unto us, now know ye that James Ritchie being absent from VA & the sd Henry Ritchie intending to go immediately to VA do by these presents impower the sd Henry Ritchie to lease or demise the sd lands or any pt/o them to such persons & for such terms & under such yearly & other rents as the sd Henry Ritchie shall think fit or to sell & convey the same ... . Wit: Will Woddrop, Robt Maitland. I

John Boman (Bowman) esqr chief magistrate of the City of Glasgow certify that personally appeared before me William Woddrop & Robert Maitland being persons well known & worthy of good credit & by solemn oath declared that they were present & did see James Ritchie & Henry Ritchie sign seal & execute this power of atty. Proved 18 Aug 1766 & recorded. Attest: John Lee clerk. (Pg 102)

22 May 1766. Deed. Thomas Bush & Mary his wife, Stephen Neale & Susannah his wife of South Farnham Parish, Essex Co for 9 pd sold to James Webb Junr of same place all their right to a certain place where formerly stood a water grist mill called Bushes Lower Mill & which is now in the possession of the sd James Webb who has lately rebuilt & repaired the same (who has a right to 1/2 thereof) together with 1 a. of land on each side of the sd run & the dam belonging to the same in the sd parish ... . Wit: Robt Mann, James Townley, William Neale, Wm Ramsey. Ackn 18 Aug 1766 by all the parties except w/o Neal & recorded. 15 Sep 1766 Susanna w/o the afsd Stephen Neale relinquished her right of dower to the sd land & recorded. Attest: John Lee clerk. (Pg 103)

19 Jul 1766. Deed. Thomas Bush & Mary his wife of South Farnham Parish, Essex Co for 40 pd sold to John Dunn of same place all their right to a 131 a. parcel of land in the sd parish being pt/o 647 a. granted by patent to Thomas Haraway bounded by John Evans & John Phillips ... . Wit: Josiah Daley (Daly), James Dunn, Stephen Neale. Ackn 18 Aug 1766 by John Bush & Mary his wife (she being first privily examined & assenting thereto) & recorded. Attest: John Lee clerk. (Pg 103)

18 Aug 1766. Deed. John Taylor & Sarah (Salley) his wife of Essex Co for 75 pd sold to Samuel Shaw of same co a 100 a. parcel of land in St. Anns Parish (except about as much land as contain 12,000 cornhills on the lower pt/o the tr adj John Garnett's land near sd Taylor's house during the sd Taylor's life) which sd tr of land was given by William Taylor to the sd John Taylor by deed dated 18 Apr 1761 bounded by the sd Taylor, John Garnett, John Lee Junr & James Gray ... . Wit: John Lee, John Matthews, James Noell, John Lee Junr. Ackn 18 Aug 1766 by John Taylor & Salley his wife (she being first privily examined & assenting thereto) & recorded. Attest: John Lee clerk. (Pg 105)

18 Aug 1766. Bond. I John Taylar of Essex Co am firmly bound unto Samuel Shaw Junr of same co for 300 pd ... whereas the sd John Taylar hath by his deed [see above] conveyed unto the sd Samuel Shaw 100 a. the condition of this obligation is such that if the sd John Taylar shall warrant & defend the right title & interest of the sd Samuel Shaw & his heirs of & in the sd land agt all & every person then this obligation to be void ... . Wit: John Lee, Jno Matthews, Jas

Noell, John Lee Junr. Ackn 18 Aug 1766 & recorded. Attest: John Lee clerk. (Pg 107)

18 Aug 1766. Deed. William Young Junr, Elizabeth his wife & Mary Young his mother of South Farnham Parish, Essex Co for 162 pd sold to James Edmondson of same place a 150 a. parcel of land in the sd parish lying on the n side of Piscattaway Cr & bounded by the lands of Man Page esqr & the waters of Piscattaway Cr, which tr of land was purch formerly by Doctor Peter Godfrey of James Boughan & by the sd Godfrey in his will devised unto his dater Masey Godfrey who afterwards died intestate leaving no issue by which means it ascended to Mary Young her sister one of the parties herein mentioned & by the sd Mary Young given to her son William herein mentioned (only reserving her life therein as may be seen by the sd deed of gift dated 17 Jul 1750) ... . Wit: Will Smith, Roy Hipkins, John Evans, Hugh Marshal. Wit to receipt: Wm Pendleton Junr, Philip Clayton Junr. Ackn 18 Aug 1766 by William Young Junr & Elizabeth his wife (she being first privily examined & assenting thereto) & as to Mary Young was fully proved & ordered to be recorded. Attest: John Lee clerk. (Pg 107)

18 Aug 1766. Deed of Gift. Mary Young of South Farnham Parish, Essex Co widow & relict of Wmson Young decd for natural love & affection hath given unto her son William Young a 107 a. tr of land in the sd parish as pt/o the land which John Lacey died seised for which the sd Mary Young obtained an escheat patent of Robert Dinwiddie esqr 13 Dec 1752 ... . Wit: Will Smith, Roy Hipkins, John Evans, Hugh Marshall. Proved 18 Aug 1766 & recorded. Attest: John Lee clerk. (Pg 108)

18 Aug 1766. Bond. William Young & Mary Young both of South Farnham Parish, Essex Co are firmly bound unto James Edmondson of same place for 334 pd ... the condition of this obligation is such that if the afsd William & Mary Young shall from time to time & at all times hereafter well & truly fulfill & keep all & every of the covenants grants articles payments conditions & agreements mentioned in an indenture bearing even date with these presents then this obligation to be void ... . Wit: Will Smith, Roy Hipkins. Ackn 18 Aug 1766 by William Young & proved by the wits as to Mary Young & recorded. Attest: John Lee clerk. (Pg 109)

30 May 1766. Deed of Mortgage. William Hathaway of Essex Co for 96 pd 13 sl now due from the sd William Hathaway unto James Ritchie & Company sold to the sd James Ritchie & Company of Glasgow in North Britain two lotts in the Town of Tappahannock where John Foster now lives also a new frame of a house which Abner Cox has got for the sd Hathaway & three sets of harnesses now in Andrew Crawford's possession ... provided that if the sd William

Hathaway shall pay to the sd James Ritchie & Company the afsd sum with interest then this indenture to be void ... . Wit: Andrew Crawford, James Shaw, Thos Montgomerie. Ackn 19 Aug 1766 & recorded. Attest: John Lee clerk. (Pg 110)

2 Sep 1766. Deed. Stephen Neale of South Farnham Parish, Essex Co & Susanna his wife for 16 pd 10 sl sold to Thomas Bush of same place all their right to 35 a. of land it being the land whereon they now live & which was allotted to the sd Stephen & Susanna in right of the sd Susanna's thirds of the lands of Bibby Bush decd her first husband ... . Wit: Frans Brizendine, Philip Cheany, Andrew Allen. Ackn 15 Sep 1766 by Stephen Neale & Susannah his wife (she being first privily examined & assenting thereto) & recorded. Attest: John Lee clerk. (Pg 110)

XXXI May 1766. Deed. Thomas Reeves & Sarah his wife of Spotsylvania Co for 20 pd sold to William Gatewood of Essex Co carpenter a messuage & 125 a. tr of land on the e side of the Main Road that goes by Piscataway Cr in South Farnham Parish & is the 1/2 of the tr of land which John Reeves by his will devised to his sisters Patience Gatewood & Ann Reeves & descended to the afsd Sarah party hereto from the sd Ann Reeves (being her only child & heir at law by her husband Francis Atwood decd) ... . Wit: Thomas Meador, Richard Bushe, Isaac Gatewood. Proved 15 Sep 1766 & recorded. Attest: John Lee clerk. (Pg 111)

3 Jun 1766. To Charles Dick, John Stewart & Charles Yates gent greeting, whereas Thomas Reeves & Sarah his wife of Spotsylvania Co have by their deed [see above] conveyed unto William Gatewood of Essex Co a tr of land and whereas the sd Sarah is unable to travel to our co court to make acknowledgment thereof, therefore we command you to repair to the sd Sarah & that privily & apart from her husband you take such acknowledgment as she shall be willing to make ... . Wit John Lee Junr clerk. 8 Jul 1766 This is to certify that we John Stewart & Charles Yates agreeable to the (above) order have examined privily and apart Sarah w/o Thomas Reeves & she acknowledged to have executed the deed of her own free will & consent. At a court held 15 Sep 1762 (sic) this commission & the commissioners return were returned & recorded. Attest: John Lee clerk. (Pg 112)

14 Jun 1766. Power of Attorney. William Ballantine, William Cuningham, William Campbell & James Hunter partners & merchants in Ayr North Britain have appointed John Ballantine Junr eldest son of the afsd William Ballantine our atty in VA & MD in North America to ask demand & call for & require from John Ballantine Senr merchant in Nomony, Westmoreland Co our factor, John Kennedy merchant in Coan Northumberland Co, Charles Hammond merchant in

Totuskey Richmond Co, John Hunter merchant at Augsburg Fairfax Co factors on our acct employed by the sd John Ballantine Senr & from all other persons whatsoever indebted to us, viz, all lands, Negroes, horses, cows, rents, goods, ships or boats of whatever kind, houses, household furniture, white servants, store debts, books, invoices of goods or any manner of stocks whatsoever belonging to us & granting power to him to sell let or dispose of any of our lands whatsoever Negroes horses, etc. ... . Wit: Hector Armour commander of the ship Hope of Ayr, Avey McGill High Street, Hugh Steel (Steell) & Thomas Duff mariners. Proved 15 Sep 1766 & recorded. Attest: John Lee clerk. (Pg 113)

18 Oct 1766 at Williamsburg. Appointment. Francis Fauquier esqr his Majesty's Lieut Governor & Commander in Chief of VA, to Thomas Roane esqr, by virtue of the power & authority to me given I hereby appoint you to be sheriff of Essex Co during pleasure ... . Ordered to be recorded. Attest: John Lee clerk. (Pg 113)

20 Oct 1766. Bond. Thomas Roane, John Upshaw & Muscoe Garnett gent are firmly bound unto our Sovereign Lord the King for 400 pd ... the condition of this obligation is such that whereas the afsd Thomas Roane is appointed sheriff of Essex Co during pleasure by commission from the Governor [see above] & if the sd Thomas Roane shall well & truly collect all quitrents fines forfeitures & Americaments accruing or becoming due to his Majesty in the sd co & shall duely account for & pay the same to the officers of his Majesty's Revenue on or before the second Tuesday in June annually & in all things truly & faithfully execute the sd office of sheriff during his continuance therein then this obligation to be void ... . Wit: None. Ordered to be recorded. Attest: John Lee clerk. (Pg 114)

20 Oct 1766. Bond. Thomas Roane, John Upshaw & Muscoe Garnett gent are firmly bound unto our Sovereign Lord the King for 1,000 pd ... the condition of this obligation is such that whereas the afsd Thomas Roane is constituted & appointed sheriff of Essex Co during pleasure by commission from the Governor [see above] & if the sd Thomas Roane shall well & truly collect & receive all officers fees & dues put into his hands to collect & duly account for & pay the same to the officers to whom such fees are due then this obligation to be void ... . Wit: None. Ordered to be recorded. Attest: John Lee clerk. (Pg 114)

11 Oct 1766. Deed. William Roane & Betty his wife of Essex Co for 67 pd 15 sl sold to John Coleman of same co a tr of land in South Farnham Parish being pt/o a tr purch by the sd William Roane of the executors of George Braxton gent decd containing 135 1/2 a. bounded by Morris Broach, Cotton Path Br, Piney Bottom Br, land that was Fawcett's, Braxton's land & Mare Br ... . Wit: Henry

Allen, Thomas Dix, Ambrose Gatewood, Ambrose Allen. Ackn 17 Nov 1766 by William Roane & Betty his wife (she being first privily examined & assenting thereto) & recorded. Attest: John Lee clerk. (Pg 115)

17 Nov 1765. Deed. William Roane of South Farnham Parish, Essex Co & Betty his wife for 104 pd 14 sl 6 pn sold to Richard Holt Junr of same place all their estate right to a part or parcel of land in the sd parish containing 188 1/2 a. it being formerly pt/o a tr of land belonging to Col George Braxton decd bounded by the fork of Piscattaway Run, Morris Brouche, Cotton Patch Br, Mare Br, Piney Bottom Br, Mr. Upshaw's land & New Quarter Tract ... . Wit: None. Ackn 17 Nov 1766 by William Roane & Betty his wife (she being first privily examined & assenting thereto) & recorded. Attest: John Lee clerk. (Pg 116)

19 Apr 1766. Deed. John Burnett of Essex Co planter for 122 pd 10 sl sold to Archd Ritchie of Tappahannock Town merchant a 245 a. tr of land whereon he now lives bounded by land of Joseph Burnett, John Burnett, John Boughan & Thomas Brooks ... . Wit: Hugh Campbell, John Tennent, Sarah Roane. Proved 15 Dec 1766 & recorded. Attest: John Lee clerk. (Pg 117)

15 Dec 1766. Deed. Francis Smith & Lucy his wife of South Farnham Parish, Essex Co for 12 pd 2 sl 1 penny 1/2 penny sold to Reubin Broocke of same place a tr of land in the sd parish on the n side of the Main Road that leads from the lower Church to Ferguson's Ordinary it being pt/o the tr of land left to him by will of his father Francis Smith decd adj John & Samuel Broocke ... . Wit: Ralph Neale, Stephen Neale, Alexander Boman. Ackn 15 Dec 1766. Attest: John Lee clerk. (Pg 118)

19 Jun 1766. Deed of Lease. John Lee the elder of Westmoreland Co gent & Mary his wife for 5 sl leased unto John Lee Junr of Essex Co two trs of land in St. Anns Parish one of which contains a plantation & 200 a. of land & was purch by the sd John Lee the elder of John Miller & Susanna his wife by deed dated 5 Mar 1749, the other tr contains 100 a. & was purch by the sd John Lee the elder of Thomas Ayres & Mary his wife by deed dated 16 Mar 1750 ... for the term of 1 year ... . Wit: Frances Smith, Richard Lee, Jno Turberville, Rev Thos Smith, Reubon Jordan. Proved 20 Oct 1766 & fully proved 19 Jan 1767 & recorded. Attest: John Lee clerk. (Pg 121)

20 Jun 1766. Deed of Release. John Lee the elder of Westmoreland Co gent & Mary his wife for 400 pd released unto John Lee Junr of Essex Co two trs of land ... [same as above] ... . Wit: Frances Smith, Richard Lee, Jno Turberville, Thos Smith, Reuben Jordan. Proved 20 Oct 1766 & fully proved 19 Jan 1767 & recorded. Attest: John Lee clerk. (Pg 121)

23 Jun 1766. To Richard Henry Lee, Richard Lee & John Turberville of Westmoreland Co gent greeting, whereas John Lee the elder of Westmoreland Co gent & Mary his wife by their deeds of lease & release [see above] conveyed unto John Lee Junr of Essex Co two trs of land, & whereas the sd Mary is unable to travel to our sd co court to make acknowledgment, therefore we command you to repair to the sd Mary & that privily & apart from her husband you take such acknowledgment as she shall be willing to make ... . Wit John Lee Junr clerk. 27 Jun 1766 Pursuant to the commission within mentioned we Richard Lee & Jno Turberville have repaired to the sd Mary Lee & her privily & apart from her sd husband have examined her touching the premises who declares that she freely & willingly relinquishes her right of dower to the lands & that she is willing the deeds be recorded. At a court held 19 Jan 1767 this commission & the commissioners return were returned & recorded. Attest: John Lee clerk. (Pg 123)

1 Nov 1766. Bill of Sale. James Davis of Essex Co for 111 pd 19 sl 8 pn sold to John Samuel of sd co Samson a Negro man, Flora a Negro woman, Amey, Betty, Ned, Lott & Lydia five mulattoes who are to serve till they arrive to lawful age, all my horses & mares (four in number), 10 cattle, hoggs & all my household furniture & my share of the crop of corn made at Portabago upon John Lee's plantation, & the increase of the sd Flora, cattle &c ... . Wit: Jno Gillon, John Lee. Proved 19 Jan 1767 & recorded. Attest: John Lee clerk. (Pg 124)

9 Mar 1767. Deed. John Gatewood & Betty his wife of Caroline Co for 30 pd sold to Philip Gatewood of same co a 55 3/4 a. tr of land bounded by Isaac & Cheyney Gatewood & a br of Hoskins's Cr ... . Wit: Jas Bowcock, William Rennolds, Chaney Gatewood. Proved 16 Mar 1767 & recorded. Attest: John Lee clerk. (Pg 124)

20 Nov 1766. Deed. Henry Picket of Augusta Co, VA for 27 pd sold to James Roy gent of Essex Co a 100 a. tr of land given by William Pickett decd unto the sd Henry Picket in his will bounded by land of the afsd Roy, David Dishman, Robert Carter esqr, William Ayres & the land of William Noell decd ... . Wit: Rd Hipkins, Muscoe Garnett, Berreman Brown. Proved 16 Mar 1767 & recorded. Attest: John Lee clerk. (Pg 125)

1 Sep 1766. Deed. Robert Parker & Sarah his wife of Essex Co for 40 pd sold to Margaret Boulware of same co a 50 a. parcel of land that the sd Robert Parker purch of Benjamin Landrum that Hugh Cary decd formerly purch of Thomas Ramsay by deed dated 14 Feb 1729/30 (excepting 1 pole square of land which the sd Landrum reserves to himself being the place where his mother Martha Landrum was buried) bounded as in the afsd conveyances ... . Wit: David

Sullivan, Thomas Gouldman, Richard Donagin. Ackn 26 Mar 1767 by Robert Parker & Sarah his wife (she being first privily examined & assenting thereto) & recorded. Attest: John Lee clerk. (Pg 127)

16 Mar 1767. Deed. Richard Hodges of South Farnham Parish, Essex Co & Betty his wife for 90 pd sold to David Loudon of same place a 60 a. tr of land which the sd Richard Hodges purch of Thomas Haile & Elizabeth his wife 14 Apr 1764 in the sd parish ... . Wit: LeRoy Hipkins, James Upshaw, Rd Hipkins. Ackn 16 Mar 1767 by Richard Hodges & Betty his wife (she being first privily examined & assenting thereto) & recorded. Attest: John Lee clerk. (Pg 128)

16 Mar 1767. Deed. Richard Hodges & Betty his wife of South Farnham Parish, Essex Co for 90 pd sold to David Loudon of same place a 165 a. parcel of land in the sd parish adj the lands of George Wright, Josiah Minter, Thomas Croxton & Joseph Burnett, it being pt/o the tr of land which the sd Richard Hodges purch of Augustine Washington & Ann his wife ... . Wit: LeRoy Hipkins, James Upshaw, Rd Hipkins. Ackn 16 Mar 1767 by Richard Hodges & Betty his wife (she being first privily examined & assenting thereto) & recorded. Attest: John Lee clerk. (Pg 129)

13 Mar 1767. Deed. John Andrews of Essex Co for 30 pd sold to Francis Davis of same co a 100 a. tr of land being the land whereon Edward Gouldman now lives bounded by Mary Seayres, Garnett's line, John Henshaw & Richard Conquest, also one Negro woman named Hannah ... . Wit: Richard Gouldman, Edward Gouldman, Thomas Gouldman. Proved 16 Mar 1767 & recorded. Attest: John Lee clerk. (Pg 130)

2 Mar 1767. Deed. Augustine & Elizabeth Garnett his wife of Essex Co for 50 pd sold to Henry Garnett of same co a water mill together with the land thereunto belonging on Occupation Cr the same left him by his grandfather James Garnett all which are now in the actual possession of the sd Henry ... . Wit: Richard Neale, James Noell Junr, James Samuel. Ackn 16 Mar 1767 by Augustine Garnett & Elizabeth his wife (she being first privily examined & assenting thereto) & recorded. Attest: John Lee clerk. (Pg 131)

17 Mar MDCCXVII. Deed. Archibald Ritchie & Charles Mortimer feofees of the Town of Tappahannock by several Acts of Assembly & for 450 lbs of tobacco sold to James Ritchie & Company merchants in Glasgow one lott or 1/2 a. of land in the sd town numbered 45 in the plan thereof the sd lot now being in the possession of the sd James Ritchie & Company ... . Ackn 17 Mar 1767 & recorded. Attest: John Lee clerk. (Pg 132)

17 Mar 1767. Deed. Benjamin Boughan of Charlot Co, VA planter for 15 pd sold to James May of Essex Co a 50 a. tr of land being all that tr of land that James Boughan Senr decd gave unto his son Abnor Boughan decd & bequeathed unto his son the sd Benjamin Boughan ... . Wit: Thomas Backer, Benja Croxton, Mary Croxton. Ackn 17 Mar 1767 & recorded. Attest: John Lee clerk. (Pg 132)

6 Apr 1767. Deed of Lease. John Lee of Essex Co gent & Susanna his wife for 5 sl leased unto Muscoe Garnett of sd co gent two trs of land in St. Anns Parish one of which sd trs contained a plantation & 200 a. of land & was purch by John Lee the elder late of Westmoreland Co gent of John Miller & Susanna his wife 5 Mar 1749, the other tr of land contains 100 a. & was purch by the sd John Lee the elder of Thomas Ayres & Mary his wife 16 Mar 1750, both which trs of land were purch by the sd John Lee of John Lee the elder by deeds of lease & release dated 19 & 20 Jun last past ... for the term of 1 year ... . Wit: Meriwether Smith, Jno Gillon, Chs Mortimer. Ackn 20 Apr 1767 & recorded. Attest: John Lee clerk. (Pg 133)

7 Apr 1767. Deed of Release. John Lee of Essex Co gent & Susanna his wife for 500 pd released unto Muscoe Garnett of sd co gent two trs of land ... [same as above] ... . Wit: Meriwether Smith, Jno Gillon, Chs Mortimer. (Pg 134)

7 Apr 1767. To Charles Mortimer, Robert Beverley & Meriwether Smith of Essex Co gent greeting, whereas John Lee of sd co & Susanna his wife have by their deeds of lease & release [see above] conveyed unto Muscoe Garnett of sd co two trs of land, & whereas the sd Susanna is unable to travel to our sd co court to make acknowledgment thereof, therefore we command you to repair to the sd Susanna & that privily & apart from her husband you taken such acknowledgment as she shall be willing to make ... . Wit John Lee clerk. 7 Apr 1767 By virtue of this commission to us directed we Chs Mortimer & Meriwether Smith have repaired to the sd Susanna Lee & her privily & apart from her sd husband have examined her touching the premises & she freely & willingly relinquishes her dower in the lands ... . At a court held 20 Apr 1767 this commission & the commissioners return were returned & recorded. Attest: John Lee clerk. (Pg 135)

6 Apr MDCCLXVII. Quit Claim. James Mills & Elizabeth his wife of Middlesex Co in consideration of the premises & for 10 sl quit claim unto James Ritchie & Company merchants in Glasgow all the dower & thirds & their right & title in three lots of land numbered 45, 51 & 52 ... whereas William Beverley late of Essex Co esqr decd did in his life time to wit 19 Mar 1744 obtain from the trustees of the Town of Tappahannock lots numbered 51 & 52 & 45 & whereas the sd James Mills on 19 May 1747 did obtain from the trustees lots

numbered 40, 51 & 52 but as the sd William Beverley never was seized or possessed of the lot numbered 40 & as the sd James Mills became possessed of the lot number 45 & not of lot numbered 40 in consequence & by virtue of the deed from the trustees afsd it is evident that the number 40 was by mistake inserted in the deed to the sd Mills instead of number 45, & whereas the sd James Mills did by his deed dated 15 Nov 1748 convey to George Gerrard the lots numbered 40, 51 & 52 & the sd Gerrard in consequence thereof became possessed of the lot number 45 & not of the lot numbered 40 the mistake afsd in numbering the lot becomes apparent & whereas the sd George Gerrard & Dinah his wife on 19 Dec 1749 conveyed to Archibald Ritchie the lots number 45, 51 & 52 endeavouring to rectify the mistake afsd as much as was in their power & the sd Archibald Ritchie hath conveyed the last mentioned lots to James Ritchie & Company afsd & whereas the sd Elizabeth was no party to the deed from the sd James Mills to the sd George Gerrard whereby it may happen that she may avail herself of her right of dower in the sd lots or some of them which is contrary to the former intentions & present sediments of the sd James Mills & Elizabeth his wife ... . Wit: Archibald Ritchie, John Mills, J. Power. Proved 20 Apr 1767 & recorded. Attest: John Lee clerk. (Pg 136)

7 Apr 1767. To Christopher Robinson, Robert Daniel & Clement Nicholson of Middlesex Co gent greeting, whereas James Mills of Middlesex Co & Elizabeth his wife by their deed of release [see above] conveyed unto James Ritchie & Company merchants in Glasgow Lots No. 45, 51 & 52 in the Town of Tappahannock, & whereas the sd Elizabeth is unable to travel to our co court to make acknowledgment thereof, therefore we command you to repair to the sd Elizabeth & that privily & apart from her husband you take such acknowledgment as she shall be willing to make ... . Wit John Lee clerk. Pursuant to the within commission to us directed we Ch Robinson & Clement Nicholson did go to the sd Elizabeth & did examine her privately & apart from her husband touching the sd deed & she did freely & voluntarily (relinquished her dower) & that she was willing the same should be recorded. At a court held 20 Apr 1767 this commission & the commissioners return were this day return'd & recorded. Attest: John Lee clerk. (Pg 136)

--- 1767. Archibald Ritchie & Mary his wife of Essex Co for 27 pd 6 sl sold to Sophia Waggoner of same co a 62 a. tr of land in South Farnham Parish and is 1/2 of the tr of land which Thomas Haile gave or sold to his son in law Mark Ball ... . Wit: Sarah Roane, John Richards, John Daly, Thomas Coleman. Ackn 20 Apr 1767 by Archibald Ritchie & Mary his wife (she being first privily examined & assenting thereto) & recorded. Attest: John Lee clerk. (Pg 137)

20 Apr MDCCLXIII. Quit Claim. Robert Beverley esqr son & heir of the Honble William Beverley for 10 sl quit claim unto James Ritchie & Company all

my estate right which I now have to a lott or 1/2 a. of land in the Town of
Tappahannock numbered 45 in the plan thereof which sd lott was laps'd in the
life time of the sd William Beverley & same has been for some time & now is in
the possession of the sd James Ritchie & Company ... . Wit: None. Ackn 18
May 1767 & recorded. Attest: John Lee clerk. (Pg 138)

23 Apr 1767. Deed. Francis Boughan & Sally his wife of South Farnham
Parish, Essex Co for 15 pd sold to Thomas Roane gent of same place a 40 a.
parcel of land whereon they now live in the sd parish bounded by Middle Br,
James Booker & John Meador ... . Wit: John Croxton, Benjn Croxton,
Benjamin Smith. Ackn 18 May 1767 by Francis Boughan & Sally his wife (she
being first privily examined & assenting thereto) & recorded. Attest: John Lee
clerk. (Pg 138)

11 Jun 1765. Deed of Mortgage. Benjamin Smith of Essex Co for 100 pd 2 sl 5
pn 3 farthings sold to Archd Ritchie of the Town of Tappahannock, Essex Co
merchant the following stock & household furniture, viz, 14 head cattle, 1 pair
oxen, 11 sheep, 2 sows, 11 shoats, 5 pigs, 1 gray 1 py'd horse, 1 bright bay mare,
3 beds & furniture, 2 iron potts, a tea kettle, 2 leather bottom & 6 flag chairs, a
copper still & worm & tub, 1 old Negro man Sampson & a young Negro man
named James, 1 large & 3 small trunks, 2 chests, an ox cart & wheels, 1
grindstone. 3 pewter dishes, 6 plates, 1 bason, 1 pair steelyards, 1 spice [?], 1
knive ... provided that if the sd Benjamin Smith shall well & truly pay unto the
sd Archibald Ritchie the afsd sum with interest on or before 1 Jul next ensuing
then this instrument of writing to be void ... . Wit: Thomas Roane, Hugh
Campbell. Proved 18 May 1767 & recorded. Attest: John Lee clerk. (Pg 139)

1 Nov 1766. Deed. John Barbee son of William Barbee now heir at law of John
Barbee & Ann his wife late decd of Essex Co he the sd John Barbee Junr now
living in Orange Co, NC for 40 pd sold to Mary Seayres widdow of Edward
Seayres decd of Westmoreland Co, VA a 100 a. parcel of land that the sd John
Barbee's grandfather held or whereon he lived bounded by the lands of Edward
Gouldman, Major Lason & the land that John Martin lately purch of Robert
Beverley esqr ... . Wit: Francis Barbee, Major Lason, Christopher Barbee,
James Gaunt, James Martin. Proved 15 Jun 1767 & recorded. Attest: John Lee
clerk. (Pg 140)

21 Nov 1766. Deed. Archibald Ritchie & Mary his wife of Tappahannock
Town, VA for 10 sl sold to James Ritchie & Company of Glasgow three lots
numbered 45, 51 & 52 ... whereas the sd Archibald Ritchie purch of George
Gerrard & Diana his wife three lotts in the sd town numbered in the plan of the
town 45, 51 & 52 on 19 Jun 1750, & whereas the sd purch was made by the sd
Archibald Ritchie in trust for the sd James Ritchie & Company & that the

purchase money to wit 50 pd 10 sl was bonafide advanced & paid by the sd company ... . Wit: Alex Cuninghame, James Shaw. Ackn by Archibald Ritchie & Mary his wife 15 Jun 1767 & recorded. Attest: John Lee clerk. (Pg 141)

15 Jun 1767. Deed. William Montague Junr gent of Essex Co for 50 pd sold to John Clowdas Junr of same co a 100 a. tr of land it being pt/o a tr of land which the sd William Mountague purch of Mrs. Susanna Parker & John Armistead gent decd ... . Wit: Lewis Mountague, Peter Mountague, Thomas Brokey. Ackn 15 Jun 1767 & recorded. Attest: John Lee clerk. (Pg 142)

10 Jun 1767. Bill of Sale. Joseph Hooker of Essex Co for 21 pd sold to John Richards of the Town of Leeds, King George Co one Negro by named of Cajah now in the possession of Donald Robertson of King & Queen ... . Wit: George Hill, William Johnson. Ackn 15 Jun 1767 & recorded. Attest: John Lee clerk. (Pg 143)

4 May 1767. To Robert Gilchrist & James Taylor of Caroline Co gent greeting, whereas John Gatewood & Betty his wife of sd co have by their deed dated 9 Mar last past conveyed unto Philip Gatewood of sd co a tr of land in Essex Co, & whereas the sd Betty is unable to travel to our co court to make acknowledgment thereof, therefore we command you to repair to the sd Betty & that privily & apart from her husband you take such acknowledgment as she shall be willing to make ... . 9 Jul 1767 at Caroline Co, in obedience to the within order we Robert Gilchrist & James Taylor Junr have examined the sd Betty Gatewood who declares that she voluntarily & of her own free will signed the deed to Philip Gatewood & was willing the same should be recorded. At a court held 20 Jul 1767 this commission & the commissioners return were returned & ordered to be recorded. Attest: John Lee clerk. (Pg 144)

20 Jul 1767. Deed. Robert Beverley esqr & Maria his wife of Essex Co for 40 barrels of corn & 1000 weight of tobacco sold to Timothy Longest of Caroline Co all their right to a 127 a. parcel of land in South Farnham Parish being pt/o a tr of land that did formerly belong to James Wall decd bounded by Augustin Garnett, Major John Lattainey, Jonathan Griffing, William Watkins & Francis Gawes ... . Wit: None. Ackn 20 Jul 1767 & recorded. Attest: John Lee clerk. (Pg 144)

30 Mar 1767. Indenture Tripartite between Archibald McCall merchant of the first part, Leonard Garnett & Catharine his wife of the second part & Augustine Garnett of the third part, whereas by an indenture of mortgage dated 4 Aug 1764 & made between the sd Leonard Garnett of the one part & the sd Archibald McCall of the other part, it is wit that the sd Leonard Garnett for 19 pd & interest from 4 Jun 1764 paid by the sd Archibald McCall did sell unto the sd

Archibald McCall a 92 a. tr of land adj John Latany & Joseph Fogg & purch by the sd Leonard Garnett of his father John Garnett Junr by deed dated 4 Jan 1764, & it was agreed by the sd parties that if the sd Leonard Garnett did well & truly pay unto the sd Archibald McCall the afsd sum & pay for whatever dealings he has had with the sd McCall he the sd Archibald McCall would at the request of the sd Leonard Garnett & at his costs & charges reconvey all the sd premises unto the sd Leonard Garnett or to whom he shall appoint, & whereas the afsd Augustine Garnett hath since purch of the sd Leonard Garnett & Catharine his wife the fee simple estate of equity of redemption of the sd Leonard Garnett in the tr of land for 48 pd, & whereas the sd Augustine Garnett hath & at the request of the sd Leonard Garnett (testified by his being a partie to these presents) paid to the sd Archibald McCall the afsd 19 pd with interest. Now this indenture wit that the sd Archibald McCall for & inconsideration of the premises & for 5 sl hath released unto the sd Augustine Garnett all his estate right which he had, now hath or which at any time hereafter he may have by means of the sd indenture of mortgage to the sd 92 a. of land ... . Wit: Richard Hipkins as to Leonard Garnett, John Garnett Junr, Joseph Noell. Ackn 20 Jul 1767 by Archibald McCall which being proved as to the execution thereof by Leonard Garnett is on the motion of sd Augustine Garnett admitted to record. On 19 Jul 1768 this deed was fully proved as to Leonard Garnett & recorded. Attest: John Lee clerk. (Pg 145)

21 Apr 1767. Deed. James Edmondson of South Farnham Parish, Essex Co & Elizabeth his wife for 182 pd 10 sl sold to Charles Bray also of sd parish a 146 a. tr of land which the sd James Edmondson purch of William Young Junr & Elizabeth his wife by indenture dated [blank] on Piscattaway Cr adj Col Mann Page ... . Wit: William Boughton, Godfrey Young, John Edmondson. Ackn 20 Jul 1767 by James Edmondson & recorded. Attest: John Lee clerk. (Pg 146)

20 Apr 1767. Power of Attorney. I John Seayres of Essex Co for divers considerations but more especially to secure to Robert Ferguson of the Town of Tappahannock merchant a debt of 206 pd 18 sl with interest that I owe to him for value received of him have appointed the sd Robert Ferguson my atty to sue & recover of every person indebted to me every sum of money & other things they shall be owing & also to take possession of all my estate & dispose thereof & apply the amount of the sales of the same to discharge of the debt afsd with interest, & I do further impower the sd Robert Ferguson to sue & eject any & every person who shall be possessed of any lands which I have or claim any right or title to either in the Cos of Lancaster, Northumberland, Gloucester, Essex, Culpepper or any other co in VA & when he has possession of the same to sell, dispose of or rent out all or any of them ... . Wit: Richard Parker, John Semple, John McGundy. Ackn 21 Jul 1767 & recorded. Attest: John Lee clerk. (Pg 148)

17 Aug 1767. Deed. Samuel Shaw Junr of St. Anns Parish, Essex Co for & in consideration of John Taylar having become security to Archibald Ritchie for goods that the sd Shaw has taken up in his store & is to take up for 2 pd 12 sl already received by the sd Samuel Shaw Junr of the sd Taylar hath sold unto the sd John Taylar of same place a 100 a. tr of land being the land that the sd Shaw bought of the sd Taylar by deed dated 18 Aug 1766, also a gun & saddle ... nevertheless if the sd Samuel Shaw Junr shall pay to the sd John Taylor the afsd sum with interest & shall truly satisfy & pay the sd Archibald Ritchie & thereby discharge & indemnify the sd John Taylar from the sd securityship then this indenture to be void ... . Wit: John Chamberlain, Benja Waggoner, Isaac Gatewood. Ackn 17 Aug 1767 & recorded. Attest: John Lee clerk. (Pg 149)

18 Aug 1767. Deed. Francis Barbee of Caroline Co, VA for 34 pd 1 penney paid by Edward Vawter of Essex Co the sd Francis Barbee acting as an executor for the estate of Ann Barbee decd late of Essex Co by virtue of her will, for & on the behalfe of the heirs of the sd Ann Barbee decd doth hereby sell unto the sd Edward Vawter 88 a. of land the sd Ann Barbee purch of John Pitts & Margaret his wife by deed dated 15 Dec 1760 bounded by Nicholas Atkinson, Edward Vawter, Benjamin Beasley decd & Martin Willard ... . Wit: John Price, Martin Willard, James Boughan, Leonard Brooke. Ackn 18 Aug 1767 & recorded. Attest: John Lee clerk. (Pg 150)

18 Aug 1767. Deed. David Loudon of Essex Co for 25 pd sold to John Baggot mariner a 60 a. tr of land which the sd David Loudon purch of Richard Hodges & Betty his wife of sd co 16 Mar last which sd tr of land was purch by the sd Richard Hodges of Thomas Hale & Elizabeth his wife then of the sd co by deed dated 14 Apr 1764, situate in South Farnham Parish ... . Wit: Jos Burnett, William Sheddon, Whitehead Coleman. Ackn 18 Aug 1767 & recorded. Attest: John Lee clerk. (Pg 151)

21 Sep 1767. Deed. James Cauthorn of South Farnham Parish, Essex Co & Elizabeth his wife for 110 pd sold to Vincent Cauthorn of same place a 45 a. parcel of land in the sd parish adj the lands of William Smith, William Young & the sd Vincent Cauthorn, it being the land devised to the sd James Cauthorn by the will of his father Richard Cauthorn decd & whereon he now lives ... . Wit: John Richards, Richard Cauthorn, Boswell Richards. Ackn 21 Sep 1767 by James Cauthorn & Elizabeth his wife (she being first privily examined & assenting thereto) & recorded. Attest: John Lee clerk. (Pg 152)

17 Jun 1767. Power of Attorney. Whereas James Ritchie & Henry Ritchie of Glasgow merchants & partners under the name & firm of James Ritchie & Company did on 13 Mar 1766 at Glasgow make & execute their power of atty to the sd Henry Ritchie with full power to transact the sd Company's affairs in VA

& to substitute one or more attys for the purposes afsd, now know ye that I the sd Henry Ritchie at present of Essex Co proposing to return to Glasgow do by virtue of the power of atty duly proved & recorded in Essex Co Court & as a partner of the sd company appoint James Anderson & William Woddrop of Essex Co, Neil McCoul of Spotsylvania Co & Thomas Montgomerie & Hugh Hamilton of Prince William Co true & lawful joint & several attys for the sd company to demise or absolutely to sell & convey any lands lots or houses to which the sd company are entitled .... Wit: Thos Hodge, Al Rose, James Shaw. Proved 21 Sep 1767 & recorded. Attest: John Lee clerk. (Pg 153)

16 Nov 1767. Deed. Ambrose Gatewood & Martha his wife of Essex Co planter for 60 pd sold to Thomas Dix of same co planter two trs of land in South Farnham Parish, the one of which tr is the land whereon the sd Ambrose Gatewood now lives bounded by Thomas Dix, Compton's line, Roane's land & Allen's land containing 141 a., the other tr is bounded by Coleman's land, Sheerwood's land, Allen's land & Moody's line containing 39 1/2 a. .... Wit: Jno Rennolds, James Booker, Richd Thos Haile, Henry Allen. Ackn 16 Nov 1767 by Ambrose Gatewood & Martha his wife (she being first privily examined & assenting thereto) & recorded. Attest: John Lee clerk. (Pg 154)

5 Oct 1767. Bond. Robert Parker & Robert Sale both of Essex Co are firmly bound each to the other in the penal sum of 1,000 pd ... whereas John Goode of Essex Co died intestate some years ago possessed of sundry slaves & left a widow (who is since dead) and two daus (who are also dead), viz, Ann Sale of whom the sd Robert Sale is son & heir at law, Elizabeth Parker of whom the sd Robert Parker is son & heir at law & whereas the sd Parker & Sale have mutually agreed to divide the sd slaves consisting of 13 in number in the following manner, that is to say, the sd Robert Parker to hold & enjoy as his absolute property the slaves named Milley, Nan, Sam, Patty, Jenny & Phoebe & their increase, & the sd Robert Sale to hold & enjoy in like manner the slaves George, Amy, Aleck, Betty, Winney, Jamey & Andrew & their increase, now the condition of this obligation is such that if the sd Robert Parker & Robert Sale & their several heirs shall stand to abide by & support & defend the agreement & division afsd then this obligation to be void .... Wit: John Matthews, R. Brooke, Jno Rowzee, John Lee. Proved 16 Nov 1767 & recorded. Attest: John Lee clerk. (Pg 155)

7 Nov 1767. Deed. James Cauthorn of South Farnham Parish, Essex Co & Elizabeth his wife for 60 pd sold to John Crow of same place a 229 a. tr of land in the sd parish adj the lands of John Crow, Joseph Mann, John Townley & Isaac Redd, it being the land which the sd James Cauthorn purch of James Mills gent .... Wit: W. Young, Henry Young, John Young, John Richards. John Corrie,

Hugh Campbell, Archibald Ritchie as to Mrs. Cauthorn. Proved 16 Nov 1767 & recorded. Attest: John Lee clerk. (Pg 156)

9 Nov ----. To Archibald Ritchie, William Montague, Charles Mortimer, Samuel Peachey, Meriwether Smith & John Corrie of Essex Co gent greeting, whereas James Cauthorn & Elizabeth his wife of South Farnham Parish, Essex Co by their indenture [see above] have sold & conveyed unto John Crow of sd co the fee simple estate of 229 a. of land, & whereas the sd Elizabeth cannot conveniently travel to our co court to make acknowledgment of the sd conveyance, therefore we do give unto you or any two or more of you power to receive the acknowledgment which the sd Elizabeth shall be willing to make before you & we do therefore command you that you personally go to the sd Elizabeth & receive her acknowledgment of the same ... . Wit John Lee clerk. In obedience to the Worshipful court we Archibald Ritchie & John Corrie have examined the sd Elizabeth privately & apart from her husband & she acknowledges her right to the premises. At a court held 16 Nov 1767 this commission & the commissioners return were returned & recorded. Attest: John Lee clerk. (Pg 157)

22 Aug 1767. Bond. Ambrose Pilkington & Isaac Hawes are firmly bound unto William Daingerfield, Francis Waring, Simon Miller, James Webb, Archibald Ritchie, William Montague, John Upshaw, Samuel Peachey, Paul Micou, Charles Mortimer, Robert Beverley, Meriwether Smith, James Roy & John Corrie gent justices of Essex Co in the penal sum of 5,000 lbs crop tobacco ... whereas the sd Ambrose Pilkington hath build a bridge over Occupatia Run at a place called Pilkington's for 900 lbs of tobacco at the charge of the sd co & hath agreed to keep the same in good & sufficient repair at his own expence for 7 years to commence from the 1st day of this instant Aug, now the condition of this obligation is such that if the sd Ambrose Pilkington shall keep the sd bridge in good & sufficient repair according to the agreement afsd then this obligation to be void ... . Wit: Henry Garnett, John Henshaw. Proved 16 Nov 1767 & recorded. Attest: John Lee clerk. (Pg 158)

24 Jun 1764. Deed of Gift. Waters Dunn of Pitsylvania Co in consideration of the premises & also 5 sl hath given unto Winefred Dunn of Essex Co all his right as son & heir at law of William Dunn decd to the tr of land where the sd William Dunn lately live & whereof he died seized & also in or to the several slaves & other estate by the sd William Dunn decd devised to the sd Henry & Alice Dunn at the death of the sd Winifred, to & for the use of the sd Winifred Dunn during her natural life ... whereas William Dunn late of Essex Co by his will devised the land whereon he lived to his son William Dunn to be delivered at the death of his wife the sd Winifred & his slaves to his son Henry & his dau Alice also to be delivered at the death of the sd Winifred & whereas it is supposed the sd land &

slaves will descend to the sd Waters Dunn as eldest son & heir at law of the sd William Dunn decd during the life of the sd Winifred whereby the sd Winifred would be left unprovided for & whereas the sd Winifred hath assigned & made over to the sd Waters Dunn all her right which she hath in to sundry lands & slaves under the will of John Waters her father & the sd Waters Dunn is moreover willing & desirous to make necessary provision for the support of his sd mother ... . Wit: J. Edmondson, Jas Edmondson, Jas Edmondson Junr. Ackn 16 Nov 1767 & recorded. Attest: John Lee clerk. (Pg 158)

XIX Oct 1767. Deed. Augustine Smith & Phebe his wife of Essex Co planter for 35 pd sold to Richard Thomas Haile of same place planter an 80 a. tr of land whereon the sd Augustine & Phebe now live being the same land that was conveyed by Henry Harper to William Smith father of the sd Augustine & by him sold to his sd son the afsd Augustine bounded by a parcel of land sold by Charles Burnett to Thomas Hutson, Thomas Burnett, Main Pocoson & the sd Richard Thomas Haile ... . Wit: John Croxton, James Allen, Thomas Croxton, Leonard Burnett. Ackn 17 Nov 1767 by the sd Phebe she being first privily examined & assenting thereto & also proved as to the sd Augustine & recorded. Attest: John Lee clerk. (Pg 159)

3 Apr 1767. Deed. James Emerson & Elry (Alice) his wife of Essex co for 230 pd sold to Archibald Ritchie merchant of sd co three lotts in the Town of Tappahannock numbered 5, 11 & 12 according to the plan of the sd town ... . Wit: Hugh Campbell, John Tennent, Fras Lodge. Proved 17 Nov 1767 & recorded. Attest: John Lee clerk. (Pg 160)

16 Nov 1767. Deed of Mortgage. James Emerson of South Farnham Parish, Essex Co for 291 pd 4 sl 10 pn 3 farthings sold to Archibald Ritchie of the Town of Tappahannock, Essex Co merchant the following slaves, viz, George, Bacckus, Ned, Sam, Dinah & her child Pat, Letty & her child Fanny, with their future increase ... if the sd James Emerson shall well & truly pay to the sd Archibald Ritchie the afsd sum with interest on or before 1 Jan next ensuing then this instrument of writing & the sale hereby made to be void ... . Wit: Hugh Campbell, John Tennent, James Stuart. Proved 17 Nov 1767 & recorded. Attest: John Lee clerk. (Pg 162)

3 Apr 1767. Bill of Sale. James Emerson of Essex Co for 230 pd sold to Archibald Ritchie of sd co merchant the following stock & household furniture, viz, 4 horses, 21 head of hogs, 33 head of cattle (4 of them oxen), 5 iron potts & hooks, 1 dutch oven, 2 copper saucepans, 2 large copper kettles, 1 fish kettle, 5 tubs, etc. & a white servant man named George Downer ... . Wit: Hugh Campbell, John Tennent, Fras Lodge. Proved 17 Nov 1767 & recorded. Attest: John Lee clerk. (Pg 163)

8 Aug 1767. Deed of Mortgage. Mark Davis of Essex Co for 88 pd 9 pn 3 farthings sold to Archibald Ritchie of the Town of Tappahannock, Essex Co merchant four slaves, viz, Phillis a wench, two boys Richmond & Anthony & one Negro girl named Nan together with their future increase ... provided that if the sd Mark Davis shall well & truly pay unto the sd Archibald Ritchie the afsd sum with interest on or before 1 Sep next ensuing then this instrument of writing & the sale hereby made to be void .... Wit: Hugh Campbell, James Stewart. Proved 17 Nov 1767 & recorded. Attest: John Lee clerk. (Pg 163)

14 Nov 1767. Deed of Mortgage. Major Lason of Caroline Co for 20 pd hath mortgaged & delivered unto Francis Barbee one Negro girl named Milley ... I am to have 3 years liberty to pay the money & the sd Francis Barbee is to have the sd girl as his own property till the money is paid, I am to pay no interest & if the sd girl should die before the money is paid the sd Barbee is not to lose his money by her death & any time within the 3 years the 20 pd being paid to Francis Barbee the sd girl is to be delivered to me again & if the money is not paid in the 3 years time then the sd Barbee may lawfully sell the girl .... Wit: Henry Garnett, Edward Gouldman. Proved 17 Nov 1767 & recorded. Attest: John Lee clerk. (Pg 164)

23 May 1767. Deed. John Smith & Mary his wife of South Farnham Parish, Essex Co for 90 pd sold to Thomas Roane of same place a messuage & 268 a. tr of land in the sd parish being the tr of land that was his father John Smith's at his death which descended to the sd John Smith as heir at law, bounded by the main run of Piscataway Cr, John Latane, Henry Kidd, Richard Thomas Haile, Crumple Quarter? Br, Stodghill's land, Farguson's line, Barker's line & Wilson's line .... Wit: James Upshaw, James Emerson, Waters Dunn, Joseph Hooker, Francis Boughan. Ackn 21 Dec 1767 by John Smith & recorded. Attest: John Lee clerk. (Pg 165)

21 Dec 1767. Bond. Thomas Roane, John Roane & James Upshaw gent are firmly bound unto our Sovereign Lord the King for 1,000 pd ... the condition of this obligation is such that if the afsd Thomas Roane sheriff of Essex Co shall well & truly collect from the inhabitants of the sd co for the ensuing year the taxes imposed on the sd inhabitants by several Acts of Assembly & pay the same according to the directions of the sd severall acts, then this obligation to be void .... Sealed & delivered in presence of Essex Co Court & ordered to be recorded. Attest: John Lee clerk. (Pg 166)

21 Dec 1767. Bond. Thomas Roane, John Roane & James Upshaw gent of Essex Co are firmly bound unto Francis Waring, Archibald Ritchie, William Mountague, John Upshaw & Charles Mortimer gent justices of Essex co for 50,000 lbs of tobacco ... whereas the afsd Thomas Roane is appointed collector

of the co levy for this present year, now the condition of this obligation is such that if the sd Thomas Roane shall well & truly collect the sd levy & pay to the several claimants their respective claimes then this obligation to be void ... . Sealed & delivered in presence of Essex Co Court & ordered to be recorded. Attest: John Lee clerk. (Pg 166)

10 Mar 1768. Deed. George Newbill & Mary his wife of South Farnham Parish, Essex Co planter for 70 pd sold to Rhodes Greenwood of same place planter a tr of land being that whereon the sd George Newbill & Mary his wife formerly lived in the sd parish on the s side of Dragon Swamp adj James Newbill Senr, William Greenwood, William Howerton, sd Rhodes Greenwood & Isiah Cole ... . Wit: William Cheaney, James Newbill, John Cheaney, William Greenwood. Ackn 21 Mar 1768 by George Newbill & Mary his wife (she being first privily examined & assenting thereto) & recorded. Attest: John Lee clerk. (Pg 167)

15 Jan 1768. Deed. James May & Elizabeth his wife of South Farnham Parish, Essex Co for 16 pd sold to George Newbill of same place all their estate right in a 50 a. parcel of land or woodland in the sd parish adj the Long Br, Harry Lane, Captain Thomas Roane, the heirs of Doctor John Clements decd (which land formerly the sd Clements purch of Jonathan Radford), John Boughan & Boughans Spring Br ... . Wit: Joseph Farguson, William Dunn (B), John Johnson, Henry Purkins Junr. Proved 21 Mar 1768 & recorded. Attest: John Lee clerk. (Pg 168)

13 Feb 1768. Deed. John Daniel & Sarah his wife & Priscilla Daniel his mother all of Essex Co for 59 pd 10 sl sold to Thomas Pitts of same co a 140 a. tr of land being all the remainder of land that the sd John Daniel holds together with the dower of the same that Priscilla Daniel his mother claims the sd land bounded by lands of Charles Taylor, Waring & Job Spearman & the main stream of Spearmans Swamp ... . Wit: Richard Nunns, James Vawter, Joshua Donohoe. Proved 21 Mar 1768 as to the sd John & Priscilla & recorded. Attest: John Lee clerk. (Pg 169)

25 Feb 1768. To Simon Miller, Paul Micou & James Roy of Essex Co gent greeting, whereas John Daniel, Sarah Daniel & Priscilla Daniel of the sd co have by a deed [see above] conveyed unto Thomas Pitts of sd co a parcel of land, & whereas the sd Sarah is unable to travel to our co court to make acknowledgment thereof, therefore we command you to repair to the sd Sarah Daniel & that privily & apart from her husband you take such acknowledgment as she shall be willing to make ... . 2 Mar 1768 Pursuant to the within order we Simon Miller & James Roy have privately examined Sarah Daniel who is willing the deed together with her acknowledgment may be recorded. At a court held 21 Mar

1768 this commission & the commissioners report was returned & ordered to be recorded. Attest: John Lee clerk. (Pg 170)

1 Sep 1767. Deed of Gift. William Fauntleroy Senr of Lunenburg Parish, Richmond Co gent for true love & paternal affection have given to my well beloved son Moore Fauntleroy of Tappahannock, Essex Co one lott of building in sd town of Tappahannock containing 1/2 a. being numbered in a plan of the sd town 16 which lott I formerly purch of James Mills gent & Elizabeth his wife ... . Wit: Wm Fauntleroy Junr, John Fauntleroy, Griffen Fauntleroy. Proved 21 Mar 1768 & recorded. Attest: John Lee clerk. (Pg 171)

19 Dec 1767. Deed. Alaman Breedlove of South Farnham Parish, Essex Co hath exchanged unto Mary Treble of same parish a 25 a. parcel of land in the sd parish adj Nathan Breedlove & the sd Mary Treble, being the land that the sd Alaman Breedlove lately purch of Nathan Breedlove ... & the sd Mary Treble in consideration thereof hath exchanged unto the sd Alaman Breedlove a 19 1/4 a. tr of land in the sd parish bounded by James Webb's mill & Breedloves Spring Br ... . Wit: Nathan Breedlove, Sarah Breedlove, Ambrose Greenhill. Ackn 21 Mar 1768 by the parties & recorded. Attest: John Lee clerk. (Pg 171)

Deed. Whereas John Gordon late of Essex Co by his will amongst other things did devise a small tr of land whereon he lived to his wife for life & after her decease to his son John Gordon, & whereas the sd John Gordon the younger was under execution at the suit of John Corrie gent & claiming benefit of the insolvent act gave in a schedule of his reversion of & in the sd small tr of land at the decease of Elizabeth Smith his step mother. Therefore a decree was made by Essex Co court that Thomas Roane sheriff should sell the sd reversion of land at publick auction & the money arising from such sale to be applyed towards the discharge of the sd execution which was accordingly done & Timothy Longest became purchaser who hath since sold it to Philip Smether ... now this indenture made --- 1768 between Thomas Roane sheriff of Essex Co of the one part & Philip Smether of sd co carpenter of the other part, wit that the sd Thomas Roane for 3 pd 12 sl paid by Timothy Longest hath sold unto the sd Philip Smether after the death of the sd Elizabeth Smith all that messuage & 50 a. tr of land whereon John Gordon decd formerly lived bounded by Stephen Munday, Col Francis Waring & James Stokes ... . Wit: None. Ackn 22 Mar 1768 & recorded. Attest: John Lee clerk. (Pg 172)

1 Sep 1767. Deed of Mortgage. John Garnett Junr of Essex Co planter for 61 pd 10 sl sold to Muscoe Garnett of same co gent the following Negroes, goods & chattels, viz, Dick, Harry & Frank, 2 cows & calves, 1 yoke of oxen, 1 cart & mare, 3 feather beds & furniture, 4 iron potts & hooks ... provided that if the sd John Garnett shall well & truly pay unto the sd Muscoe Garnett ... . Wit: John

Matthews, Jno Gillon, James Davis. Proved 18 Apr 1768 & recorded. Attest: John Lee clerk. (Pg 173)

23 Oct 1767. Deed of Mortgage. John Loyd (Loyde) of St. Anns Parish, Essex Co for 34 pd 12 sl 6 pn 1/2 penny sold to Muscoe Garnett of same parish a 50 a. tr of land in the sd parish bounded by George Strang, Robert Beverley, Anna Noell, Caleb Rice Noell & Nicholas Faulkoner, also one grey horse called Fox ... provided that if the sd John Loyd shall pay unto the sd Muscoe Garnett the afsd sum with interest then this indenture to be void ... . Wit: Reuben Garner, Jno Gillon, James Davis, John Lee. Ackn 18 Apr 1768 & recorded. Attest: John Lee clerk. (Pg 174)

22 Aug 1767. Deed. John Andrews of Essex Co being moved by the [below considerations] for the natural love & affection of the children of his son James Andrews doth sell unto Muscoe Garnett of same co gent one Negro man slave named James & one Negro girl named Judy & her increase & all the estate right which he has to his father's estate in the hands of his mother in law to & for the following uses & purposes & to no other use & purpose whatsoever that is to say for the support & maintainance of the sd John Andrews during his life & for the payment of all his just debts that may be now due or that hereafter may be due by & with the consent of the sd Muscoe Garnett & after the death of the sd John Andrews to the use & behoof of the children of the sd James Andrews to be divided among them & their heirs ... whereas the sd John Andrews has been frequently imposed upon by several evil disposed persons who have taken advantage of him & by that means have deprived him unjustly of most pt/o his substance & he being apprehensive that he shall soon come to want the necessities of life unless he secures some pt/o his substance in such manner as shall prevent the like advantage being taken of him for the future & being also minded to secure some pt/o his estate to his grandchildren after his death ... . Wit: John Lee, J. Gillon, James Davis, John Henshaw. Proved 18 Apr 1768 & recorded. Attest: John Lee clerk. (Pg 175)

26 Dec 1753. Deed. Augustine Ramsay of St. Anns Parish, Essex Co for 5 pd 10 sl sold to Cornelius Noell of same place a 50 a. tr of land whereon Elizabeth Evans now liveth bounded by a parcel of land the sd Noell formerly purch of the sd Ramsay, sd Noell's line, Hawkins's line & Cattlet's line ... . Wit: John Noel (Noell), Jas Noel (Noell), John Tucker, William Brown. Fully proved 18 Apr 1768 & on the motion of Anna Noell was admitted to record. Attest: John Lee clerk. (Pg 176)

15 Apr 1768. Deed. Meriwether Smith of South Farnham Parish, Essex Co for 50 pd sold to Robert Mann of same place a 147 a. tr of land in the sd parish which was purch by the sd Smith of Francis Jones & Richard Jeffries separately

adj Webb's Mill & the Beaver Dam ... . Wit: None. Ackn 19 Mar 1768 & recorded. Attest: John Lee clerk. (Pg 177)

12 Apr 1768. Power of Attorney. This is to certify that Henry Ford of Amelia Co being married to Frances Simco dau to Thomas Simco decd (late of Essex Co) do make John White my atty to act & do in my behalf receive buy or sell anything concerning the estate of Thomas Simco & whatever the sd White acts or does shall stand good in law. Wit: William Ford (Foord), Francis White. Proved 18 Apr 1768 & recorded. Attest: John Lee clerk. (Pg 178)

21 Jan 1768. Bill of Sale. I William Davis of Essex Co for 33 pd sold unto Alexander Saunders of sd co my Negro lad named David ... . Wit: William Gibbs, Leonard Croutcher. Proved 19 Apr 1768 & recorded. Attest: John Lee clerk. (Pg 178)

1 Dec 1767. Power of Attorney. William Stranhan late of the Town of Fredericksburg, VA now of the City of London merchant have appointed James Mercer atty at law in the Town of Fredericksburg, VA, John Mitchel, Henry Mitchel & James Dunsanson all merchants in the sd town my attys to ask demand require sue for & recover or receive all & every such debt sums of money goods merchandize goods estate & things due or to grow due to me ... . Wit: Muscoe Livingston, Joseph Richardson. Proved 18 Apr 1768 & recorded. Attest: John Lee clerk. (Pg 178)

XX Apr 1768. Deed. Robert Farish of Caroline Co acting executor of the will of Joseph Stevens decd for 706 pd sold to Archibald Ritchie of the Town of Tappahannock, Essex Co eight lotts in the Town of Tappahannock ... whereas the sd Joseph Stevens in his life time & at the time of his death was seised of eight lotts or half acres of land with the messuage & improvements thereon in the Town of Tappahannock numbers 17, 18, 21, 22, 25, 26, 29 & 30, the four first mentioned being the square whereon the sd Archibald now lives & fronting the Main Street of the sd town & the Publick Square & the last four lotts being the square whereon the stables of the sd Archibald now stand which sd eight lotts were purch by the sd Joseph of William Fauntleroy & by the sd Fauntleroy from James Mills late of the sd town & the sd Joseph being so seised made his will dated 3 Aug 1765 which is duly proved & recorded in Caroline Co whereby the sd Joseph did order & direct that his lotts & improvements at Hobbs Hole should be sold & the money arising should be divided amongst several of his children therein named & by the will did appoint his loving friends John Baylor & Edmund Pendleton esqrs & Robert Farish party hereto his executors the sd Robert only taking upon himself the burthen of the execution of the sd will, & whereas the sd Robert Farish by virtue of the sd power & authority & in pursuance of the direction of the sd will did on XIX Nov 1766 expose to sale at publick vendue the sd eight lotts & the sd Archibald Ritchie being the last & highest bidder for 706 pd ... . Wit: None. Ackn 20 Apr 1768 & recorded. Attest: John Lee clerk. (Pg 179)

7 Nov 1767. Deed of Gift. Sophia Waggoner of South Farnham Parish, Essex Co for love, good will & affection have given to my loving son Thomas Coleman & his heirs a 62 a. tr of land which I purch of Capt Ritchie, & if the sd Thomas Coleman should die before me or die without issue the land before given to return to me at my disposal & also I am not to be debarred of living on the afsd land & working it during my natural life ... . Wit: Nathan Waggener, Thomas Armstrong, George Coleman, Benja Waggener. Fully proved 16 May 1768 & recorded. Attest: John Lee clerk. (Pg 180)

10 Apr 1768. Deed. John Gray & Sarah his wife & Mary Gray the sd John Gray's mother of Essex Co for 75 pd sold to John Rowzee of same co a tr of land containing by a survey made by Edward Vawter on purchase of the land 100 a. adj the land of the sd John Rowzee lives upon, a br that divides the land of John Gray from his brother William Gray & James Noell ... . Wit: Thomas Newman, William Gray, Richd Rowzee. Ackn 16 May 1768 by John Gray & Mary his wife (she being first privily examined & assenting thereto & recorded. Attest: John Lee clerk. (Pg 181)

19 Sep 1767. Deed of Mortgage. Robert Tompkins of Gloucester Co for 188 pd 15 sl 8 pn sold to Archibald Ritchie of the Town of Tappahannock, Essex Co merchant the following vessel, viz, a schooner on the stocks of my own land called the Paragon as per a register obtained for sd vessel together with her sails rigging anchors cables boats & all other materials thereunto belonging ... provided that if the sd Robert Tompkins shall well & truly pay unto the sd Archibald Ritchie the afsd sum with interest on or before 1 Sep next ensuing then this instrument of writing & the sale hereby made to be void ... . Wit: Hugh Campbell, James Stewart, John Tennent. Proved 16 May 1768 & recorded. Attest: John Lee clerk. (Pg 182)

18 Jan 1768. Bill of Sale. Whereas Peter Samuel late guardian of me William Samuel did by his bond dated 5 Feb 1759 bind himself & his heirs in the penalty of 200 pd unto James Colquit who intermarried with my mother Sarah the widow of my decd father John Samuel upon condition that the sd James Colquit should in right of his sd wife surrender up to me the sd William Samuel all my sd mother's right of dower in & to the lands whereof my father died seised, also those following slaves, York, Cate, Winey, Judy, Pegg, Ned, Betty, Milley & Davy, provided & also upon this condition to be performed on the pt/o me the sd William Samuel that is to say when I the sd William Samuel should arrive to lawful age should secure unto the afsd James Colquit one Negro wench named

Moll & her increase also to deliver up to the sd James Colquit all my right to the personal estate of my sd father & moreover to pay unto him the sd James Colquit in full of his right in the lands afsd the sum of 10 pd as by the sd bond, & whereas I the sd William Samuel am now of full age & being fully satisfied with the agreement made by my sd guardian with the sd James Colquit do by these presents for the consideration above mentioned which on my part I ackn to have received sell & make over unto the sd James Colquit the afsd Negro wench Moll & her increase from the date of the afsd bond also the personal estate afsd ... . Wit: Samuel Hawes, Amb Pilkinton, Isaac Hawes, James Shaddock, Henry Samuel, William Gibson. Proved 29 Jun 1768 & recorded. Attest: John Lee clerk. (Pg 183)

9 May 1768. Deed of Mortgage. Ambrose Hundley (Hunley) of Essex Co for 79 pd 10 sl 2 pn 1/2 penny sold to James Ritchie & Company of Glasgow in North Britain a square sterned schooner built in Gloucester by John Gale burthen about 34 tons which sd vessel is not entirely finished & also two slaves named Orra & Sarah together with their increase also one bay horse & one red cow & all the household furniture now in my possession ... provided that if the sd Ambrose Hundley shall pay to the sd James Ritchie & Company the afsd sum with interest then this indenture to be void ... . Wit: Al Rose, James Shaw, Will Woddrop. Proved 20 Jun 1768 & recorded. Attest: John Lee clerk. (Pg 183)

16 Jan 1768. Deed. Rice Noell & Tabitha his wife of Essex Co for 55 pd sold to Caleb Noell of same co a 100 a. tr of land whereon the sd Rice Noell now lives in St. Anns Parish on the n side of a br that runneth between the house where Rice Noell now lives & Cornelius Noell's land bounded by Nicholas Faulconer, Cornelius Noell, Merriday Brown & John Sale it being all the land I hold upon the n side of that br ... . Wit: Augustine Garnett as to Rice Noell, Nicholas Faulconer, Richard Noell. Ackn 20 Jun 1768 by Rice Noell. Attest: John Lee clerk. (Pg 184)

22 Nov 1767. Deed of Mortgage. Lucy Munday of Essex Co for 20 pd sold to James Mills merchant of Middlesex Co a 260 a. tr of land adj the lands of James Banks, John Clements & William Dunn (son of the inspector William Dunn) all of the co afsd, 130 a. of which land the sd Lucy Munday heired? by the death of a brother the other 130 a. was bought by her husband James Munday of her sister Peggy Pagget ... provided that if the sd Lucy Munday shall well & truly pay unto the sd James Mills the afsd sum with interest then this indenture to be void ... . Wit: James Lang, Henry Clements, Philemon Gatewood, John Corrie, proved 20 Jun 1768 & recorded. Attest: John Lee clerk. (Pg 185)

XIX Oct MDCCLXVII. Deed. John Biddlecomb & Sarah his wife of Essex Co for 25 pd sold to John Henshaw of same co a 72 a. tr of land which the sd Sarah

Biddlecomb purch of Joseph Bowler bounded by Simon Golding, sd John Henshaw & the main run of Popomon Swamp ... . Wit: Alexr Anderson, Cornelius Sale, James Bates, Thomas Landrum, John Rose. Fully proved 20 Jun 1768 & recorded. Attest: John Lee clerk. (Pg 186)

20 Nov 1767. To John Rose & Henry Rose of Amherst Co greeting, whereas John Biddlecomb & Sarah his wife of Amherst Co have by their deed [see above] conveyed unto John Henshaw of Essex Co a parcel of land in Essex Co, & whereas the sd Sarah is unable to travel to our sd co court to make acknowledgment thereof, therefore we command you to repair to the sd Sarah & that privily & apart from her husband you take such acknowledgment as she shall be willing to make touching the premises ... . Wit John Lee Junr clerk. XVIII Jan MDCCLXVIII at Amherst by virtue of this commission to us directed we John Rose & Henry Rose did go to the dwelling house of the sd Sarah Biddlecome & having examined her privily & apart from John Biddlecome her husband & do certify that she declared that she voluntarily & freely acknowledges the conveyance & that she was willing the same should be recorded. At a court held 20 Jun 1768 this commission & the commissioners report was returned & recorded. Attest: John Lee clerk. (Pg 187)

21 Jun 1768. Deed of Assignment. John Ritchie & Company merchants & partners in North Britain (by William Woddrop their atty) for 400 pd have assigned, transferred & made over to James Edmondson of Essex Co gent a mortgage so far as it relates to a 480 a. tr of land ... whereas James Dycke seised in a 480 a. tr of land on the brs of Hoskins Cr did on 16 Oct 1764 execute an indenture of mortgage to the sd James Ritchie & Company for the consideration therein mentioned which sd mortgage is now duly recorded in the co records ... . Wit: None. Ackn 21 Jun 1768 & recorded. Attest: John Lee clerk. (Pg 187)

14 Jul 1768. Articles of Agreement between Constance Bond of South Farnham Parish, Essex Co widow & relict of William Bond decd on the one part & William Bond her son of sd parish of the other part, whereas there is a marriage shortly intended to be had & solemnized between Philip Pendleton of King & Queen Co & the afsd Constance Bond & in order to prevent any disputes that shall or may hereafter arise concerning the sd Constance Bond's title in right of dower or otherwise of in or to the sd William Bond decd's lands & all his other estate the sd William Bond her son doth hereby agree to deliver up to the sd Constance one Negro woman named Sarah & one Negro girl named Criss?, one black leather trunk, one small red trunk & her side saddle in lieu thereof of which the sd Constance doth agree to accept as full satisfaction in right of dower as afsd & at the decease of the sd Constance it is the true intent & meaning of these presents that the afsd two Negroes with their future increase shall return to the sd William Bond & his heirs forever, the sd William Bond paying all the

debts which are now owing from the sd estate to all & every person whatsoever who shall have a lawful claim agt the same. Wit: Joshua Boughton, Thomas Boughton, Alexr Saunders. Proved 18 Jul 1768 & recorded. Attest: John Lee clerk. (Pg 188)

29 Jul 1767. Deed of Gift. Mary Clements of Essex Co at her death by virtue of John Clements' will for love & affection hath given to Pitman Clements her son of sd co these following Negroes, viz, Vocina, Beck & Beck's son Jack, also my gold buttons, my chain & two chair houses with the harness belonging thereto, also the best bed & furniture in my house forever ... . Wit: Fras Lodge. Proved 18 Jul 1768 & recorded. Attest: John Lee clerk. (Pg 188)

9 Jul 1768. Deed. Thomas Haddon of Essex Co marriner & Mary his wife for the severall uses & purposes herein after mentioned & for 5 sl have sold to Alexander Smith the equal 1/2 pt/o a tr of land near the upper Church in South Farnham Parish wherein the sd Mary w/o the sd Thomas & Betty w/o William Porter & sister to the afsd Mary are now jointly seized ... to remain to the only proper use & behoof of the sd Thomas Haddon & Mary his wife & the survivor of them during their & each of their natural life & after their death then to the use of the right heirs of the sd Thomas Haddon by the sd Mary his wife for want of such heir to the use of the right heirs of him the sd Thomas Haddon ... . Wit: Thomas Meador, Philip Smether, Reuben Meador, John Meador. Ackn 19 Jul 1768 by Thomas Haddon & Mary his wife (she being first privily examined & assenting thereto) & recorded. Attest: John Lee clerk. (Pg 189)

15 Aug 1768. Bill of Sale. I Sarah Gibson of Essex Co do hereby bargain set over & deliver unto William Gibson of same co one Negro man slave called Buck for & in consideration of the sum of 100 pd ... . Wit: James Shaddock, William Rennolds, James Rennolds Junr. Proved 15 Aug 1768 & recorded. Attest: John Lee clerk. (Pg 190)

18 Jun 1768. Deed. Frances Davis of Essex Co for 53 pd 10 sl sold to John Henshaw of same co her 107 a. tr of land bounded by the land of the sd John Henshaw, Henry Garnett, Sear's land, land formerly Morgan's & Gouldmans Swamp ... . Wit: Henry Garnett, Richd Rowzee, John Livingston, Edward Gouldman, Thomas Gouldman, Daniel Noell Junr. Proved 15 Aug 1768 & recorded. Attest: John Lee clerk. (Pg 190)

18 Jun 1768. Deed. John Clark of Essex Co for 25 pd sold to John Henshaw of same co a 40 a. tr of land pt/o the tr of land which the afsd John Clark now lives on & which was left unto the sd John Clark by the will of his father Edward Clark decd, bounded by the sd John Henshaw, Henry Garnett & Gouldman's Swamp ... . Wit: Richd Rowzee, Thomas Gouldman, John Livingston, Daniel

Noell Junr, Henry Garnett, Edward Gouldman. Proved 15 Aug 1768 & recorded. Attest: John Lee clerk. (Pg 192)

23 Jul 1768. Deed. Williams Amis & Hannah his wife of Essex Co for 100 pd sold to William Brooke Junr now a resident of Middlesex Co all their estate right to a 150 a. parcel of land in South Farnham Parish which sd tr of land was formerly the property of Thomas Pane decd bounded by the land of Capt William Montague, Samuel Montague & the orphans of Leonard Hill & Thomas Watts decd ... . Wit: Henry Vass, Reuben Bush, Phil Broocke. Proved 15 Aug 1768 as to the sd William Amis & ordered to be certified & ackn by the sd Hannah being first privily examined & assenting thereto & ordered to record & on 19 Sep 1768 ackn by William Amis & admitted to record. Attest: John Lee clerk. (Pg 193)

4 Feb 1764. Deed. LeRoy Hipkins & Grisel his wife of South Farnham Parish, Essex Co for 1,050 pd sold to Luke Covington of same place a plantation & 880 a. tr of land being the land & premises purch by Benjamin Smith decd of LeeRoy Peachey on 7 Aug 1758, also all that other plantation & tr of land given to the sd Benjamin Smith by his father Col Joseph Smith decd as by his will dated 7 May 1728, & the sd Benjamin Smith by his will dated 26 Aug 1760 did give all his lands &c to his wife Grisel & her heirs forever, the sd plantations containing 1,050 a. of land on Piscattaway Cr in the sd parish ... . Wit: Thomas Roane, Wm Webb, Isaac Williamson. Ackn 16 Aug 1768 & LeRoy Hipkins & admitted to record. Attest: John Lee clerk. (Pg 194)

20 Feb 1764. To Thomas Roane & John Upshaw gent greeting, whereas LeRoy Hipkins & Grisel his wife have by their deed [see above] conveyed unto Luke Covington of Essex Co a parcel of land, & whereas the sd Grisel is unable to travel to our sd co court to make acknowledgment thereof, therefore we command you to repair to the sd Grisel & that privily & apart from her husband you take such acknowledgment as she shall be willing to make touching the premises ... . Wit John Lee Junr clerk. 21 Feb 1764 by virtue of this commission to us directed we Thomas Roane & John Upshaw did repair to the sd Grisel & having examined her privily & apart from LeRoy her husband do certify that she declared that she voluntarily & freely acknowledges the conveyance & that she was willing the same should be recorded. At a court held 26 Aug 1768 this commission & the commissioners report was returned & recorded. Attest: John Lee clerk. (Pg 195)

29 Aug 1768. Deed of Gift. Mary Lee of Westmoreland Co widow for love & affection & 5 sl have given to John Lee & Susanna his wife & Hancock Lee their son of Essex Co all her right of dower in the lands specified in the recited deeds ... whereas John Lee late of Westmoreland Co formerly of Essex Co decd

did in his life time by deed convey unto the sd John Lee party hereto a 320 a. tr of land in St. Anns Parish purch by the decd John Lee of John Noell? & others & did also by one other deed in Dec 1765 convey unto the sd John Lee & Susanna his wife for their lives & to the survivor the remainder in fee to the sd Hancock Lee one other tr of land in the sd parish whereon the sd John Lee decd then lived containing 906 a. .... . Wit: Rev. Mr. Thos Smith, Philip Smith, Solomon Robinson. Proved 19 Sep 1768 & further proved 20 Sep 1768 & fully proved 21 Dec following & ordered to be recorded. Attest: John Lee clerk. (Pg 196)

31 Aug 1768. Deed of Release. John Smith of Northumberland Co gent & Mary his wife for 5 sl have released unto John Lee of Essex Co all their right title & interest in & to the slaves ... whereas John Lee late of Essex Co gent did convey unto the sd John Lee party hereto one Negro woman named Agga & a Negro boy named Simon & to Susanna w/o the sd John Lee one girl named Silla for the consideration in the several conveyances expressed which sd Negroes were pt/o the sd Mary's dower in the estate of her first husband Jessee Ball gent decd the reversion of which the decd John Lee had purch of James Ball gent the heir at law & the sd John Smith & Mary his wife being willing to release unto the sd John Lee any right or title that they or either of them may have in the sd slaves ... . Wit: Thomas Smith, Philip Smith. Proved 19 Sep 1768 & recorded. Attest: John Lee clerk. (Pg 197)

27 Jul 1768. Deed. William Covington of South Farnham Parish, Essex Co & Sarah his wife & Elizabeth Covington widow of Richard Covington decd & mother of the sd William Covington (she having a just & lawful right by virtue of her marriage dower to 1/3 pt/o the tr of land herein mentioned) for 30 pd sold to Heritage Howerton of the same place planter a tr of land in the sd parish bounded by sd William Covington's Spring Br on the side of a swamp that runs between him & the sd Heritage Howerton & sd Williams Covington's other pt/o his land that he is now living upon, being pt/o the tr of land that the sd William Covington lawfully claimed by the death of his father Richard Covington containing 20 a. .... . Wit: Robert Read, Henry Crutcher, Thomas Covington. Ackn 18 Sep 1768 by William Covington & Sarah his wife (she being first privily examined & assenting thereto) & ackn by Elizabeth Covington & admitted to record. Attest: John Lee clerk. (Pg 197)

XVI Aug 1768. Deed. Isaac Scandrett of South Farnham Parish, Essex Co for 5 sl sold to George Stone of same place three Negroes namely Sue & her dau Lucy also one young Negro woman Bell & their increase during his natural life & after his decease my will & desire is that the afsd Negroes be divided between his two sons William Scandrett Stone & Isaac Stone to hold them in like manner but in case they should have issue to descend to their children & if it should happen that either should dye without issue the survivor to have the whole & if both should dye without issue then to descend to my dau Judith Scandrett. Wit: John Seayres, John Landrum. Proved 19 Sep 1768 & recorded. Attest: John Lee clerk. (Pg 198)

19 Apr 1768. To Thomas Williams & Stephen Cooke of Amelia Co gent greeting, whereas Henry Ford & Frances his wife of co afsd have by a deed dated 12 Apr 1768 sold & conveyed to William Cole of Essex Co the fee simple estate of & in all that 50 a. parcel of land in Essex Co & the sd Frances through the infirmity of her health cannot travel to the court of Essex Co to make such acknowledgment as in that case is required as we have received information, we have given you power to receive the acknowledgment which the sd Frances shall be willing to make to you concerning the premises, therefore we command that you personally repairing to the sd Frances you take her acknowledgment afsd ... . Wit John Lee clerk. 20 Aug 1768 at Amelia Co agreeable to this commission we have personally repaired to the sd w/o Henry Ford & she saith that the conveyance from her is her voluntary act. At a court held 19 Sep 1768 this commission & the commissioners certificate were returned & ordered to be recorded. Attest: John Lee clerk. (Pg 199)

7 May 1768. Deed of Mortgage. Leonard Garnett of St. Anns Parish, Essex Co sold to John Garnett Junr of same place all my estate whatsoever, viz, 5 head of cattle, 10 head of hogs with their future increase, 2 feather beds & furniture, gun, 1 large trunk, 2 small trunks, 1 chest, 2 tables, cheers & violin, loom, 2 wheels, saws, bars & boxes, pewter of most kinds, iron & wooden ware of ditto with every known thing or commodity of my property not remembering to mention ... the condition of the above is such that if the sd Leonard Garnett shall well & truly pay to the sd John Garnett the full & just sum of 33 pd 1 sl on or before 25 Dec next for value received then this to be void ... . Wit: John Garnett, Edwin Garnett. Proved 21 Nov 1768 & recorded. Attest: John Lee clerk. (Pg 199)

2 Nov 1768. Deed of Gift. Rhodes Greenwood & Ann his wife of South Farnham Parish, Essex Co planter for 5 sl but more especially for natural love & affection doth give unto their son James Greenwood of same place planter a 100 a. tr of land ... whereas the sd Rhodes Greenwood hath by an instrument of writing for his will made this present year bequeathed to the sd James Greenwood a 100 a. tr of land in the sd parish on the s side of Dragon Swamp bounded by Capt James Webb, Luke Covington, James Newbill Junr, William Greenwood, sd Rhodes Greenwood & Isaiah Cole, it being the tr of land that the sd Rhodes Greenwood purch of George Newbill, & whereas the sd Rhodes Greenwood since the (making) of the sd will hath come to a resolution to give unto the sd James Greenwood the afsd tr of land as is mentioned in the sd will with quiet publick & peaceable possession from the date of these presents ... . Wit: Robert Read, John Greenwood, William Newbill, William Greenwood.

Ackn 21 Nov 1768 by Rhodes Greenwood & Ann his wife (she being first privily examined & assenting thereto) & recorded. Attest: John Lee clerk. (Pg 200)

-- Oct 1768. Deed of Gift. James Samuel of Essex Co for natural love & affection have given unto my children Rachel, William & Rose the Negroes goods chattels furniture household stuff & utensils herein after mentioned, to wit, to my dau Rachel a Negro woman named Peg & her increase, 5 head of cattle, 1 horse, 5 head of sheep, 8 hogs, 1 bed & furniture, 1 pot & 1/3 pt/o all the rest & residue of my household furniture. To my son William a Negro man named Bob, 5 head of cattle, 1 horse, 5 head of sheep, 8 hogs, 1 bed & furniture, 1 pot, my waggon & 1/3 pt/o all the rest of my household furniture. To my dau Rose a Negro man named Alick, 5 head of cattle, 1 horse, 5 head of sheep, 8 hogs, 1 bed & furniture, 1 pot & the remaining 1/3 pt/o all my household furniture ... know ye further that for 5 sl to me in hand paid by Elizabeth Short my mother in law have given unto the sd Elizabeth Short the following Negro slaves, to wit, Mill, Sam, Winney & Will & 1 horse & the increase of the Mill & Winney ... . Wit: Thomas Boulware, Edward Gouldman, Jno Gillon. Ackn 21 Nov 1768 & recorded. Attest: John Lee clerk. (Pg 201)

12 Apr 1768. Deed. Henry Ford & Frances his wife & Elizabeth White of Amelia Co for 20 pd sold to William Cole of Essex Co a 50 a. tr of land bounded by the lines of Elizabeth Hanes, William Parr, William Cole Junr & William Cole ... . Wit: William Ford, Robert Read, LeeRoy Cole. Proved 18 Apr 1768 by the oaths of John White & William Ford two of the wits & ordered to be certified & on 21 Nov following was fully proved by LeRoy Cole & ordered to be recorded. On 18 Sep 1769 the deed & receipt were proved by Robert Read & ordered to be certified. Attest: John Lee clerk. (Pg 202)

3 Nov 1768. Deed. Elizabeth Allen widow &c of John Allen of Essex Co decd for natural love & affection hath given unto her son Henry Allen of same co all her right & title of dower which she hath or claimeth of in or to the tr of land whereon the sd Henry now dwells in South Farnham Parish ... . Wit: James Pamplin, Jeremiah Burnett, John Ball. Fully Proved 21 Nov 1768 & recorded. Attest: John Lee clerk. (Pg 202)

21 Nov 1768. Deed of Gift. Isaac Hawes of Essex Co for 5 sl but more especially for natural love & affection hath given unto my son Samuel Hawes of same co a 50 a. tr of land I bought of Saddler & also a 100 a. tr pt/o the tr I now live on adj the corner of Sadler's, Sorrel's line & Pilkington's line ... . Wit: Frans Waring, William Waring, Lawson Waring. Ackn 21 Nov 1768 & recorded. Attest: John Lee clerk. (Pg 203)

1 Nov 1768. Deed of Gift. Benjamin Dunn of Essex Co planter for natural love & affection hath given to his son Philip Dunn of same co planter all that messuage & 50 a. tr of land whereon the sd Philip now lives bounded by Marlow's line, Cabin Br, Croucher's line & Dragon Swamp ... . Ackn 21 Nov 1768 & recorded. Attest: John Lee clerk. (Pg 204)

28 Apr 1768. Deed. Mary Davis of South Farnham Parish, Essex Co for 186 pd 10 sl sold to Alexander Smith of same place a 200 a. tr of land in the sd parish whereof Robert Mills late of sd parish was possessed who by deed of gift dated 10 Jun 1709 confirmed the same to his son John Mills & the sd John afterwards intermarrying with the sd Mary Davis by his will dated 26 Dec 1719 devised to her by the name of Mary Mills bounded by the lands of John Smith, land of [blank] McDuff called Mohokeny, Robert Paine Waring, the heirs of Tortle McLeod decd, the sd Alexander Smith now in possession of the sd Mary Davis, Gilsons Cr & John Smith ... . Wit: William Edmondson, Geo Stone, Robt P. Waring, Thos Wyld. Proved 21 Nov 1768 & recorded. Attest: John Lee clerk. (Pg 205)

Appointment. John Blair esqr President of his Majesty's Council & Commander in Chief of VA. To William Montague esqr by virtue of the power & authority to me committed I do hereby constitute & appoint you to be sheriff of Essex Co during pleasure ... . Nov Court 1768 the above commission was ordered to be recorded. Attest: John Lee clerk. (Pg 206)

21 Nov 1768. Bond. William Montague, William Roane & James Edmondson are firmly bound unto our Sovereign Lord the King for 500 pd ... the condition of this obligation is such that whereas the afsd William Montague is appointed sheriff of Essex Co during pleasure [see above], therefore if the sd William Montague shall well & truly collect all quit rents fines forfeitures & Americiaments accrueing or becoming due to his Majesty in the sd co & shall duly account for & pay the same to the officers of his Majestys revenue for the time being on or before the second Tuesday in Jun annually & shall in all other things duly & faithfully execute the sd office of sheriff during his continuance therein then this obligation to be void ... . Sealed & delivered in presence of Essex Co court & ordered to be recorded. Attest: John Lee clerk. (Pg 206)

21 Nov 1768. Bond. William Montague, William Roane & James Edmondson are firmly bound unto our Sovereign Lord the King for 1,000 pd ... the condition of this obligation is such that whereas the afsd William Montague is appointed sheriff of Essex Co during pleasure [see above], therefore if the sd William Montague shall well & truly collect & receive all officers fees & dues put into his hands to collect & duly account for & pay the same to the officers to whom such fees are due respectively at such times as are prescribed & limited by law

& shall well & truly execute & due return make of all process & precepts to him directed & pay & satisfy all sums of money & tobacco by him received by virtue of such process to the persons to whom the same are due & in all other things shall truly & faithfully perform the sd office of sheriff during the time of his continuance therein then this obligation to be void ... . Sealed & delivered in presence of Essex Co court & ordered to be recorded. Attest: John Lee clerk. (Pg 207)

19 Nov 1768. Deed. Morris Broach & Sarah his wife of Essex Co planter for 21 pd 15 sl sold to Joseph Ryland of same co planter a 29 a. parcel of land being between the trs of the sd Morris Broach & Joseph Ryland & is pt/o the land purch by the sd Morris Broach of George Braxton gent decd ... . Wit: William Crow, Richard Brown, Richard Ryland. Ackn 19 Dec 1768 & recorded. Attest: John Lee clerk. (Pg 207)

18 Jan 1769. Deed. William Watkins of Halifax Co shoemaker & Mary his wife for 40 pd sold to William Howerton of South Farnham Parish, Essex Co planter a 100 a. parcel of land in South Farnham Parish bounded by Roger Shackleford, the heirs of Griffing Purkins decd, James Kidd, John Crow & James Townley, it being the land & plantation whereon the sd William Watkins & Mary his wife formerly lived ... . Wit: Heritage Howerton, James Parron, William Shepherd. Proved 20 Feb 1769 & admitted to record. Attest: John Lee clerk. (Pg 208)

19 Jan 1769. To Samuel Peachy, Mer. Smith & James Webb Junr of Essex Co gent greeting, whereas William Watkins & Mary his wife of Halifax Co have by their deed [see above] conveyed unto William Howerton of Essex Co a 100 a. tr of land, & whereas the sd Mary is unable to travel to our co court to make acknowledgment thereof, therefore we command you to repair to the sd Mary & that privily & apart from her husband you take such acknowledgment as she shall be willing to make ... . Wit John Lee clerk. 21 Jan 1769 by virtue of the within commission to us directed Samuel Peachy & James Webb Junr did repair to the sd Mary Watkins & privily & apart from her husband examined her touching the premises who declared that she makes the acknowledgment freely & is willing the same shall be recorded. At a court held 28 Feb 1769 the commission & the commissioners report were returned & ordered to be recorded. Attest: John Lee clerk. (Pg 210)

13 Jan 1769. Deed. Pitman Clements of South Farnham Parish, Essex Co for 3 pd sold to Archebald McCall & James Edmondson of same place a 2 a. tr of land in the sd parish on Hoskins's Cr bounded by Gatewoods Cr & Atwoods Swamp which divides the land bought by Jas Edmondson of James Dyke from Pitman Clements & John Edmondson Junr ... . Wit: Francis Lodge, Mace Clements,

George Ranken, Lauchr Mackintosh. Ackn 20 Feb 1769 & recorded. Attest: John Lee clerk. (Pg 210)

Wm Woddrop factor for James Ritchie & Company came into court & ackn to have received of Thos Haddon full satisfaction for the sum due on a mortgage made by the sd Haddon & uxor to the sd Ritchie & Company. This release was ackn 21 Feb 1769 & admitted to record. Attest: John Lee clerk. (Pg 213)

XXI Nov 1768. Articles of Agreement between Covington Searles of Essex Co ship carpenter of the first part & Mary Faulkner of same co widow of the second part & Alexr Midleton of Essex Co ship wright of the third part, whereas the sd Mary Faulkner is seised in fee of & in two trs of land & also is possessed in her own right of 7 head of black cattle, 13 head of hogs & sundry household goods & chattles, & whereas a marriage is intended (by Gods Grace) & shortly to be had & solemnized between the sd Covington Searles & the sd Mary Faulkner, it is therefore agreed by & between the sd parties in manner following (that is to say) that notwithstanding the sd marriage, he the sd Covington Searles shall not nor will intermeddle with or have any right, title or interest either in law or equity in or to any pt/o the lands or personal estate afsd, or in or to any pt/o the rents profits or increase of the same nor shall he the sd Covington Searles intermeddle with or have any right title or interest in or to any debts due or demands that is now due or hereafter to become due to the sd Mary Faulkner, but the same shall be & remain to & for the sole & separate use & benefit of the sd Mary Faulner & shall be accounted reckoned & taken as a separate & distinct estate of & from the estate of the sd Covington Searles & no ways liable or subject to him or to the payment of his debts, but shall with the profits or increase that shall be hereafter gotten or made, be ordered, deployed & employed to such persons & to & for such use & purposes as the sd Mary shall & may direct & order, either by her will or direction whatsoever, & it is further agreed that the sd Covington Searles & all such estate that he is possessed of or hereafter may acquire shall not be answerable for any debts dues or demands that the sd Mary Faulkner at this time is in arrears or at any time hereafter may contract, or be liable to pay, now shall the sd Mary Faulkner claim any dower or share at any time hereafter of in or to any lands or other estate that the sd Covington Searles may in any manner require, but the same shall be & remain to his sole use & to the sole disposition of the sd Covington Searles free & clear from any incumbrance whatever on account of the marriage afsd. Wit: Vincent Jackson, Alexander Midleton, William Mark Faulkner. Ackn by Searles & proved by Alexander Middleton & Wm Faulkner as to Faulner 21 Feb 1769 & recorded. Attest: John Lee clerk. (Pg 213)

22 Dec 1741. To Major Thomas Waring, Essex. Sir, I have recd your letter by my son Henry in answer to which I am fully resolved to give my son all the

[blank] that he now has unless Belfield &c should get them from me in that case I will give other Negroes full as good & I intend to increase the number next year. I will give him 500 a. of land in Spotsylvania & hope in a little time I shall be able to get him the whole profits of the clerks place as I find my son has a great value for your dau. I am very well pleased that it should be a match & I think the sooner the better & without much ceremony. I pray God bless us in our intended proceeding & believe that I sincerely am your most affect(ionate) friend & servant. John Robinson. At a court held 21 Feb 1769 on the motion of John Robinson by Jack Power an atty at law presenting this letter & desiring that it might be admitted to record & the court being satisfied that it is the proper handwriting of the late John Robinson esqr do order the same may be recorded. Attest: John Lee clerk. (Pg 215)

8 Mar 1769. Deed of Gift. Thomas Beale of Lunenburg Parish, Richmond Co gent for 5 sl hath given to John Beale of same place gent two trs of land in South Farnham Parish which sd lands were conveyed to the sd Thomas Beale by indenture dated 4 Jul 1757 made between William Beale of Richmond Co gent & Harwar his wife & Thomas Beale ... . Wit: Will Beale Junr, Richd Parker Junr, Reuben Beale, Simon Vile. Ackn 19 Mar 1769 & recorded. Attest: John Lee clerk. (Pg 215)

XVI Aug 1768. Deed. Luke Covington of South Farnham Parish, Essex Co & Sarah his wife for 1,050 pd sold to LeRoy Hipkins of same place two trs of land being upon Piscattaway Cr containing 1,050 a. being the same trs of land purch by the sd Luke Covington of the afsd LeRoy Hipkins & Grizel his wife 20 Feb --- . Wit: W. Roane, John Seayres, Thomas Ley, John Hipkins. Ackn 20 Mar 1769 by Luke Covington & recorded. Attest: John Lee clerk. (Pg 216)

17 Feb 1769. To Thomas Roane, John Upshaw & James Webb Junr gent of Essex Co greeting, whereas Luke Covington & Sarah his wife have by their deed [see above] conveyed two trs of land containing 1,050 a. in South Farnham Parish unto LeRoy Hipkins of Essex Co, & whereas the sd Sarah is unable to travel to our co court to make acknowledgment thereof, therefore we command you to repair to the sd Sarah & that privily & apart from her husband you take such acknowledgment as she shall be willing to make ... . Wit John Lee clerk. 17 Feb 1769 by virtue of the within commission to us directed we Thomas Roane & John Upshaw did go to the sd Sarah & her separately & apart from Luke Covington her husband examin'd touching the premises who said she did freely & voluntarily relinquish her right of dower in the sd trs of land & desired it should be recorded. At a court held 20 Mar 1769 this commission & the commissioners report was returned & order'd to be recorded. Attest: John Lee clerk. (Pg 219)

20 Mar 1769. Deed. John Gordon & Rachel his wife of Essex Co taylor for 25 pd sold to Isaac Jordan of same co carpenter a 47 a. 2 rods 30 perches parcel of land in South Farnham Parish bounded by the dividing line between the sd Jordan & Thomas Gordon which the sd Jordan & Gordon purch of the sd John Gordon & Rachel his wife, corner of Davis & Clark's corner, which sd parcel of land is 1/2 of the tr of land devised to the sd John Gordon party hereto by the will of his father William Gordon late of sd co decd ... . Wit: None. Ackn 20 Mar 1769 by John Gordon & Rachel his wife (she being first privily examined & assenting thereto) & admitted to record. Attest: John Lee clerk. (Pg 219)

20 Mar 1769. Deed. John Gordon & Rachel his wife of Essex Co taylor for 25 pd sold to Thomas Gordon of same co carpenter a 47 a. 2 rods 35 perches parcel of land in South Farnham Parish bounded by West Br of Webbs Mill Swamp, the dividing line of Isaac Jordan & Thomas Gordon's lands purch of the afsd John Gordon & Rachel his wife, which sd parcel of land is 1/2 of the tr of land devised to the John Gordon by the will of his father William Gordon late of sd co decd ... . Wit: None. Ackn 20 Mar 1769 by John Gordon & Rachel his wife (she being first privily examined & assenting thereto) & admitted to record. Attest: John Lee clerk. (Pg 221)

21 Feb 1769. Deed of Mortgage. William Meredith (Meridith) of King & Queen Co for 5 pd sold unto Pitman Clements one Negro man slave named George ... provided that whereas the sd Pitman Clements have become special bail for the sd William Meredith in a suit depending between the sd Wm Meredith def & Archibald McCall plt, if the sd William Meredith doth keep the sd Pitman Clements harmless & indemnified from all loses, damages & expences that he may sustain by reason of such special bail then these presents to be & remain of non effect ... . Wit: Richd Holt Junr. Proved 22 Mar 1769 & recorded. Attest: John Lee clerk. (Pg 223)

13 Jan 1769. Bond. Archibald McCall & James Edmondson (Edmonson) both of South Farnham Parish, Essex Co are firmly bound unto Pitman Clements of same place for 25 pd ... the condition of this obligation is such that whereas Pitman Clements hath this day made us deeds for a point of land at ye mouth of Gatewood's Swamp containing 2 a. for the use of a mill, & whereas the dam will overflow & deprive him of some of his marsh, now if the sd Archibald McCall & James Edmondson will now & at all times give Pitman Clements free leave & authority to cut & carry away four stacks of hay from Dykes large marsh now in the possession & property of James Edmondson then this obligation to be void ... . Wit: Fras Lodge, Mace Clements. Proved 22 Mar 1769 & recorded. Attest: John Lee clerk. (Pg 223)

A plot of 198 a. of land being pt/o the estate of Nichos Lasen decd laid off in three equal parts among the children 6 Jan 1764 & the widow's dower laid off as directed by the gent appd for that purpose 15 Mar 1769. Surveyed at the request of Mr. Upshaw & Mr. Rennolds by Richard Brown. [Drawing not included here] (Pg 224)

Explanation: 2 1/4 a. were laid off out of the lotts assigned to Miss Eliza Lason (who owns 2/3 parts) to John Rennolds in pt/o his wife's dower & the 22 a. is allowed to be the other pt/o Mr. Rennolds's wife's dower out of the lot assigned to John Upshaw in right of his wife. Corner to Rennolds & Fauntleroy on Northside Road, adj Pagett's orphans, Waring's line, Rennolds's line, Mr. Upshaw's lot. Pursuant to an order of the court we have laid off & assigned to John Rennolds in right of his wife her dower in the land of Nicholas Lason decd her first husband. Given under our hands 15 Mar 1769, Frans Waring, Thos Roane, W. Roane. (Pg 225)

At a court held 20 Mar 1769 this division of the lands of Nicholas Lason decd & the reports hereto annexed were returned & ordered to be recorded. Attest: John Lee clerk. (Pg 225)

-- Mar 1769. Deed. John Edmondson Junr of South Farnham Parish, Essex Co for 25 pd sold to Isaac Kidd of same place a plantation & 50 a. parcel of land on the s side of Piscattaway Cr in the sd parish which land was granted to Daniel Taylor by Thos Edmondson & Constant his wife by deed of feoffment dated 17 May 1729, afterwards devised to Henry Purkins Taylor by the will of his father Daniel Taylor who granted it to Thos Edmondson (father of the sd John Edmondson Junr) by deed of feoffment dated 22 Jan 1757, afterwards devised to the sd John Edmondson Junr (party hereto) by the will of his father Thos Edmondson, adj Thos Bryant, Glady Swamp & William Gatewood ... . Wit: Phillip Kidd, Pitman Clements, John Mann. Ackn 21 Mar 1769 & recorded. Attest: John Lee clerk. (Pg 226)

18 Oct 1768. Deed. Thomas Farmer & Sarah his wife of Bedford Co, VA for 55 pd sold to David Pitts the younger of Essex Co a 160 a. tr of land bounded by Gray's land, Smithers Spring Br & Gilsons Swamp ... . Wit: Thomas Pitts, Reuben Garnett, Lunsford Pitts. Proved 20 Mar 1769 & ordered to be certified & on 17 Apr following was fully proved & admitted to record. Attest: John Lee clerk. (Pg 227)

23 Aug 1768. Deed. John Loyd (Loyde) for 28 pd & Ruth Loyd (Loyde) & George Strang for 5 sl to each of them paid (all of St. Anns Parish, Essex Co) sold to Muscoe Garnett of same parish all their estate right in a 50 a. tr of land mentioned in the devise in the sd parish ... whereas John Strang by his will dated

7 Sep 1716 among other things devised as followeth, "I give unto my grandchild John Loyd one piece of land called the Little Ridge adj John Merrit & to his mother during her life & in case he dying without heir to fall to my son George Strang, the sd John Loyd not hindering my son George of getting any timber he has occation of" ... . Wit: John Lee, Richd Noell, George Loyde, Martha Loyd. Proved 20 Mar 1769 & certified, & on 17 Apr following was fully proved & recorded. Attest: John Lee clerk. (Pg 229)

23 Aug 1768. Deed. George Strang of St. Anns Parish, Essex Co planter for 34 pd sold to Muscoe Garnett of same parish a 68 a. tr of land whereon the sd George Strang now lives which tr of land was devised to him by the will of his father John Strang decd dated 11 Sep 1716 ... reserving the use of the sd land to the sd George Strang during his natural life ... . Wit: John Lee, Richd Noell, George Loyde, Martha Loyd. Proved 20 Mar 1769 & certified, at on 17 Apr following fully proved & recorded. Attest: John Lee clerk. (Pg 231)

21 Mar 1769. Deed of Mortgage. John Richards of the Town of Leeds in King George Co merchant & Susanna his wife for 200 pd sold to Charles Mortimer of the Town of Tappahannock in Essex Co gent two lotts or 1/2 acres of ground numbered [numbers not given] in the Town of Tappahannock on the Main Street adj to the waterside whereon is a brick house & other houses ... provided that if the sd John Richards shall well & truly pay unto the sd Charles Mortimer the 200 pd with interest on or before 21 Mar 1776 then this present bargain & sale to be void ... . Wit: Richd Parker, John Lee, Chs Mortimer Junr, John Burns, Sarah Grafton, John Dickue. Ackn 17 Apr 1769 by John Richards & admitted to record. Attest: John Lee clerk. (Pg 232)

22 Mar 1769. To Robert Beverley, Henry Garnett & Griffing Boughan of Essex Co gent greeting, whereas John Richards & Susanna his wife of King George Co have by their deed [see above] conveyed unto Charles Mortimer of Essex Co the houses & lotts in the Town of Tappahannock where Doctor John Brockenbrough lately lived, & whereas the sd Susanna is unable to travel to our co court to make acknowledgment thereof, therefore we command you that you repair to the sd Susanna & her privily & apart from her sd husband whether she willingly relinquishes her right of dower in the lands ... . Wit John Lee clerk. 15 Apr 1769 by virtue of this commission to us directed we Henry Garnett & G. Boughan did personally go to the sd Susanna w/o the sd John Richards & we did examine privately & apart from her sd husband & she declared that she consented to the same willingly & was willing the same should be recorded. At a court held 17 Apr 1769 this commission & the commissioners report were returned & ordered to be recorded. Attest: John Lee clerk. (Pg 234)

A list of freeholders that voted in the election of burgesses for Essex Co on 9 Jul 1765.

Candidate John Lee: Richard Corbin esqr, Mann Page esqr, James Upshaw, Thomas Beal, Charles Mortimer, Thomas Boulware, William Mountague, James Gray, John Upshaw, Thomas Roane, Rice Jones, Barnet Gaines, John Daniel, Richard Noell, John Harper, Mace Picket, Nicholas Atkinson, James Atkinson, Robert Clark, Robert Sale, John Lee, John Edmondson, John Patterson, Newman Miskell, John Samuel, Samuel Piles, Reuben Noell, Thomas Bradbourn, George Newbell, Isaac Jordan, Robert Brooke, William Young, John Corrie, John Richards, Caleb Lynsey, Rodes Greenwood, Morish Brooke, William Cox, Meriwether Smith, John Richards, Isaac Williamson, William Williamson, Thomas Williamson, James St. John, Smith Young, Daniel Stodgell, Richard Hipkins, Samuel Peachy, Humphrey Davis, John Price, James Clark, Thomas Games, John Oneal, William Daingerfeild, John Clements, Isaac Scandret, Samuel Hawkins, Andrew Crawford, Mark Davis, John Andrews, Thomas Ayres, Roger Shackleford, James Samuel, John Davis, Thomas Brooke, Foster Samuel, John Bastin, Thomas Faver, William Bowler, Thomas Turner, Lott Noell, John Bougton, The Rev. John Matthews, Daniel Noell, James Webb (red head), Thomas Cauthorn, Richard Cauthorn, John Howerton, William Cole, James Reynolds, Paul McCou, James Roy, John Mitchell, John Goode, Thomas C. Dickerson, William Hawkins, Oswell Byrum, Cornelious Noell, William Dobson, James Bowler, John Connerley, Leonard Harrison, Allaman Breedlove, William Dunn, John Williamson, William Bond, Thomas Cox, John Byrum, Peter Trible, Isual Hawes, John Hodges, Mark Ball, Thomas Barker, John Cooper, Edward Murray, David Pitts Junr, Drury Daubins, John Belfeild, Theodirick Bland, John Vass, John Rowzee, John Brooke, Thomas Clark, Benja Dunn, John Harper, Ambrose Pinckleton, James Martin, James Colquet, William Young Junr, Caleb Elliot, John Gray, James Bates, Edward Bowmer, Thomas Cox Junr, Ephraim Sheapard, Thomas Sale, Peter Samuel, Samuel Henshaw, John Bush, John Webb, Thomas Brooke, Stark Bowler, Samuel Davis, Robert Cole, James Key, Henry Cauthorn, Samuel Johnson, Nathaniel Dunn, James Medley, William Amiss, Henry Cox, John Rodding, Jonathan Dunn, John Edmondson, Thomas Dix, Ezekle Byrum, Even Davis, John Burk, Richard Burk, Richard Hodges, William Mitchell, John Clark, Andrew Allen, Abraham Mountague, Jonathan Shearwood, Griffin Johnson, John Burnet, Nathaniel Breedlove, John Sullivan, Joseph Gatewood, Benjamin Bowler, Haraway Owen, Henry Woodbanks, Thomas Sullivan, John Crutchfield, Josiah Cole, Henry Croucher, Thomas Dennet, William Watkins, Thomas Thorp, John Dunn, John Ball, Martin Willard, Luke Covington, Francis Smith, Richard Jeffres, William Ayres,, William Dunn Junr, James Davis, John Taylor, Simon Gouldin, James Landrum, Ralph Rowzee, Thomas Watts, Reuben Shelton, Greensby Evans, James Mills,

Stephen Neal, John Mitchel, James Webb, Muscoe Garnett, Joseph Reves, James Campbell, James Jones, Henry Vass, John Blott, Leonard Hill, Thomas Butler, John Sale, Nicholas Faulkner, Cornelius Sale, Francis Boughan, John Smith, Thomas Newman, David Dishman, Joseph Tinsley, James Shaddock, Ambrose Greenhill, James Sullivan, The Rev. Thomas Smith, Richard Hill, John Castle, Theophilus Faver, William Thomas Junr, Robert Parker, Thomas Gouldman, Richard St. John, Henry Kidd, Richard Meadows, Joseph Mann, Francis Jones, Thomas Upshaw, Samuel Allen, John Hill, Francis Graves, John Haynes, Thomas Oneal, Phill Kidd, Joseph Minter, Joshua Boughton, James Stokes, Henry Motley, Henry P. Taylor, Edmond Padget, William Bowler, John Burnet Junr, Oliver Howard, Thomas Dunn, William Fletcher, Heretage Howerton, Alexander Saunders, Thomas Newbell, Henry Gardner, Thomas Coghill, Major Lason, Thomas H. Brooke, Jacob Shearwood, John Croxton, Richard Thomas Hale, Thomas Croxton, William Covington, David Pitts, Major John Boughan, Richard Brown, Henry Brown, Samuel Smith, Throughsebulus Minor, William Greenwood, Robert Rennolds, Francis Brizendine, Phill Cheyney, John Brizendine, Thomas Bush, William Gatewood, Ralph Neal, Edmund Ball, James Cauthorn, Vincent Cauthorn, Isaac Kidd, John Brooke, Benja Smith, George Moody, Archd McCall, Thomas Cole, James Booker, William Dunn (B), Joseph Ryland, Samuel Noell, Charles Taylor, Alexander Anderson, Meridith Brown, John Williams, James Noell, Isaac Williams, Abner Ball, William Gray, John Henshaw, Ambrose Cox, James Webb Junr, James Medley, William Clark, William Howerton, Bartholomew Clark, Robert Hundley, John Smither, Mereday Brown, Leroy Hipkins, Robert Beverley, Archd Ritchie.

Candidate Francis Waring esqr: William Mountague, Rice Jones, Richard Noell, John Harper, Mace Picket, Nicholas Atkinson, James Atkinson, Robert Clark, John Byrum, Peter Trible, Josiah Macteer, Isaac Hawes, John Hodges, Mark Ball, Henry Street, John Sadler, Thomas Barker, John Cooper, Edward Murray, David Pitts Junr, John Edmondson, John Patterson, Newman Miskell, Reuben Noell, Thomas Bradbourn, George Newbell, Isaac Jordan, Rodes Greenwood, William Cox, Drury Daubins, Richard Phillips, John Biddlecum, John Vass, John Brooke, Richard Street, Joseph Burnet, George Wright, Thomas Clark, Benjamin Dunn, John Harner, Ambrose Gatewood, Isaac Williams, William Williamson, Thomas Williamson, James St. John, Augustine Smith, Robert Smith, William Roane, Daniel Stodgell, William Porter, Griffing Boughan, Thomas Fogg, Thomas Munday, John Caragan, Robert Jones, John Price, James Clark, Thomas Games, John Oneal, William Gordon, William Daingerfeild, John Clements, Isaac Scandret, Samuel Hawkins, Thomas Ayres, Francis Raysey (sic) Junr, Roger Shackleford, James Samuel, John Davis, Thomas Brooke, John Smith, Thomas Faver, John Fauntleroy, William Edmondson, Edward Vawters, Thomas Turner, Lott Noell, John Bougton,

William Johnson, James Webb, Thomas Cauthorn, Richard Cauthorn, John Howerton, William Cole, James Rennolds, John Mitchell, John Goode, Thomas C. Dickerson, William Hawkins, Oswell Byrum, Cornelius Noell, William Dobson, James Bowler, John Connerley, Leonard Harrison, Allaman Breedlove, William Dunn, John Williams, William Bond, Thomas Cox, James Colquet, George Strang, William Young Senr, Caleb Elliot, John Gray, James Bates, Edward Bowman, Thomas Cox Senr, Ephraim Sheapard, Samuel Henshaw, Edward Rowsey, James Allen, John Bush, John Webb, Thomas Brooke, James Davis Junr, Stark Bowler, Samuel Davis, Robert Cole, William Cole, James Key, Samuel Johnson, Nathaniel Dunn, William Marlow, James Medley, William Amiss, Henry Cox, Thomas St. John, John Rodding, Jonathan Dunn, John Edmondson, Thomas Dix, Erckle Byrum, Even Davis, John Burk, Ambrose Wright, Richard Burk, Richard Hodges, William Mitchell, John Clark, Jonathan Shearwood, Griffin Johnson, John Burnet, Nathaniel Breedlove, John Sullivan, Joseph Gatewood, Benja Bowler, John Turner, Haraway Owen, Henry Woolbanks, Thomas Sullivan, John Crutchfeild, Josiah Cole, Rice Noell, Henry Croutcher, Thomas Dennet, William Watkins, Thomas Thorp, James Dyke, John Dunn, John Ball, Martin Willard, Francis Smith, Richard Jeffres, William Ayres, Alexander Middleton, William Dunn Junr, Simon Gouldin, James Landrum, Thomas Watts, Reuben Shelton, Greensby Evans, Stephen Neal, John Mitchel, Chaney Gatewood, Joseph Fogg, Joseph Reves, John Webb, James Jones, Leonard Hill, Benja Fisher, Isaac Gatewood, John Sale, Nicholas Faulkoner, Francis Boughan, John Smith, David Dishman, James Tinsley, Ambrose Greenhill, James Sullivan, Richard Hill, John Castle, Theophilus Faver, William Thomas Junr, Robert Parker, Thomas Gouldman, Richard St. John, Henry Kidd, Reuben Waggoner, Richard Meadows, Joseph Mann, Francis Jones, John Crow, John Dickerson, Thomas Upshaw, Samuel Allen, John Meadows, Thomas Oneal, Phill Kidd, Reuben Meadows, Joseph Minter, Joshua Boughton, James Stokes, John Garnet Junr, Henry Motley, John Loyd, Henry P. Tayler, Edmond Paget, William Bowler, John Burnet, Oliver Howard, John Gatewood, Augustine Owen, Thomas Dunn, William Fletcher, Heretage Howerton, Thomas Newbell, Major Lason, Thomas H. Brooke, Jacob Shearwood, James Boughan, Richard Hale, Thomas Croxton, William Covington, David Pitts, Major John Boughan, Richard Brown, Henry Brown, James Edmondson, Thomas Loyd, Throughsibulus Minor, Benja Jones, Richard Jones, Stephen Munday, William Gatewood, Robert Rennolds, Francis Brizendine, Phill Cheyney, John Brizendine, Thomas Bush, William Greenwood, Ralph Neal, Edmund Ball, Benjamin Waggoner, Nathaniel Waggoner, Thomas Meadows, Josiah Minter, Isaac Kidd, John Brooke, Benja Smith, George Moody, Archd McCall, Thomas Cole, John Rennolds, James Booker, William Dunn (B), John Lateney, Henry Purkins, Joseph Ryland, James Banks, John Williamson, James Noell, William Ramsey, Isaac Williams, Abner Ball, Charles Bray, Ambrose Cox, James

Medley, William Howerton, Thomas Hadden, Francis Garnett, John Smither, Leroy Hipkins.

Candidate Robert Beverley esqr: Richard Corbin esqr, Mann Page esqr, James Upshaw, Thomas Beal, Charles Mortimer, Thomas Boulware, James Gray, John Upshaw, Thomas Roane, Barnet Gaines, John Daniel, Robt Sale, Josiah Macteer, Henry Street, John Sadler, John Turner, Rice Noell, James Dyke, Luke Covington, Alexander Middleton, John Lee, John Samuel, Samuel Piles, Robert Brooke, William Young, John Corrie, John Richards, Caleb Lynsey, Morish Brooke, Meriwether Smith, John Richards, Richard Phillips, John Belfield, Theodireck Bland esqr, John Rowzee, Richard Street, George Wright, Ambrose Gatewood, Ambrose Pinckleton, James Martin, Smith Young, William Roane, William Porter, Griffin Boughan, Richard Hipkins, Thomas Fogg, Thomas Munday, John Carragan, Samuel Peachey, Humphrey Davis, William Gordon, George Strang, Thomas Sale, Peter Samuel, Edward Rowzee, James Allen, James Davis Junr, William Cole, Henry Cauthorn, Ambrose Wright, Andrew Allen, Abraham Mountague, Andrew Crawford, Mark Davis, John Andrews, Francis Ramsey Junr, Foster Samuel, John Bastin, John Smith, William Bowler, John Fauntleroy, William Edmondson, The Rev. Alexander Gruden, Edward Vawters, The Rev. John Matthews, William Johnson, Daniel Noell, John Meadows, Paul Mecou, James Roy, James Davis, John Taylor, Ralph Rowzee, James Mills, James Webb Junr, Muscoe Garnett, Philip Gatewood, Chancy Gatewood, James Campbell, John Webb, Henry Vass, John Blatt, Benja Fisher, Isaac Gatewood, Thomas Butler, Cornelius Sale, Thomas Newman, James Shaddock, The Reverend Thos Smith, John Crow, John Hill, Francis Graves, John Haynes, Reuben Meadows, John Garnett, John Loyd, Agustine Owen, Alexander Saunders, Henry Gardner, Thomas Coghill, James Edmondson, Samuel Smith, Thos Loyd, Benja Jones, Richard Jones, Stephen Munday, James Cauthorn, Vincent Cauthorn, John Rennolds, John Latteney, Henry Purkins, Samuel Noell, Charles Taylor, Alexander Anderson, Meridith Brown, James Banks, William Ramsey, William Gray, Charles Bray, John Henshaw, James Webb, William Clark, Thomas Haddon, Francis Garnett, Robert Hundley, Mereday Brown, John Lee Junr, Archd Ritchie.

Candidate William Daingerfield esqr: Augustine Smith, Robert Smith, Robert Jones, William Marlow, Thomas St. John, Reuben Waggoner, John Dickerson, John Gatewood, Benja Waggoner, Nathaniel Waggoner, Joseph Burnet, James Boughan, Thomas Meadows, Josiah Minter, Francis Warring.

Candidate John Upshaw esqr: John Lee Junr, Robert Beverley esqr.
Candidate Thomas Roane esqr: Phill Gatewood, Francis Warring.

Essex Co Sct. 9 Jul 1765, Archibald Ritchie sheriff. Recorded Apr Court 1769.
Attest: John Lee clerk. (Pg 235-242)

A poll taken for the electing burgesses in Essex Co at Tappahannock on
Thursday 24 Nov 1768 by Samuel Peachey gent he being first sworn as the law
directs, viz,

       Candidate Col Francis Waring: John Reynolds, Joseph Burnet, Mace
Picket, James Clark, Peter Samuel, John Farguson, Henry Cox, John Gray,
Daniel Stockdill, John Oneal, Isaac Jordan, Thomas Gordan, George Newbill,
James St. John, John Goode, James Medley, William Daniel, Isaac Hawes,
James Webb Senr, Henry Woolbanks, John Shanault, Ambrose Howard, James
Clark, Ellerson Nowel, William Fletcher, Samuel Piles, James Calkit, John
Edmondson, Griffing Boughan, Thomas C. Dickerson, James Jones, Major
Leson, John Conduit, James Garnett, Richard Holt, Covington Searles, Joseph
Reaves, Thomas Meadows, Richard Meadows, Thomas Coleman, Reuben
Meadows, John Rhodding, John Kerrigan, Richard Holt Junr, John Coleman,
Jonathan Shearwood, Hugh Willson, John Coleman, Thomas Munday, Francis
Vaughn, Ralph Rowzee, Alex Smith, James Rennolds, Job Spearman, John
Conniley, Griffin Johnson, William Mitchell, James Allen, Thomas Dix, John
Gordon, Benja Jones, Richard Jones, Elias Harrison, Thomas Sullivan, William
Edmondson, Francis Ramsey, Maurice Brush, William Bowler, Cornelius Sale,
James Landrum, John Spindle, John Ball, Threcibulus Minor, John Clark,
George Wright, John Bastean, John Croxton, Oliver Howard, Joseph Ryland,
Thomas Croxton, Thomas Coleman, Reuben Meadows, John Rhodding, John
Kerrigan, Richard Holt Junr, John Coleman, Jonathan Shearwood, Hugh
Willson, John Coleman, Thomas Munday, Francis Vaughn, Ralph Rowzee, Alex
Smith, James Rennolds, Job Spearman, John Conniley, Griffin Johnson, William
Mitchell, James Allen, Thomas Dix, John Gordon, Benja Jones, Richard Jones,
Elias Harrison, Thomas Sullivan, William Edmondson, Francis Ramsey,
Maurice Brush, William Bowler, Cornelius Sale, James Landrum, John Spindle,
John Ball, Threcibulus Minor, John Clark, George Wright, John Bastean, John
Croxton, Oliver Howard, Joseph Ryland, Thomas Croxton, Rogger Shackleford,
Samuel Allen, William Young, Benja Waggoner, John Mitchell, Edward
Rowzee, Henry Croutcher, Robert Hundley, John Garnett, George Strang,
Samuel Shaw, Caleb Elliot, Richard Hipkins, Thomas Sale, Benja Fisher,
Andrew Gatewood, Edward Vawter, Jeremiah Bizwell, Alexr Anderson,
Thomas Oneal, Wm Ayres, James Davis, Robt Clark, Andrew Waggoner, Caleb
Noell, Joseph Tinsley, Robt Mann, Philip Smither, Wm Dobson, Robt Sale,
James Noell, John Fogg, Charles Mecks, Theophilus Faver, Thomas Bradbourn,
Robert Rennolds, Marlow Thorp, Nathan Waggoner, Stephen Munday, Ralph
Neal, Augustine Compton, Thomas Ayre, Thomas Newman, Thomas Dean,
John Meadows, Edward Davis, John Richards, James Bates, Harraway Owin,

Nathan Breedlove, Nicholas Atkerson, Richard Jeffries, Leonard Hill, Richard Hill, James Sullivan, Bartho Nowell, Bartho Clark, Martin Willard, Benja Smith, David Pitts Junr, John Boughton, Samuel Hoskins, John Matthews, William Tureman, Thomas Dunn, John Gatewood, Alaman Breedlove, John Tureman, Stark Bowler, Charles Taylor, Henry Kidd, Erasmus Jones, William Watkins, John Castle, John Taylor, Abner Ball, Thomas Upshaw, John Hill, William Waller, Nathan Dunn, Richard Brown, Henry Street, John Smither, John Patterson, James Stoaks, William Clark, Pitman Clements, John Edmondson, Thomas Lee, William Cole, Josiah McTire, John Saddler, William Gatewood, Thomas Allen, John Smith, Thomas Newbell, William Gatewood Junr, John Webb, John Blott, William Webb, John Crow, Edmond Pasquet, Timothy Longast, John Tate, Thomas Andrews, Henry Purkins, Tandy Dix, Richard T. Hale, Henry Allen, John Burnet, Robert Smith, Thomas Broocke, Joseph Gatewood, John Gatewood, Thomas Wood, Thomas Dennet, Thomas Turner, Samuel Henshaw, John Price, Robert Parker, Simon Golddin, Ambrose Pilkington, William Bonds, John Edmondson, John Howerton, Thomas Faver, Cheaney Gatewood, Nicho Faulkoner, John Loyde, Lott Noell, Ambrose Greenhill, James Croxton, Josiah Minter, Jacob Shearwood, William Marlow, Peter Montague, Thomas Fogg, William Gray, Philip Kidd, Rick Burk, Evan Davis, Henry Vass, John Dayley, John Williamson, John Baughn, Archillis Garnett, George Gains, William Dunn, David Pitts, William Thomas, Alexander Middleton, James Atkerson, Thomas Gouldman, Benja Bowler, Paul McCou, William Thomas, Isaiah Cole, Thomas Butler, Archd McCall, Reuben Noell, John Crutchwell, John Latane, William Ramsey, Samuel Haws, William Hathaway, Robert Waring, William Dunn, Benja Dunn, Heritage Howerton, James Booker, James Banks, Augustine Garnett.

Candidate Capt Mer. Smith: Joseph Burnet, Samuel Coats, Peter Samuel, John Oneal, John Upshaw, Thomas Cox, John Goode, James Medley, Thomas Williamson, Ellerson Noell, Wm Fletcher, Samuel Piles, James Shaddock, James Jones, John Hodges, John Cooper, James Garnett, John Roddin, Williamson Young, John Harper, Rhodes Greenwood, Alexander Smith, Philip Dunn, Griffin Johnson, William Mitchell, John Dickerson, William Edmondson, John Williamson, Thomas Cox Junr, Alex Cruden, Charles Mortimer, John Tayloe esqr, John Bastean, Thomas Gaines, Richd Hodges, Rogger Shackleford, William Young, Joshua Boughton, Henry Croutcher, Robt Hundley, Ezekiel Byrum, Robt Clark, John Owin, Robt Mann, John Samuel, John Byrum, James Campbell, Charles Wecks, Theophilus Faver, Thomas Bradford, Robert Rennolds, Marlow Thorp, Ephraim Sheperd, John Haynes, Ralph Neal, Alex Bowmer, Thos Haddon, Richard St. John, William Covington, Thomas Smith, Robert Brooke, John Rowzee, Philip Cheaney, Thomas Broocke, Haraway Owin, Nathan Breedlove, John Richards, John Young, Wm Broockes, Nicho Atkerson, Peter Trible, Richd Jeffries, Caleb Lynsey, Thomas Cauthorn,

Bartho Clark, Marlow Woolard, John Boughton, Charles Saunders, Robert Beverley, William Shepherd, John Matthews, Ezekiel Byrum, Robt Clark, John Owin, Robt Mann, John Samuel, John Byrum, James Campbell, Charles Wecks, Theophilus Faver, Thomas Bradford, Robert Rennolds, Marlow Thorp, Ephraim Sheperd, John Haynes, Ralph Neal, Alex Bowmer, Thos Hadden, Richard St. John, William Covington, Thomas Smith, Robert Brooke, John Rowzee, Philip Cheaney, Thomas Broocke, Haraway Owin, Nathan Breedlove, John Richards, John Young, Wm Broockes, Nicho Atkerson, Peter Trible, Richd Jeffries, Caleb Lynsey, Thomas Cauthorn, Bartho Clark, Marlow Woolard, John Boughton, Charles Saunders, Robert Beverley, William Shepherd, John Matthews, William Greenwood, William Tureman, Henry Gardner, William Mountague, Smith Young, John Brooke, Alaman Breedlove, Stark Bowler, Charles Taylor, Erasmus Jones, John Cheaney, William Williamson, John Patterson, William Clark, John Evans, Richard Phillips, James Webb Junr, John Broocke, Titus Farguson, Thomas Allen, Francis Graves, Alexr Saunders, Thomas Newbell, William Gatewood, Vincent Cauthorn, John Webb, John Corrie, John Webb Junr, John Blott, Thomas H. Broocke, John Brizendine, Thomas Andrews, Thomas Dennit, Isaac Williamson, John Price, John Mitchell, William Howerton, William Cheaney, Francis Brizendine, William Bond, Thomas Bush, William Bowmer, William Porter, Anglia Vawter, Lot Noell, Samuel Davis, Philip Kidd, Evan Davis, William Smith, Henry Vass, John Williamson, Merridy Brown, Luke Covington, George Gaines, David Pitts, William Thomas, James Atkerson, Thomas Goldman, Benjamin Bowler, Henry Cauthorn, Leonard Broocke, Oswald Byrum, William Thomas, Thomas Butler, Abra Mountague, Reuben Bush, John Lee, John Crutchwell, Thomas Bowler, James Davis, James Webb Junr, Samuel Peachey, Christopher Broocke, James Boughn, William Young, William Dunn, Herritage Howerton.

Candidate Capt William Roane: John Reynolds, Samuel Coats, Mace Picket, James Clark, John Farguson, Henry Cox, John Gray, Daniel Stockdill, John Upshaw, Isaac Jordan, Thomas Gordan, Thomas Cox, George Newbill, James St. John, William Daniel, Isaac Haws, James Webb, Henry Woolbanks, John Shanault, Ambrose Howard, Thomas Williamson, James Clark, James Shaddock, James Calket, John Edmondson, Griffing Boughan, Thos C. Dickerson, Major Leson, John Hodges, John Cooper, John Conduit, Richard Holt, Covington Searles, Joseph Reaves, Thomas Meadows, Richard Meadows, Thomas Coleman, Reuben Meadows, Richard Holt, John Coleman, Jonathan Shearwood, Hugh Wilson, John Coleman, Thomas Munday, Francis Boughan, Ralph Rowzee, John Harper, Rhodes Greenwood, James Rennolds, Job Spearman, Philip Dunn, John Conniley, John Dickerson, James Allen, Thomas Dix, John Gorden, Benja Jones, Richard Jones, Elias Harrison, Thomas Sullivan, John Williamson, Francis Ramsey, Thomas Cox Junr, Maurice Brush, William Bowler, Cornelius Sale, James Landrum, John Spindle, John Ball, Threcibulus

Minor, John Clark, George Wright, John Croxton, Oliver Howard, Joseph
Ryland, Thomas Gaines, Thomas Croxton, Richard Hodges, Samuel Allen,
Benja Waggoner, John Coleman, Jonathan Shearwood, Hugh Wilson, John
Coleman, Thomas Munday, Francis Boughan, Ralph Rowzee, John Harper,
Rhodes Greenwood, James Rennolds, Job Spearman, Philip Dunn, John
Conniley, John Dickerson, James Allen, Thomas Dix, John Gorden, Benja
Jones, Richard Jones, Elias Harrisson, Thomas Sullivan, John Williamson,
Francis Ramsey, Thomas Cox Junr, Maurice Brush, William Bowler, Cornelius
Sale, James Landrum, John Spindle, John Ball, Threcibulus Minor, John Clark,
George Wright, John Croxton, Oliver Howard, Joseph Ryland, Thomas Gaines,
Thomas Croxton, Richard Hodges, Samuel Allen, Benja Waggoner, Benjamin
Waggoner, John Mitchell, Edward Rowzee, John Garnett, George Strang,
Samuel Shaw, Caleb Elliot, Richard Hipkins, Thomas Sale, Benja Fisher,
Andrew Gatewood, Edward Vawter, Jeremiah Bizwell, Alexr Anderson,
Thomas Oneal, William Ayres, James Davis Junr, Ezekiel Byrum, Andrew
Waggoner, Caleb Noell, Joshua Tinsley, John Samuel, John Byrum, Philip
Smither, William Dobson, Robert Sale, James Noell, Richard Noell, John Fogg,
John Haynes, Nathan Waggoner, Stephen Munday, Alexr Bomer, Augustine
Compton, Thomas Haddin, Thomas Ayre, Thomas Newman, James Roy,
Thomas Dean, John Meadows, Richd, St. John, William Covington, Edward
Davis, John Rowzee, James Bates, Leonard Hill, Richard Hill, James Sullivan,
Berry Noell, Benjamin Smith, David Pitts Junr, William Shepherd, Samuel
Hoskins, William Greenwood, John Brooke, Thomas Dunn, John Gatewood,
John Turner, Henry Kidd, William Watkins, John Castle, John Taylor, Abner
Ball, John Cheaney, Thomas Upshaw, John Hill, William Waller, Nathan Dunn,
Richard Brown, Henry Street, John Smither, James Stoakes, John Evans,
Richard Phillips, Pitman Clements, John Edmondson Junr, Thomas Lee, William
Cole, Josiah McTyre, John Saddler, Titus Farguson, William Gatewood, Francis
Graves, John Smith, John Corrie, Thomas Broocke, John Brizendine, Wm
Webb, John Crow, Edmund Pasquet, Timothy Longast, John Sale, Henry
Purkins, Tandy Dix, Richard T. Hale, Henry Allen, John Burnett, Robert Smith,
Thomas Broocke, Joseph Gatewood, John Gatewood, Thomas Wood, Isaac
Williamson, Thomas Turner, Samuel Henshaw, John Mitchell, Robert Parker,
Simon Golddin, Ambrose Pilkington, William Howerton, William Cheaney,
Francis Brizendine, Thomas Bush, William Bowmer, William Porter, John
Edmondson, John Howerton, Thomas Faver, Cheaney Gatewood, Nicho
Faulkoner, John Loyd, Anglia Vawter, Ambrose Greenhill, James Croxton,
Josiah Minter, Jacob Shearwood, Samuel Davis, William Marlow, Peter
Montague, William Gray, Rick Burk, John Dayley, John Baughn, Merriday
Brown, Luke Covington, Achilles Garnett, William Dunn, Alexr Middleton,
Paul Mecou, Henry Cauthorn, Leonard Broocke, Oswald Byrom, Charles Bray,
Isaiah Cole, Abra Montague, Reuben Bush, Archd McCall, Reuben Noell, John
Latane, William Ramsey, Christopher Broocke, Samuel Haws, James Baughn,

William Hathaway, Robert Waring, Benja Dunn, James Boocker, James Banks, Augustine Garnett.

Candidate Richd Parker: John Herrigan, Williamson Young, Alexander Cruden, Charles Mortimer, John Tayloe esqr, Joshua Boughton, John Owin, James Campbell, Ephraim Shepherd, James Roy, Thomas Smith, Robert Brooke, Philip Cheaney, Thomas Brooke, John Richards, John Richards Junr, John Young, William Broocke, Peter Trible, Caleb Lynsey, Thomas Cauthorn, Charles Saunders, Robt Beverley, Henry Gardner, William Mountague, Smith Young, William Williamson, James Webb Junr, John Broocke, Alexander Saunders, Vincent Cauthorn, John Webb, William Smith, Charles Bray, John Lee, Thomas Boulware, James Davis, James Webb Junr, Samuel Peachy, William Young.

Essex Sct. William Montague esqr high sheriff of sd co made oath before me that the foregoing is a true copy of the poll taken at the election of burgesses for the sd co on 24 Nov last. Given under my hand 17 Apr 1769, Meriwether Smith. Recorded in May Court 1769. Attest: John Lee clerk. (Pg 243-248)

25 Nov 1768. Deed Poll. These are to certify that I Edward Donohoe do give unto Francis Donohoe 1/2 my right of the Negroes & 1/2 the dower which shall or might descend to me after my mothers death for a valuable consideration to me in hand paid by the afsd Francis Donohoe. Wit: Robt Parker, James Adkinson, Thomas Gouldman. Proved 15 May 1769 & recorded. Attest: John Lee clerk. (Pg 248)

25 Nov 1768. Power of Attorney. I Edward Donohoe of Bedford Co have appointed my son Francis Donohoe of Essex Co my atty granting to my sd atty full power & authority to administer on that pt/o my mother's thirds after her death as shall fall to me by the will of my father Patrick Donohoe ... . Wit: Robert Parker, James Adkinson, Thomas Gouldman. Proved 15 May 1769 & recorded. Attest: John Lee clerk. (Pg 248)

12 Dec 1768. Deed. John Burnett & Caty his wife of Mecklenburg Co for 122 pd 10 sl sold to Archibald Ritchie of Essex Co merchant a 245 a. tr of land bounded by the land of Joseph Burnett, John Burnett, John Boughan & Thomas Brooke ... . Wit: John Chamberlain, Jos Burnett, Jeremiah Burnett. Fully proved 16 May 1769 & recorded. Attest: John Lee clerk. (Pg 249)

12 Nov 1768. To John Potter & John Kemp of Mecklenburg Co gent greeting, whereas John Burnett & Cathrine his wife have by their deed [see above] conveyed unto Archibald Ritchie of Essex Co 245 a. of land in Essex Co, & whereas the sd Cathrine is unable to travel to our co court to make

acknowledgment thereof, therefore we command you to repair to the sd Cathrine & that privily & apart from her sd husband you take such acknowledgment as she shall be willing to make ... . Wit John Lee clerk. 12 Dec 1768 at Mecklenburg Co in persuance of the within dedimus we John Kemp (Camp) & John Potter justices have this day examined the within named Kathrine Burnett privately & apart from her sd husband touching her right of dower in the lands & we do certify that the sd Kathrine doth freely relinquish her right of dower therein ... . At a court held 16 May 1769 this commission & the commissioners report were this day returned & ordered to be recorded. Attest: John Lee clerk. (Pg 251)

19 Nov 1768. Power of Attorney. I Muscoe Livingston of London mariner master of the Baltick merchant have constituted Archibald Ritchee of VA merchant, James Mills of VA merchant & Muscoe Garnett of VA merchant my attys to attach, seize, hold & retain all such goods, chattles, merchandize & effects as shall be found in the possession custody or care of any person whatsoever in VA or MD of & belonging to John Day of London merchant whether the same be in any warehouse cellar or other place of safety whatsoever & to sell & absolutely dispose of all such goods, chattles, merchandize & effects or a competent part thereof to satisfy the debt of 400 pd &c or whatever sum shall appear to be due & owing to me from the sd John Day ... . Wit: John Livingston, Jno Staples. Pub: Nov 1768. Proved 16 May 1769 & recorded. Attest: John Lee clerk. (Pg 252)

19 Jun 1769. Deed. Isaac Williamson & his wife Frances of South Farnham Parish, Essex Co for 9 pd 10 sl sold to Richard Williamson of same place a 30 a. tr of land in the sd parish adj on the brs of Piscataway Cr & bounded by Gordon's land, Turner's land, Hay's land & Clark's land ... . Wit: John Webb. Wit to receipt: Robt Mann. Ackn 19 Jun 1769 by Isaac Williamson & Frances his wife she being first privily examined & assenting thereto & recorded. Attest: John Lee clerk. (Pg 253)

19 Jun 1769. Deed. Edward Dobyns & Frances Davis of Hanover Parish, King George Co for 40 pd sold to John Broocke Junr of South Farnham Parish, Essex Co a 100 a. tr of land in South Farnham Parish bounded by Andrew Allen, the other pt/o the sd tr which the sd Broocke purch of Richens Dobyns, Cheaney's land, Francis Brizendine & Andrew Allen ... . Wit: Andrew Allen, Thomas Broocke, Wm Bomar. Ackn 19 Jun 1769 & admitted to record. Attest: John Lee clerk. (Pg 255)

19 Jun 1769. Deed. John Sadler & Elisabeth his wife for 60 pd sold to Richard Street of sd co a 93 a. tr of land bounded by Thos Clark, sd Sadlar, Josiah McTire, Causway Swamp & Abraham Mountague ... . Wit: A. Mountague,

Henry Street, Joseph Patterson. Ackn 19 Jun 1769 by John Sadler & Elizabeth his wife (she being first privily examined & assenting thereto) & recorded. Attest: John Lee clerk. (Pg 257)

16 Jun 1769. Deed. William Shepard & Catharine his wife of South Farnham Parish, Essex Co for 105 pd sold to John Evans of same place all their estate right in a 100 a. parcel of land in the sd parish bounded by Robert Cole, John Haines, Ephraim Shepherd & Cheyneys Bridge Swamp, which sd parcel of land formerly belonged to his father Jeremiah Shepherd & as heir at law the sd William Shepperd now posseseth it ... . Wit: William Young Junr, Henry Young, Isaac Webb, Henry Vass. Ackn 19 Jun 1769 by William Shepherd & Catharine his wife (she being first privily examined & assenting thereto) & recorded. Attest: John Lee clerk. (Pg 259)

16 Jun 1769. Deed. William Shephard (Shepherd) & Catharine his wife of South Farnham Parish for 235 pd 5 sl sold to William Young Junr of same place all their estate right in a 225 a. parcel of land in the sd parish bounded by Thomas Newbill, Francis Smith, Alexander Bomar, William Cheyney & Cheyneys Bridge Swamp, which parcel of land being pt/o that tr of land which formerly belonged to his grandfather William Cheyney & as heir at law the sd William Sheppard now posseseth it whereon the sd William Shephard & Catharine his wife now liveth ... . Wit: John Evans, Henry Young, Isaac Webb, Henry Vass. Ackn 19 Jun 1769 by William Shepherd & Catharine his wife (she being first privily examined & assenting thereto) & recorded. Attest: John Lee clerk. (Pg 261)

19 Jun 1769. Deed. Williamson Young of Essex Co for 250 pd sold to John Richards of sd co gent a 129 3/4 a. tr of land in South Farnham Parish devised to the sd Williamson Young by his father Williamson Young decd by his will dated 22 Apr 1749 ... . Wit: Bosk Richards, John Evans, Henry Young, Isaac Webb. Ackn 19 Jun 1769 & recorded. Attest: John Lee clerk. (Pg 262)

9 Dec 1768. Deed. John Young of Granville Co, NC & Rachel his wife for 280 pd sold to Henry Young of Essex Co, VA a 220 a. parcel of land adj William Gatewood, Philemon Young, Philemon Gatewood, John Webb & Rappahannock River ... . Wit: Samuel Peachey, W. Young, James Webb Junr, John Richards. Proved 19 Jun 1769 & recorded. Attest: John Lee clerk. (Pg 264)

10 Dec 1768. To Samuel Peachey, Meriwether Smith & James Webb Junr of Essex Co gent greeting, whereas John Young & Rachel his wife of NC by their deed [see above] conveyed to Henry Young of VA a 220 a. tr of land, & the sd Rachel through the infirmity of her health cannot travel to our co court to make such acknowledgment as in that case is required as we have received

information, we therefore have given you power to receive & take the acknowledgment which the sd Rachel shall be willing to make concerning the premises, therefore we command you that you personally repairing to the sd Rachel you take her acknowledgment ... . Wit John Lee clerk. 10 Dec 1768 by virtue of the within commission the sd Rachel being seperately & apart from her husband examined did declare that she freely & voluntarily acknowledged the sd indenture, certified by Samuel Peachey & James Webb Junr. At a court held 19 Jun 1769 this commission & the commissioners report were returned & ordered to be recorded. Attest: John Lee clerk. (Pg 265)

25 Mar 1769. Deed. John Evans of South Farnham Parish, Essex Co planter for 265 pd sold to Charles Evans of same place mariner a 186 a. parcel of land in the sd parish adj the lands of John Webb, Leonard Hill decd, James Evans, Richard Philips, John Dunn, John Evans Junr, William Young Junr & Phil Gatewood, which sd tr of land was the property of John Evans the elder decd & by him devised to his son Greensbe Evans & the sd Greensbe Evans devised 1/2 thereof to his brother Micajah Evans father to the afsd John Evans party to these presents who dying intestate the same descended to the sd John Evans as heir at law, & the other 1/2 to the afsd John Evans as by the devises afsd ... . Wit: Richard Phillips, Curtis Hardy (Hardee), Elizabeth Evans. Ackn 19 Jun 1769 & recorded. Attest: John Lee clerk. (Pg 265)

18 Apr 1769. Deed of Gift. William Daingerfield Senr of Essex Co for love & affection have given to Elizabeth Daingerfield the following Negro slaves, to wit, Old Lydia, Frank, Lydia, Betty, Else, Judy, Nell with all their children & grandchildren now living, as also Jack the son of Lydia & Ben ... . Wit: Robinson Daingerfield. Proved 18 Apr 1769 by Robinson Daingerfield a wit & ordered to be certified. On 19 Jun 1769 this deed was again produced in court & William Daingerfield gent of Spotsylvania Co being sworn deposeth & saith that it is signed with the proper handwriting of William Daingerfield decd & some of the court being satisfied with the truth thereof the same is ordered to be recorded. Attest: John Lee clerk. (Pg 267)

24 Dec 1768. Deed. Griffing Boughan of St. Anns Parish, Essex Co gent & Mary his wife for 10 pd sold to John Richards of the Town of Leeds, King George Co merchant a 2 a. piece of land on the s side of Rappahannock River bounded by Thomas Bridgforth an orphan & sd Boughan's land ... . Wit: Philip Richards, Edward Matthews, Reuben Noell. Proved 19 Jun 1769 & ordered to be certified, on 20 Jun 1769 the sd Boughan personally came into court & ackn this deed which is admitted to record. Attest: John Lee clerk. (Pg 268)

30 Dec 1768. To Simon Miller, Robert Beverley & Henry Garnett of Essex Co gent greeting, whereas Griffing Boughan & Mary his wife have by their deed

[see above] conveyed unto John Richards a 2 a. piece of land, & whereas the sd Mary is unable to travel to our co court to make acknowledgment thereof, therefore we command you to repair to the sd Mary & that privily & apart from her sd husband you take such acknowledgment as she shall be willing to make ... . Wit John Lee clerk. 14 Jun 1769 By virtue of the within commission to us directed we Simon Miller & Henry Garnett did personally go to the sd Mary w/o the sd Griffin Boughan & her did examined privately & apart from her sd husband & she declared that she relinquished her right to the sd 2 a. of land & that she was willing the same should be recorded. At a court held 19 Jun 1769 this commission & the commissioners report were returned & ordered to be recorded. Attest: John Lee clerk. (Pg 268)

19 May 1769. Agreeable to order of Essex Court directed to us Charles Mortimer & John Corrie have in presence of the sheriff laid off the prison bounds so as to include the following houses &c, the Publick Square, Archibald Ritchie, Whitlock's house, Doctor Mortimer's shop, Emerson's new ordinary & Ramsay's ordinary. This report was on 29 Jun 1769 returned & recorded. Attest: John Lee clerk. (Pg 269)

11 Jul 1769. Deed. William Howerton & Mary his wife of South Farnham Parish, Essex Co for 25 pd sold to John Harper of same place shoemaker 1/2 of a 100 a. tr of land that the sd William Howerton formerly purch of William Watkins in the sd parish adj the lands of Roger Shackleford, Isaac Kidd, John Crow, James Townley & Reedy Swamp ... . Wit: Heritage Howerton, George Newbill, Robert Read. Ackn 17 Jul 1769 by William Howerton & Mary his wife (she being first privily examined & assenting thereto) & recorded. Attest: John Lee clerk. (Pg 270)

11 Jul 1769. Deed. John Harper & Margret his wife of South Farnham Parish, Essex Co for 25 pd sold to William Howerton of same place a 50 a. parcel of land in the parish afsd adj Roger Shackleford, Heritage Howerton, Covingtons Swamp, sd William Howerton & James Newbill Senr, it being the tr of land whereon the sd John Harper formerly lived ... . Wit: Heritage Howerton, George Newbill, Robert Read. Ackn 17 Jul 1769 by John Harper & Margret his wife (she being first privily examined & assenting thereto) & recorded. Attest: John Lee clerk. (Pg 272)

7 Jul 1769. Deed. John Garnett & Esther his wife of Essex Co for 58 pd 10 sl sold to Thomas Gouldman of same co a 78 a. tr of land bounded by the main run of Occupatia Swamp & Capt John Lee ... . Wit: Edward Vawter, Achilles Garnett, Rice Garnett, John Greensteed. Proved 17 Jul 1769 & recorded. Attest: John Lee clerk. (Pg 274)

17 Jul 1769. Deed. Mark Davis of St. Anns Parish, Essex Co for 40 pd sold to Cornelius Sale of same place a 70 a. tr of land whereon the sd Mark Davis now lives in the sd parish ... . Wit: John Sale, James Bates, Mereday Brown. Proved 17 Jul 1769 & recorded. Attest: John Lee clerk. (Pg 276)

18 Aug 1769. Deed. Leroy Hipkins of St. Anns Parish, Essex Co for 51 pd 10 sl sold to John Rodden of South Farnham Parish, Essex Co a 103 a. tr of land in South Farnham Parish it being that pt/o that tr of land that Benjamin Smith purch of William Peachey gent bounded by Isaac Williams, Goode's land, the run formerly called Parrys Run whereon the bridge formerly called Fishers now stands & Turner's land ... . Wit: Robt Mann, Robert Brooking, Smith Young. Ackn 21 Aug 1769 & admitted to record. Attest: John Lee clerk. (Pg 277)

14 Jul 1769. Deed. Robert Beverley of St. Anns Parish, Essex Co gent & Maria his wife for 122 pd 2 sl sold to Rice Noell of same place planter a tr of land part in St. Anns Parish & the remainder in Drysdale Parish, Caroline Co, containing by a survey made by Robert Broocke surveyor of Essex Co 301 1/2 a. bounded by James Upshaw & Fauntleroy's corner ... . Wit: None. Ackn 21 Aug 1769 by Robert Beverley & admitted to record. Attest: John Lee clerk. (Pg 279)

31 Dec 1768. Deed. Philip Gatewood & Susanna his wife of Caroline Co for 109 pd sold to Hannah Martin widow of Chesterfield Co a 218 a. tr of land bounded by Twyman's line, Edward Davis, Cook's corner, McMehan's corner & Joseph Gatewood ... . Wit: Sally Rennolds, Richard Brown, Andrew Gatewood, John Upshaw. Proved 21 Aug 1769 & recorded. Attest: John Lee clerk. (Pg 280)

11 Apr 1769. To Robert Green, Williams Williams & James Slaughter of Culpeper Co gent greeting, whereas Philip Gatewood & Susanna his wife late of Caroline Co have by their deed [see above] conveyed unto Hannah Martin widow of Chesterfield Co 218 a. of land, & whereas the sd Susanna is unable to travel to our sd co court to make acknowledgment thereof, therefore we command you to repair to the sd Susanna & that privily & apart from her husband you take such acknowledgment as she shall be willing to make ... . Wit John Lee clerk. Pursuant to the within commission to us directed we Robt Green & James Slaughter did personally go to the sd Susannah Gatewood w/o Philip Gatewood & did examine her seperate & apart from the sd Philip & she declared she did acknowledge the conveyance freely & that she was willing the same should be recorded. At a court held 21 Aug 1769 this commission & the commissioners report were returned & ordered to be recorded. Attest: John Lee clerk. (Pg 282)

XXI Aug 1769. Deed. John Upshaw & Mary his wife of South Farnham Parish, Essex Co planter for 33 pd sold to John Rennolds of same parish planter all that messuage & 66 a. tr of land in the sd parish adj the sd Rennolds's Rock Land Tract & bounded by Fauntleroy's land ... whereas Nicholas Lason formerly of Essex Co was in his lifetime seised & possessed of a 200 a. tr of land in Essex Co & being so seised died intestate leaving Betty his widow, Richard his only son & heir, Hannah, Mary & Elizabeth his daus. Richard the son died in his minority, the sd tr of land then devolved upon the three daus in coparcenary incumber'd with their mother's dower. Mary one of the daus intermarried with John Upshaw at whose instance the sd tr of land was divided & he in right of his wife became entitled to 1/3 pt/o the sd tr which he agreed & hath sold with its incumbrance of dower to John Rennolds who intermarried with Betty the widow & relict of sd Nicholas Lason .... Wit: None. Ackn 21 Aug 1769 by John Upshaw & Mary his wife (she being first privily examined & assenting thereto) & admitted to record. Attest: John Lee clerk. (Pg 282)

14 Apr 1769. Articles of Agreement. Whereas it is a mutual contract & agreement made between Thos Brooke of South Farnham Parish, Essex Co of the one part & Elizabeth Wiley of the same place of the other part, wit that there is shortly a marriage agreed to be solemnised between the afsd parties & the sd Eliza Wiley has in her own right & possession at the time of signing these presents several slaves & household goods &c which the sd Thos Brooke is willing & agreed should be disposed of at the time limited hereafter which is the desire of the sd Eliza Wiley (that is to say) at the death of the sd Eliza Wiley if she shou'd die before her intended husband, the Negro wench named Pegg & her child named Jessee shall return to her brother Robert Clark & that a Negro boy named Bristow return to her brother John Clark & that a Negro girl named Doll return to her niece Susanna Patterson & that one bed & furniture be given & delivered to her niece Jane Patterson, & that all the remainder of the slaves & personal estate shall be to the only use & behoof of the sd Thos Brooke during his natural life, but at his death (if he should out live the sd Eliza Wiley) they are then to return & be divided amongst the persons hereafter named; except 10 pd which is to be divided between my two nieces Mary & Eliza Clark daus of my brother Thos Clark decd (that is to say) my brothers Robt Clark & John Clark, my nieces Susanna Patterson & Jane Patterson & my nephew John Ouor, & further if that the Negro wench Pegg should have any increase before the death of the sd Eliza Wiley that the sd Eliza Wiley shall have the whole disposal of the same; & that if any debts is agt the estate of John Wiley decd they are to be discharged & satisfyed out of that pt/o the estate that the sd Brooke is to have for life, & this is a mutual contract & agreement between us & we further desire this instrument of writing may be recorded, & we do bind ourselves to each other in the sum of 1,000 pd to stand to & abide by this contract & agreement. Wit:

Philip Mountague, John Broocke Junr, Lewis Mountague. Proved 21 Aug 1769 & admitted to record. Attest: John Lee clerk. (Pg 284)

1 Aug 1769. Deed. George Turner of Hallifax Co, NC for 34 pd sold to Thomas Dunn Junr of Essex Co a 73 a. tr of land in South Farnham Parish it being the land where the sd Thos Dunn now lives & the same tr of land that James Turner decd gave to his son George Turner on the s side of Dunn's & Edmondson's Mill Run, bounded by Thomas Dennet, orphan of Fras Brown, road leading from Webbs ordinary to the bridge formerly called Mathews, Richard Brown, John Webb, Thos Turner & William Dunn (B) ... . Wit: Benjamin Dunn, Thomas Dennet, Richard Brown, Benjamin Dunn Junr. Fully proved 21 Aug 1769 & recorded. Attest: John Lee clerk. (Pg 286)

23 Aug 1769. Deed. LeRoy Hipkins of Caroline Co for 138 pd sold to William Fletcher of South Farnham Parish, Essex Co a 76 a. tr of land in South Farnham Parish bounded by Fishers Bridge, Ramsay's land, Gordon's land, Dunn's land, Turner's land & Mill Swamp ... . Wit: Luke Covington, Ambrose Wright, Richard Brown. Ackn 18 Sep 1769 & recorded. Attest: John Lee clerk. (Pg 288)

8 Jul 1769. Deed. Mary Morgan of Middlesex Co widow for 40 pd sold to James Banks of Essex Co planter a 121 1/4 a. tr of land in South Farnham Parish adj the lands now belonging to the sd Banks whereon he now lives bounded by Wm Dunn, the road that leads from Piscataway Old Mill Bridge, Clements corner & Munday's land ... . Wit: W. Roane, James Booker, Thomas Wood, William Dunn (B). Fully proved 18 Sep 1769 & recorded. Attest: John Lee clerk. (Pg 289)

23 Aug 1769. Deed. LeRoy Hipkins of Drysdale Parish, Caroline Co for 298 pd 12 sl 6 pn sold to Ambrose Wright of South Farnham Parish, Essex Co all his estate right in two parcels of land containing 298 a. in South Farnham Parish, one dividend whereof containing 299 1/4 a. (sic) where Benja Smith did live which was purch by Joseph Smith of Benja Fisher on the e side of Fishers Mill Cr & on the s side of Piscataway Cr bounded by Byrum's land ... the other dividend of land is pt/o a tr of land purch by the afsd Benjamin Smith of Peachey & is bounded by the road on Good's line, the Mill Dam, the Old Mill House & Fishers Bridge ... . Wit: Luke Covington, Sarah Covington, Richd Brown. Ackn 18 Sep 1769 & recorded. Attest: John Lee clerk. (Pg 291)

28 May 1769. Deed of Lease. Muscoe Garnett of St. Anns Parish, Essex Co gent & Grace Fenton his wife for the rents & covenants herein after mentioned have farm lett unto Frances Bizwell w/o Jeremiah Bizwell of same co a tr of land which the sd Jeremiah & Frances by their deed dated 15 Apr last conveyed unto

Thomas Thorpe (Tharp) & which sd land is now in possession of the sd Muscoe Garnett by a deed to him made by the sd Thomas Thorp & Eliza his wife dated 27 May instant ... during the life of the sd Frances she the sd Frances paying unto the sd Muscoe Garnett on 1 Jan in every year during the sd term one pepper corn if demanded, & is agreed by & between the sd parties that the sd Frances shall & may have all the liberties & priviledges on the sd land as if she held the same as an estate in dower & no more ... . Wit: R. Brooke, John Lee, Richard Rowzee, Thomas Boulware. Ackn 18 Sep 1769 by Muscoe Garnett & recorded. Attest: John Lee clerk. (Pg 294)

24 May 1765. Bill of Sale. Thomas Moor of Dorsett Co, MD for 117 pd 1 sl 4 pn sold to Archibald Ritchie of Essex Co, VA a small sloop called the Hannah & Rachell with her sails riging anchors & kables thereto belonging ... . Wit: William Muir, Joseph Warwick, Edward Pearson. The bill of sale hereto annexed was proved 18 Oct 1769 & at the motion of Levin Todd is admitted to record. Attest: John Lee clerk. (Pg 295)

25 May 1765. Then received from Thomas Moor of Dorsett Co, MD a bill of sale [see above] for his sloop called the Hannah & Rachell with her sails riging anchors kables &c thereto belonging in consideration of a sum of money already paid by the sd Ritchie mentioned in the bill of sale delivered me in behalf of the sd Ritchie but provided Thomas Moore makes the following payments, viz, 1/3 of the money to be paid by 1 Jul, another 1/3 by 1 Sep & the remaining 1/3 by 25 Nov 1765 with all costs & charges that may attend the sd bill of sale. In case the afsd Thomas Moor complys with the above I William Muir do hereby oblige myself in behalf of the sd Ritchie to take no advantage of the bill of sale. Proved 18 Oct 1769 by Archibald Ritchie to be the hand wiring of the sd Muir & on the motion of Levin Todd is admitted to record. Attest: John Lee clerk. (Pg 296)

24 Jun 1769. Deed. Elizabeth Smether of St. Anns Parish, Essex Co for 5 sl sold to David Pitts the younger of same parish a tr of land the reversion of which my son John Smether hath this day agreed to sell & convey unto the sd David Pitts as by his bond to the sd Pitts of equal date with these presents ... to be laid off out of the tr of land on which the sd Elizabeth Smether now lives agreeable to the directions & true intent & meaning of the sd bond ... it is agreed by & between the parties that the sd Eliza Smether shall have & enjoy so much of the 100 a. of land within mentioned as is now inclosed around her dwelling house during her life & to make use of firewood from any pt/o sd land as well as to get rail timber provided the rails are not carried or permitted to be carried off the sd land by the sd Elizabeth Smether ... . Wit: John Lee, Jno Gillon, Ann Hudson, John Smether. Proved 18 Sep 1769 & ordered to be certified. Fully proved 16 Oct 1769 & recorded. Attest: John Lee clerk. (Pg 296)

24 Apr 1769. Deed. Thomas Upshaw of St. Anns Parish, Essex Co for 36 pd sold to Thomas Sthreshly of South Farnham Parish, Essex Co a messuage & 110 a. tr of land on the n side of Jillsons Swamp adj Tamzin Upshaw, Mary Fogg, Thomas Upshaw, Rennolds's land & Beverleys Mill Swamp, which sd tr is pt/o that dividend of land which formerly belonged to William Upshaw father to the sd Thos Upshaw & will'd by the sd Wm Upshaw to the sd Thomas Upshaw .... Wit: James Hambleton, John Hambleton, Thos Graves, Wm Hill. Proved 16 Oct 1769 & certified. Fully proved 17 Oct 1769 & recorded. Attest: John Lee clerk. (Pg 298)

15 Dec ----. Alexander Gilchrist dyster in Old Rain, Elizabeth Gilchrist spouse to John Durno of Calie & Margaret Gilchrist spouse to George Watt in Little Flender brother & sisters german of John Gilchrist late merchant in Toppac or Hobb's Hole on the River Rappahannock in VA as also the sd John Durno & George Watt husbands of the sd Eliza & Margaret Gilchrist for our several interest & taking burden on us for our sd spouses all with joint & unanimous consent & assent & Isobell Maitland in Kirktown of Premnay relict of the decd Adam Gilchrist in Kirktown who was also brother german of the sd John Gilchrist & extrix dative decerned to him by the Commissary of Aberdeen upon 8 Nov now last past for herself & for behoof of Adam, Lilias & James Gilchrist her infant children procreated of the marriage betwixt her & the sd decd Adam Gilchrist, whereas the sd John Gilchrist died sometime ago in VA leaving behind him certain sums of money goods & effects which are not yet uplifted or received by us & as we are his only surviving nearest relations & have a just right & title to whatever sums of money & all other subjects & effects which did belong or may have belonging to him at the time of his decease, therefore we the sd Alexr, Elizabeth & Margaret Gilchrist, the sd John Durno, George Watt & Isobell Maitland have appointed Alexander Crudon Minister of the Gospell at Hobb's Hole near Tappa on the River Rappahannock VA our atty to ask demand sue for recover & receive of & from John Corrie merchant in the Town of Tappa or Hobb's Hole on the River Rappahannock in VA with whom the sd John Gilchrist carried on a copartnery or company trade for some years before his death the whole stock which belonged to the sd John Gilchrist in the joint trade carried on by him & the sd John Corrie with the haile shares & proportions of profits arising from the sd copartnery to which he was entitled or had right & all claims or demands thereby competent to him or his heirs .... Wit: John Paterson, John Durno. 15 Dec 1763 I John Duncan of Mosstown esqr present provost & chief majestrate of the City of Aberdeen in North Britain do certify & attest that Alexr, Elizabeth & Margaret Gilchrist, John Durno, George Watt & Isobell Maitland did on 13th instant personally appear before me & ackn they signed the preceding pages .... Alexr Carnegie conjt recorder. Proved 18 Oct 1769 & on the motion of John Corrie is admitted to record. Attest: John Lee clerk. (Pg 299)

25 Jul 1766. We, Archibald Ritchie in behalf of John Corrie surviving partner of John Gilchrist & Wm Snodgrass in behalf of the Rev. Alexr Cruden atty for the heirs of John Gilchrist decd have this day settled & examined the books of the sd Gilchrist & Corrie & find a ballance due from John Corrie to John Gilchrist of 33 pd 2 sl. This settlement is on the sd Corrie's motion admitted to record 18 Oct 1769. Attest: John Lee clerk. (Pg 303)

17 Jul 1769. Release. I Alexr Cruden atty in fact for John Durno of Aberdeen heir at law of John Gilchrist decd who was a partner in trade with John Corrie late of Tappahannock but now of Richmond Co ackn to have received from the sd John Corrie 33 pd 2 sl being the ballance of principal stock & profits found by settlement made 25 Jul 1766 to be due to the heir of the sd John Gilchrist & have released & acquitted the sd John Corrie from the sd accts lately depending between the sd Gilchrist & Corrie ... . Wit: Philemon Gatewood. This release is on the motion of sd Corrie admitted to record 18 Oct 1769. Attest: John Lee clerk. (Pg 303)

Pursuant to an order of the Co Court of Essex dated Jun 1767 we the subscribers did on 20 Aug following make publick sale of the land in the sd order mentioned & which as the estate of the late Major Brooke was struck off to Thomas Sale & Richard Rowzee on 12 months credit for 254 pd with interest of 14 pd 8 sl 2 pn, total 268 pd 8 sl 1/2 pn. The 4th pt/o the sd 268 pd 8 sl 2 pn we allott to Mrs. Catharine Rose a dau of sd Brooke's 67 pd 2 sl 1/2 pn, to John Rowzee who intermarried with Susanna another dau 67 pd 2 sl 1/2 pn, to Thos Sale who intermarried with Molly another dau 67 pd 2 sl 1/2 pn & to Edward Vass who intermarried with Elizabeth another dau 67 pd 2 sl 1/2 pn. Given under our hands this 10 Oct 1769, Robert Beverley, Rd Brooke. This sale of the land of Robert Brook decd & the division of the purch money were returned & ordered to be recorded 18 Oct 1769. Attest: John Lee clerk. (Pg 303)

5 May 1769. Bill of Sale. John Smith for 30 pd sold to Francis Boughan, Mary Smith, Alice Smith & John Smith Junr the Negroes Jack & Milley ... provided that if the sd John Smith do well & truly save the sd Frans Boughan, Mary Smith, Alice Smith & John Smith harmless & indemnified in a certain bond passed by them to Wm Roane for the delivery of a Negro girl Mille or pay 30 pd then this writing to be void ... . Wit: W. Roane, Daniel Stodghill. Proved 20 Nov 1769 & recorded. Attest: John Lee clerk. (Pg 304)

18 Sep 1769. Deed. Mary Treble of South Farnham Parish, Essex Co for 60 pd sold to Peter Treble of same parish a 119 a. tr of land in the same parish on the brs of Capt Archibald Ritchie & Capt James Webb Junr's mill run bounded by Olemond Breadlove, Coate's land, Robert Mann, Wm Williamson, Isaac Kidd, John Mann & Nathan Breadlove ... . Wit: Robt Mann, Richd Brown, Sarah

Breadlove. Ackn 20 Nov 1769 & admitted to record. Attest: John Lee clerk. (Pg 305)

4 May 1769. Deed of Mortgage. John Smith of Essex Co for 12 pd sold to James Dunn of same co one Negro man named Jack upon condition that if the sd John Smith do pay & discharge a certain debt due from him to the exors of John Bush decd for 6 pd besides interest & costs of a suit commenced agt him & the afsd James Dunn on a bond passed by them & John Dunn who were his securities for the sd debt & save & keep the sd James Dunn harmless & fully indemnifyed then this present deed to be void ... . Wit: James Stodghill, Daniel Stodghill. Proved 20 Nov 1769 & recorded. Attest: John Lee clerk. (Pg 306)

18 Dec 1769. Deed. James Oneale & Frances his wife of Essex Co planter for 17 pd sold to William Prosser of Essex Co a parcel of land pt/o a tr of land formerly held by Willm Brizendine containing 50 a. ... . Wit: Archd McCall, William Miskell, Henry Clements. Ackn 18 Dec 1769 by James Oneal & Frances his wife (she being first privily examin'd & assenting thereto) & admitted to record. Attest: John Lee clerk. (Pg 307)

10 Nov 1769. Deed. William Marshal & Ann his wife of Caroline Co for 48 pd sold to Alexr Smith a 96 a. tr of land adj the land where Garret Fitzsimons decd formerly lived & land that was before purch by John Ayres of William Winston ... it being all that land which was purch by Torkel McLeod of Waters Dunn ... . Wit: John Semple, LeRoy Hipkins, Edmd Pendleton Junr, Al Rose. Ackn 18 Dec 1769 by William Marshall & admitted to record. Attest: John Lee clerk. (Pg 308)

10 Nov 1769. To James Taylor, Saml Hawes & Wm Buckner gent justices of Caroline Co greeting, whereas Wm Marshall & Ann his wife by an indenture [see above] conveyed a 96 a. tr of land unto Alexr Smith, & whereas the sd Ann cannot conveniently (come) to our co court to make her personal acknowledgment, we do therefore authorize & require you to go to the sd Ann & her examine separate & apart from her sd husband & receive such acknowledgment as she shall be willing to make ... . Wit John Lee clerk. 12 Nov 1769 at Caroline, pursuant to the above commission we Sam Hawes & William Buckner did this day examine Ann Marshall w/o the sd Wm Marshall & she did freely ackn the sd indenture. At a court held 18 Dec 1769 this commission & the commissioners report was returned & recorded. Attest: John Lee clerk. (Pg 310)

11 Jan 1770. Indenture Tripartite between Mary Harbin of St. Anns Parish, Essex Co of the first part, John Lee gent of the sd parish of the second part & Mertilles Harbin, Elizabeth Harbin & Lucy Harbin children of the sd Mary

Harbin of the third part, wit that the sd Mary Harbin for natural love & affection which she hath & doth bear unto her sd children & also for 5 sl paid by the sd John Lee hath assigned & set over unto the sd John Lee three Negro slaves, to wit, Bob, Ben & Sarah & the increase of the sd Sarah, subject nevertheless to the trusts hereafter mentioned, that is to say, in trust as to the sd Bob to suffer the sd Mary to enjoy the same during her natural life & then to the use of the sd Mertilles, but if the sd Mertilles should die before his mother then to the sd John Lee in trust & for the use of the sd Elizabeth & Lucy to be divided at their mother's death, & further in trust as to the sd slave Ben to suffer & permit the sd Mary to enjoy the same during her natural life and then to the use of the sd Elizabeth, but if the sd Eliza shou'd die before her mother without issue living then to the sd John Lee in trust to & for the use of the sd Lucy, & further in trust as to the sd slave Sarah to suffer the sd Mary to enjoy the same during her natural life & then to the use of the sd Lucy, but in case the sd Lucy shou'd die before her mother without issue living then the sd slaves to return to the mother, in case any of the sd slaves shou'd die in the lifetime of the sd Mary then the remaining pt/o them to be divided at her death between the sd Mertilles, Elizabeth & Lucy or their heirs, & further that the increase which the sd slave Sarah may have during the life time of the sd Mary shall & are to be divided at the death of the sd Mary between the afsd Mertilles, Elizabeth & Lucy or the heirs of the sd Eliza & Lucy ... . Wit: Jno Gillon, Reuben Garnett. Proved 15 Jan 1770 & recorded. Attest: John Lee clerk. (Pg 311)

23 Dec 1769. Power of Attorney. I Nathan Waggener of Essex Co have appointed my trusty & well beloved brother Benjamin Waggener of co afsd my atty to ask demand recover & receive for me & in my name & to my use & behoof & giving by these presents to my sd atty my sole & full power & authority to sue arrest implead imprison & condemn any person owing or being indebted to me in any sum of money ... . Wit: Richard Allen, Rachel Waggene(r), Elener Armstrong. Fully proved 15 Jan 1770 & recorded. Attest: John Lee clerk. (Pg 312)

15 Mar 1770. Deed. John Lee gent & Susanna his wife of St. Anns Parish, Essex Co for 22 pd sold to John Samuel of same place a 22 a. parcel of land in the sd parish as by a survey made Edward Vawter deputy surveyor of sd co ... . Wit: Jno Gillon, Wm Ferguson, John Sale, Reuben Garnett. Ackn 19 Mar 1772 by John Lee & admitted to record. Attest: John Lee clerk. (Pg 313)

13 Apr 1769. Deed. Sarah Thorp of St. Anns Parish, Essex Co widow for 50 pd sold to Thomas Thorp of same parish a tr of land now in her possession ... whereas Thomas Thorp late of sd co decd father of the sd Thomas Thorp party hereto in & by his will dated 1 Apr 1767 did devise as follows "I lend unto my loving wife Sarah Thorp all my estate during her life or widowhood for the

support & schooling of what children I have living with me unmarried at my decease, if she my sd loving wife shou'd marry or depart this life before my youngest dau Frances Thorp comes of age or married my will is my exors keep the estate together till she my sd dau do come of age or marry, then I give unto my son Thomas Thorp all the land whereon I now live" and whereas the sd Sarah having duly proved the will afsd & being desirous to dispose of the sd lands during her widowhood the better to enable her to school & maintain the testator's children according to the directions of the sd testator ... . Wit: Richard Rowzee, Thomas Boulware, John Taliaferro, Robt Brooke. Proved 19 Mar 1770 & certified. Fully proved 20 Aug 1770 & recorded. Attest: John Lee clerk. (Pg 314)

13 Mar 1770. Deed. John Samuel & Catharine his wife of St. Anns Parish, Essex Co for 7 pd 10 sl sold to John Lee of same parish gent a 7 a. 66 square poles tr of land as by a survey made by Edward Vawter deputy surveyor of sd co bounded by a br of Assage Swamp which divides the lands of Peter & John Samuel ... . Wit: Jno Gillon, Wm Ferguson, John Sale, Reuben Garnett. Fully proved 19 Mar 1770 & recorded. Attest: John Lee clerk. (Pg 315)

13 Mar 1770. Deed. Peter Samuel of St. Anns Parish, Essex Co for 14 pd 8 sl 9 pn sold to John Lee of same parish a 10 1/2 a. parcel of land bounded by Assages Br, sd Samuel, sd Lee's line, & the late James Samuel, Assages Swamp & the beginning br which divides this & the land of John Samuel ... . Wit: Jno Gillon, Wm Ferguson, John Sale, Reuben Garnett, John Samuel. Fully proved 19 Mar 1770 & recorded. Attest: John Lee clerk. (Pg 316)

19 Mar 1770. Deed. John Smether & Ann his wife of South Farnham Parish, Essex Co for 30 pd sold to David Pitts the younger of St. Anns Parish, co afsd a tr of land (being pt/o the tr on which Elizabeth Smether now lives & by her conveyed to the sd Pitts for her life) containing 100 a. by a survey made by Edward Vawter in St. Anns Parish bounded by sd Pitt's line, Gray's line, Upshaw's line & Richard Noell (except 40' square at the old grave yard for a burial place) ... . Wit: None. Ackn 19 Mar 1770 by John Smither & recorded. Ackn -- May following by Ann Smether w/o the sd John Smether (she being first privily examined & assenting thereto) & recorded. Attest: John Lee clerk. (Pg 317)

A poll at an election of burgesses for Essex Co at the Court House on Friday 15 Sep 1769 per Thomas Boulware clerk.

Candidate William Roane: John Upshaw, Thomas Boulware, John Lee, Hon. John Tayloe esqr, James Campbell, Rev. Alexr Cruden, James Upshaw, Archd Ritchie, Mace Picket, Rhodes Greenwood, Heritage Howerton, Thomas

Wood, Richard Hodges, Francis Waring, Thos Upshaw, Henry Woolbanks, James Booker, Thomas Coats, Wm Bond, Wm Mountague, John Owens, John Richards, Rev. John Matthews, John Boughan, Wm Chiney, Alexr Bowmer, Charles Mortimer, Wm Daingerfield, Roger Shackleford, Wm Boulware, Robt Brooke, Ambrose Wright, Wm Howerton, John Taylar, Robt Beverley esqr, Joseph Gatewood, John Richards S.F., Joshua Booton, James Clark, Luke Covington, Wm Covington, Thomas Sthreshly, James Webb, Saml Shaw, John Vass, Geo Newbill, Saml Hoskins, Oliver Howard, Wm Greenwood, Isaac Jordan, Augustine Garnett, Alexr Saunders, John Chiney, Thomas Meador, Reuben Meador, Wm Gatewood, John Turner, John Crow, John Goode, Joseph Fogg, Jas Colquet, Jas Jones, Wm Tureman, Richard St. John, Thos Miller, Richd Holt Junr, James Stokes, Jas Clark Junr, Henry Crutcher, John Broocke, Isaac Wmson, Wm Wmson, Isaac Haws, Richd Noel, John Byrum, Meraday Brown, Richd Wmson, Hugh Marshal, Thos Cauthorn, Benja Fisher, John Harper, John Edmondson, Wm Dobson, Benja Jones, Wm Dunn, Francis Brizendine, John Samuel, Stephen Munday, Geo Strang, Philip Chiney, Oloman Breedlove, Thos Greensted, John Mitchel, Wm Montague, Robt P. Waring, Thomas Newman, John Ferguson, Joseph Burnett, Thomas Gaims, Hugh Wilson, John Rodden, Vincent Coleman, John Burnett, Thomas Broocks, Francis Ramsay, Joseph Mann, James Vaughan, John Blatt, Richd Jeffres, Ellison Noel, Angus Vawter, Lott Noel, Jas Munday, Rev. Thos Smith, Jas Davis Junr, Danl Stodghil, Thos Cox Junr, Martin Willard, Wm Bowmer, Nicholas Atkinson, Robert Sale, Henry Vass, Vincent Cauthorn, Thomas Pitts, John Castle, John Price, James Bates, Ephraim Shepherd, John Smether, Wm Hathaway, Jas Webb, Thomas Bradburn, John Rowzee, Muscoe Garnett, Robt Rennolds, John Corrie, Chs Evans (dispd), Jas Davis, Thos Turner, Benja Dunn, Jas Rennolds, Jas Medley, Robt Cole, Henry Young (dispd), Henry Cox, Jas Croxton, Thos Dix, Peter Montague, Wm Ramsay, John Townley, John Boughan Junr, Andrew Allen, Alexr Middleton, Jas Samuel, Saml Dishman, John Gordon, Ricker Burk, Thos H. Broocks, Nathal Dunn, Benja Smith, Thomas Dennett, William Smith, Wm Cole, Jas Shaddock, Ambrose Greenald (dispd), Thomas Coleman, Thos St. John, John Dickerson, John Meador, Thomas Gordon, John Coleman, Andrew Gatewood, Saml Davis, Jacob Sharewood, Thomas Allan, John Ball, Peter Samuel, Jas Noel, Morias Broach, Thos Sale, Theophilus Faver, Richd Jones, Saml Haws, Joshua Tinsley, Benja Waggener, John Gatewood, Robt Smith, John Conoley, Thos Parrin, Wm Fletcher, Wm Watts, John Burk, Isaac Kidd, John Beal, John Edmondson Junr Sd, Richd Holt, Thos Gouldman, Simon Golding, Majer Lason, Bernd Noel, Thos Ley, Edward Rowzee, Rice Noell, Wm Garrard, John Patterson, Richd Meador, Isaiah Cole, Peter Treble, Thos Faver, Henry Allen, Erasmus Jones, John Dayley, John Chenault, Chs Braw, Jas Sullivan, John Fogg, Josiah Minter, Augustine Compton, Ezekle Byrum, Jas Allen, Waters Dunn, Thos Dunn Junr, Wm Watkins, Wm Dunn (white), Jonathan Sharewood, Jos Warnick, Thos

Haddon, Richd Phillips, Chs Tayler, Wm Thomas, Thresibulus Minor, Timothy
Longest, Richd Brown, Ozwell Byrum, David Pitts Junr, John Carnal, Jeremiah
Bizwell, Jas Webb, Ambrose Pilkington, Edwin Motley, Wm Webb, John
Spindle, Wmson Young (dispd), Henry Street, Wm Broocks, Caleb Noell,
Cornelius Sale, Ralph Rowzee, John Gray, Josiah Mctire, Robt Parker, Thomas
Croxton, Edward Davis, Thomas Coghill, Richd Thos Haile, John Latane, Henry
Kidd, Abner Ball, Wm Thomas Junr, John Croxton, Nathan Waggener, Richd
Hill, Wm Gatewood, John Sadler, Leroy Hipkins, Wm Young Senr, Chiney
Gatewood, Achilles Garnett, Jos Ryland, Henry Purkins, Jas Banks, Wm Gray,
John Edmondson younger, Robt Oglesby (dispd), Gilbert Tureman (dispd),
Berriman Brown (dispd).

Candidate Meriwether Smith: John Upshaw, Thomas Boulware, John
Lee, Hon. John Tayloe esqr, James Campbell, Rev. Alexr Cruden, James
Upshaw, Archd Ritchie, Rhodes Greenwood, Thomas Wood, James Booker,
Thomas Coats, Wm Bond, Wm Mountague, John Owens, John Richards, Rev.
John Matthews, Wm Chiney, Alexr Bowmer, Charles Mortimer, Wm
Daingerfield, Roger Shackleford, Robert Brooke, Ambrose Wright, Wm
Howerton, Thomas Andrews, Robert Beverley, John Richards, Joshua Booton,
Wm Broockes, Luke Covington, Thomas Sthreshly, Humphrey Davis, John
Vass, Marmaduke Thorp, Thomas Thorp, Wm Greenwood, James Oneal,
Augustine Garnett, Alexr Saunders, John Chiney, Wm Gatewood, Robt Mann,
John Booton, John Crow, John Goode, James Jones, Wm Tureman, James
Medley, Richd St. John, Thos Miller, Henry Crutcher, John Broocks, Saml Piles,
Richd Noel, Meraday Brown, Hugh Marshel, Thos Cauthorn, John Harper, John
Hodges, Wm Dunn, Frans Brizendine, Thos Wmson, John Samuel, Philip
Chiney, Wm Montague, Robt P. Waring, John Brizendine, Evan Davis, Henry
Cauthorn, Thos Gaines, John Blatt, Richd Jeffress, Robt Clark, Ellison Noell,
Angus Vawter, Lott Noel, Rev. Thos Smith, Wm Bowmer, Henry Vass, Vincent
Cauthorn, Thos Pitts, John Price, Ephraim Shepherd, Jas Webb Junr, Philip
Kidd, Thos Bradburn, John Rowzee, Muscoe Garnett, Robert Rennolds, John
Corrie, Charles Evans (dispd), James Davis, Jas Medley, Thos Dean, Robt Cole,
Henry Young (dispd), Thomas Dix, Peter Montague, John Cooper, Andrew
Allen, Alexr Middleton, Thos H. Broocks, Saml Montague, John Wmson, Thos
Dennett, Thos Bush, John Haynes, Wm Smith, Wm Cole, John Bastin, John
Webb Hayes, Griffing Johnson, Nathan Breedlove, Wm Mitchel, Peter Samuel,
Cornelius Noel, James Noel, Thomas Sale, Theophilus Faver, Ralp Neal, Thos
Parrin, Wm Fletcher, Wm Watts, Wm Johnson, Isaac Kidd, Charles Saunders,
John Beal, Rice Noel, John Patterson, Edmund Pagett, Isaiah Cole, Peter Treble,
Saml Peachie, Erasmus Jones, John Dailey, Wm Watkins, Thos Hadden, Chs
Tayler, Wm Thomas, John Rodden, Thomas Broocks, John Broocks Junr, Jas
Webb, Titus Farguson, Edwin Motley, John Wmson, Reuben Bush, Thos
Newbel, Haraway Owen, Wm Broocks, Cornelius Sale, Josiah McTyre, Edward

Davis, Thomas Coghill Junr, Thomas Butler, John Kerchivalle, Wm Young Junr,
Wm Thomas Junr, Richd Street, Wm Young (S), Nicholas Faulconer, Wm
Porter, Henry Gardner, Gilbert Tureman (dispd).

Candidate James Edmondson: Mace Picket, Richd Hodges, Francis
Waring, Thomas Upshaw, Henry Woolbanks, John Boughan M, Wm Boulware,
John Taylor, Joseph Gatewood, Thomas Andrews, James Clark, Wm Broocks,
James Webb, Samuel Shaw, Humphrey Davis, Marmeduke Thorp, Thomas
Thorp, Geo Newbel, Saml Hoskins, Oliver Howard, James Oneal, Isaac Jordan,
Thos Meador, Reuben Meador, Robt Mann, John Booton, John Turner, Joseph
Fogg, Jas Colquet, Jas Medley, Richd Holt Junr, Jas Clark Junr, Jas Stokes,
Isaac Williamson, Wm Williamson, Saml Piles, Isaac Hawes, John Byrum,
Richd Wmson, Benja Fisher, John Edmondson, Willm Dobson, Benja Jones,
John Hodges, Thos Wmson, Stephen Munday, George Strang, Oloman
Breedlove, Thos Greenstead, John Mitchel, Thomas Newman, John Ferguson,
Joseph Burnett, John Brizendine, Evan Davis, Henry Cauthorn, Hugh Wilson,
John Rodden, Vincent Coleman, John Burnett, Thomas Broocks, Francis
Ramsay, Joseph Mann, James Vaughan, Robt Clark, Jas Munday, Thos Fogg,
Jas Davis Junr, Danl Stodghil, Thos Cox Junr, Thos Cox Junr, Martin Willard,
Nicholas Adkinson, Robt Sale, John Castle, James Bates, John Smether, Wm
Hathaway, Philip Kidd, Thos Turner, Benja Dunn, Jas Rennolds, Thos Dean,
Henry Cox, James Croxton, John Cooper, Wm Ramsay, John Townley, John
Baughan, Jas Samuel, Saml Dishman, John Gordon, Ricker Burk, Nathal Dunn,
Benja Smith, John Wmson, Thos Bush, John Haynes, James Shaddock,
Ambrose Greenald (dispd), John Bastin, Thos Coleman, John Webb Hayes,
Thomas St. John, John Dickerson, John Meador, Thomas Gordon, John
Coleman, Andrew Gatewood, Samuel Davis, Griffing Johnson, Nathan
Breedlove, Jacob Sharewood, Thos Allen, John Ball, Wm Mikhel, Cornelius
Noell, Morias Broach, Ralph Noel, Richd Jones, Saml Hawes, Joshua Tinsley,
Benja Waggener, John Gatewood, Robt Smith, John Conoly, Wm Johnson, John
Burk, Charles Saunders, John Edmundson S.F., Richard Holt, Thos Gouldman,
Simon Golding, Majer Lason, Bernard Noell, Thomas Ley, Edward Rowzee,
Wm Garrard, Richard Meader, Edmund Pagett, Henry Allen, Saml Peachie, John
Chernault, Charles Braw, Jas Sullivan, John Fogg, Josiah Minter, Augustine
Compton, Ezekle Byrum, Jas Allen, Waters Dunn, Thos Dunn Junr, Wm Dunn
(W), Jonathan Sharewood, Joseph Warwick, Richd Phillips, Thresibulus Minor,
Timothy Longest, Richd Brown, Ozwell Byrum, David Pitts Junr, John Rodden,
Thos Broocks, John Carnal, Jerah Bizwell, John Broocks Junr, Titus Ferguson,
Ambrose Pilkington, John Wmson, Reuben Bush, Wm Webb, John Spindle,
Wmson Young (dispd), Thos Newbel, Henry Street, Haraway Owen, Caleb
Noel, Ralph Rowzee, John Gray, Robt Parker, Thos Croxton, Richd Thomas
Haile, John Latane, Henry Kidd, John Kerchivalle, Abner Ball, Wm Young Junr,
John Croxton, Nathan Waggener, Richd Hill, Wm Gatewood Senr, John Sadlor,

Leroy Hipkins, Richd Street, Chiney Gatewood, Nicholas Faulconer, Achilles Garnett, Wm Clark, Jos Ryland, Wm Porter, Henry Purkins, Henry Gardner, Jas Banks, Wm Gray, John Edmondson younger, Berriman Brown (dispd), Robt Oglesby (dispd).

19 Mar 1770. William Montague gent sheriff for Essex Co came this day before me & made oath that the [above] is a true copy of the poll by him taken at the last Election of Burgesses for the sd co. Certified under my hand John Upshaw. Recorded Mar Court 1770. Attest: John Lee clerk. (Pg 318-324)

21 Aug 1769. Deed of Mortgage. John Davis of Essex Co have sold unto Mary Davis of same co 2 cows & calves, 2 heiphers, 15 hogs young & old, 2 feather beds & furniture, 1/2 doz. flag chairs & sundry other household & kitchen furniture for 13 pd 16 sl which I stand justly indebted to her for value received ... the condition of this bill is such that if the afsd John Davis doth well & truly pay unto the sd Mary Davis the full & just sum of 13 pd 16 sl with interest at or upon 25 Dec next then this bill of sale to be null & void ... . Wit: Lawson Waring, Wm Waring, Robt P. Waring. Proved 16 Apr 1770 & recorded. Attest: John Lee clerk. (Pg 324)

15 Jan 1770. Deed. Pitman Clements exor of John Clements gent decd for 64 pd 10 sl pursuant to the will of sd decd John Clements gent sold to Josiah Minter (both of South Farnham Parish, Essex Co) a 129 a. tr of land in the parish afsd bounded by the Main Road, William Snodgrass merchant, land that was formerly call'd Tyler's which now is in the possession of William Ramsay, Macall's land where Wm Snodgrass now lives, land Arthur Tate decd purch of James Boughan, land of Doctor John Clements decd, James Banks formerly Tyler's land, land William Dunn's purch of Tyler & land that was call'd the afsd Tyler's a corner of Peaches which now is the afsd Dunn's & Smith's ... . Wit: John Rennolds, William Edmondson, Joseph Fargason. Ackn 16 Apr 1770 & recorded. Attest: John Lee clerk. (Pg 325)

30 Sep 1766. Bond. John Ballendine of Prince William Co, John Taylor & James Ewell of Lancaster Co & Wm Montague of Essex Co gent are firmly bound unto the Honourable Col Phil Lud Lee L.L.D. of Stratford for 20,000 pd ... Whereas the afsd Phil Lud Lee has leased to the before mentioned John Ballendine for 21 years from 1 Jan 1764 all his estate in Fairfax & Loudoun Cos excepting such exceptions as is therein expressed, now the condition of this obligation is that if the afsd John Ballendine or John Taylor of James Ewell or Wm Mountague or their heirs &c jointly & severally keep & perform all the sd lease fully & compleatly except the payment of the rent of 500 pd a year then this obligation to be void ... . Wit: Jesse Ball, James Selden, Christ James, Thomas Bennet, Margaret Mountge. Proved 30 Apr 1767 at a general court held

at the capitol by the oaths of Jesse Ball & James Seldon & ordered to be recorded. Attest: Ben Waller clerk. 21 Nov 1768 at Tappa Thomas Bennett being summoned as a wit to prove this bond as to Wm Montague declares on oath that he did not see the sd Montague execute the same which on the motion of the sd Montague is ordered to be certifyed. 16 Apr 1770 at Tappa this bond on the motion of the Honble Philip Ludwell Lee esqr was ordered to be recorded. Attest: John Lee clerk. (Pg 327)

9 Mar 1769. Power of Attorney. Robert Ferguson late of Essex Co, VA now of Ayr in North Britain merchant being confident of the fidelity & abilities of John Lee esqr clerk of Essex Co & David Cochran of Newcastle in Hanover Co, VA merchant have appointed them my attys to ask demand sue for levy & recover from all & every person that are due me or my factors any sums of money & all & every debt goods merchandizes & every other subject matter & thing due addebted & oweing to me or my factors afsd by any person in VA, MD or any other of his Majestys Dominions in America ... . Wit: John Murdock, David Limond. 9 Mar 1769 I David Bannatyne esqr present Lord Provost of the Burgh of Ayr in the Co of Ayz in North Britain do hereby certify that personally appeared before me & John Murdock & David Limond both writers in Ayr afsd subscribing wits to the executing the power of atty that Robert Ferguson granter of the power of atty did sign seal & execute & deliver the sd power of atty ... . At a court held -- Apr 1770 this letter of atty & the testimonial hereto annex'd were presented in court by the sd Lee & on his motion they are admitted to record. Attest: John Lee clerk. (Pg 328)

17 Apr 1770. Articles of Agreement entered into & concluded between Robert Beverley esqr of the one part & Thomas Wyld Junr of the Town of Tappa sadler of the other part, whereas the sd Robert Beverley on 1 Oct 1767 sold to the sd Wyld four lotts or 1/2 acres of land within the limits of the sd town situate near the Court House but no deed of conveyance hath been executed for the sd lotts & whereas the sd Wyld has made some improvements on the sd lotts but is utterly unable to pay the consideration money viz 150 pd the sd Wyld is desirous of delivering up to the sd Robert Beverley the sd lotts with improvements thereon on 1 Dec next ensuing he the sd Robt Beverley agrees to [?] the property & possession of the sd lotts on the terms following viz that in consideration of the sd Wyld's releasing & acquitting the sd Robert Beverley of all accts claims & demands whatsoever & in consideration of his delivering up all the sd lotts & improvements at the time afsd he the sd Robert Beverley doth oblige himself to pay to the sd Thomas Wyld 60 pd on 25 Apr 1771, now the sd Thomas Wyld for & in consideration of the sd 60 pd hath released & quit claim all his right title in law or equity to the sd lotts to the sd Robert Beverley forever, & be it understood that every thing contained in the preamble of this writing is equally obligatory

on each party. Ackn by Robert Beverley esqr & Thomas Wyld 17 Apr 1770 & recorded. Attest: John Lee clerk. (Pg 330)

21 May 1770. Deed. William Young & Elizabeth his wife of South Farnham Parish, Essex Co gent for 23 pd sold to James Webb Junr of same place a 23 a. 69 square poles parcel of land in the sd parish bounded by Webb's & Young's land & Capt Smith's line ... . Wit: Wm Webb, John Webb Junr, Reuben Garnett. Ackn 21 May 1770 by William Young & Elizabeth his wife (she being first privily examined & assenting thereto) & admitted to record. Attest: John Lee clerk. (Pg 330)

21 May 1770. Deed. James Webb Junr & Mary his wife of South Farnham Parish, Essex Co gent for 23 pd sold to William Young of same parish a 23 a. 69 square poles parcel of land in the sd parish bounded by sd Young's & John Patterson decd's lands ... . Wit: Wm Webb, John Webb Junr, Reuben Garnett. Ackn 21 May 1770 by James Webb Junr & Mary his wife (she being first privily examined & assenting thereto) & admitted to record. Attest: John Lee clerk. (Pg 332)

-- May 1770. Deed. Benja Wagener of South Farnham Parish, Essex Co for 334 pd 12 sl sold to R. P. Waring of same parish planter a 239 a. tr of land on the n side of Hoskins's Cr in the sd parish bounded by sd Waring's land, Nathan Wagener (Wagoner), Richd Meador & Thos Smith, which sd land by the will of Benja Wagener decd was given & devised to his son Benja Wagener party hereto ... . Wit: John Rennolds, Thos Haile Junr, John Davis. Ackn 21 May 1770 & recorded. Attest: John Lee clerk. (Pg 333)

10 May 1770. Deed. William Dobson & Elizabeth his wife of Essex Co for 27 pd 19 sl 6 pn sold to Nicholas Faulconer taylar of same co a 93 1/3 a. tr of land in St. Annes Parish bounded by Richd Noell, John Garnett, Thomas Loyd, Nicholas Faukconer Senr father to the sd Nichos & sd William Dobson's plantation ... . Wit: Thomas Boulware, John Greensteed, Thomas Whitlock. Ackn 21 May 1770 by William Dobson & Elizabeth his wife (she being first privily examined & assenting thereto) & admitted to record. Attest: John Lee clerk. (Pg 335)

21 May 1770. Deed. John Belfield of Richmond Co, VA gent & Ruth his wife, Theodorick Bland of Prince George Co, VA gent & Frances his wife & Meriwether Smith of Essex Co gent & Elizabeth his wife for 130 pd sold to Archibald Ritchie of Essex Co gent three parts in four of all those three lotts or 1/2 acres of land in the Town of Tappahannock which are known in the plat of the sd town by the numbers 7, 13 & 31, & also all their estate right whatsoever in the premises ... . Wit: None. Ackn 21 May 1770 by John Belfield &

Meriwether Smith & admitted to record. Proved 21 Feb 1774 & commissions for the privily examination of the within named Ruth Belfield & Frances Bland & the certificates of their acknowledgment thereon are ordered to be recorded. Attest: W. Young dep clerk. (Pg 338)

1 May 1770. To Theophilus Field & Nathaniel Harrison gent justices of Prince George Co greeting, whereas Theodorick Bland & Frances his wife, John Belfield & Meriwether Smith by an indenture [see above] have conveyed to Archibald Ritchie the fee simple estate of & in three lots or 1/2 acres of land in the Town of Tappahannock Numbers 7, 13 & 31, & whereas the sd Frances cannot conveniently travel to our co court to make her personal acknowledgment we do therefore authorize & require you to cause to come before you the sd Frances & her examine separate & apart from her sd husband & receive such acknowledgment as she shall be willing to make ... . Wit John Lee clerk. 29 Apr 1771 at Prince George, by virtue of the within commission this indenture hereunto annexed was ackn by the within named Frances Bland who being first privately examined declared she did the same freely & that she is willing the same shall be recorded. Theo Feild, Nathl Harrison. Truly recorded. Attest: John Lee clerk. (Pg 340)

14 Jun 1770. To William Brockenbrough, Williamson Ball & Richard Barnes of Richmond Co gent greeting, whereas John Belfield gt & Ruth his wife of Richmond Co & others have by an indenture [see above] conveyed three parts in four of three lotts or 1/2 acres of land containing 1 1/2 a. & numbered 7, 13 & 31 in the Town of Tappahannock, whereas the sd Ruth is unable to travel to our co court to make acknowledgment thereof, therefore we command you to repair to the sd Ruth & that privily & apart from her husband you take such acknowledgment as she shall be willing to make ... . Wit: John Lee clerk. 5 Jun 1771 at Richmond, by virtue of the within commission this indenture hereunto annexed was ackn by the within named Ruth Belfield who being first privately examined separate & apart from her husband declared she did the same freely & that she is willing the same shall be recorded. Wm Brockenbrough, Richard Barnes. Truly recorded. Attest: John Lee clerk. (Pg 340)

17 Mar 1770. Deed. John Williamson & Winifred (Wineford) his wife of South Farnham Parish, Essex Co for 22 pd 10 sl sold to Henry Dunn of same parish an 80 a. tr of land, marshes & swamp on the South Br of Piscattaway Cr called Dunns Mill Swamp in the sd parish bounded by John Edmondson, Thos Henry Broockes, Allens Quarter & Mary Marlows, which sd 80 a. of land the sd John Williamson bought of Thomas Mason & reference being had unto a survey made by James Wood 10 Dec 1732 may more fully appear ... . Wit: Benja Dunn, Wm Dunn, Philip Dunn. Ackn 21 May 1770 by John Williamson & Winifred his

wife (she being first privily examined & assenting thereto) & admitted to record. Attest: John Lee clerk. (Pg 341)

8 Jan 1770. Deed. James Davis & Elizabeth his wife of Essex Co for 11 pd sold to Samuel Davis of St. Anns Parish, Essex Co a messuage & 11 a. tr of land in the sd parish bounded by Samuel Davis, Jolsons Cr, Wm Webb & Fauntleroy's land, which tr of land is pt/o a dividend which formerly belonging to Samuel Davis decd & by him devised to his son James by his will & by the sd James conveyed to the afsd Samuel Davis party to these presents ... . Wit: John Daly, William Webb, Henry Woolbanks. Proved 17 Apr 1770 & certified. Fully proved 21 May following & recorded. Attest: John Lee clerk. (Pg 343)

7 Apr 1770. At the request of Thomas Haddon & Elizabeth Allen surveyed & divided 197 a. of land in South Farnham Parish on the s side of Daingerfields Mill Pond, adj Nicholas Faulkconer, sd Allen's, sd Haddon's, Waters Dunn, Wm Gatewood & Alexr Smith. By Richard Brown. [Drawing not included here]. Pursuant to an order of court we have divided the tr of land between Thomas Hadden & William Porter in right of their wives as in the platt expressed. Given under our hands 16 Apr 1770 John Upshaw, W. Roane. This report was returned 20 May 1770 & on the motion of Thos Haddon & Wm Porter is ordered to be recorded. Attest: John Lee clerk. (Pg 345)

21 May 1770. Deed. Francis Waring of St. Ann Parish, Essex Co for 13 pd sold to Alexander Smith of South Farnham Parish same co a 13 a. tr of land in the parish afsd pt/o Greenhill's tr bounded by the sd Smith's (lately Waggoner's), Waggoner's land & Hobbs Hole Road ... . Wit: James Campbell, John Brockenbrough, James Lang. Ackn 21 May 1770 & recorded. Attest: John Lee clerk. (Pg 347)

21 May 1770. Deed. Whereas William Sthreshly decd formerly of Essex Co was in his life time possessed of a 300 a. tr of land whereon he lived, & whereas the sd William Sthreshly died intestate leaving Sukey his widow who was intitled to dower in the afsd land & she having since intermarried with James Upshaw, now they the sd James & Sukey having made an agreement to sell & relinquish all their right of dower of & in the sd tr of land to Thomas Sthreshly son & heir of the sd William ... this indenture James Upshaw & Sukey his wife of South Farnham Parish, Essex Co for 50 pd have sold to Thomas Sthreshly a messuage & right of dower of & in all the lands above mentioned ... . Wit: Thomas Roane. Ackn 21 May 1770 by James Upshaw & Sukey his wife (she being first privily examined & assenting thereto) & admitted to record. Attest: John Lee clerk. (Pg 348)

21 May 1770. Deed. John Edmondson & Caty his wife of Essex Co for 44 pd 5 sl sold to James Booker of same co a messuage & tr of land adj the lands of Thomas Miller & the sd James Booker being pt/o the tr of land the sd John Edmondson now lives on lying on the w side of Middle Br containing 59 a. ... . Wit: James Edmondson, Thomas Wood, William Dunn B. Ackn 21 May 1770 by John Edmondson & Caty his wife (she being first privily examined & assenting thereto) & admitted to record. Attest: John Lee clerk. (Pg 349)

16 Oct 1769. Deed. Thomas Sthreshly & Patty his wife of Essex Co for 45 pd sold to James Noell Senr of St. Anns Parish same co a messuage & 110 a. tr of land in the sd parish bounded by Jelsons Swamp, Tamzin Upshaw, Mary Fogg, Mrs. Rennold's land & Beverleys Mill Swamp, which sd tr of land is pt/o a dividend which formerly belonged to William Upshaw decd & by him devised to his son Thomas by his will & by the sd Thos conveyed to the sd Thomas Sthreshly ... . Wit: Leonard Sale, John Fogg, Richard Hambleton. Ackn 21 May 1770 by Thomas Sthreshly & Patty his wife (she being first privily examined & assenting thereto) & recorded. Attest: John Lee clerk. (Pg 351)

15 Feb 1770. Indenture. Robt Brooking of King & Queen Co gent guardian of James Coleman infant orphan of Robert Spilsby Coleman late of Essex Co decd with the consent & approbation of the worshipful court hath put & bind the sd James Coleman unto John Richards merchant of King George Co untill he shall arrive to the age of 21 he being born 4 Jul 1754 ... the sd John Richards doth covenant to & with the sd Robt Brooking gent (to & for the use of the sd ward) that he will teach him the art & mistery of a merchant ... . Wit: None. Ackn 21 May 1770 & recorded. Attest: John Lee clerk. (Pg 353)

21 May 1770. Deed. Leroy Hipkins of Caroline Co for 95 pd sold to Saml Gresham of Essex Co a 195 a. tr of land in South Farnham Parish bounded by William Fletcher, Ambrose Wright, Deep Landing Gut, Piscataway Cr, Josiah Minter & Wm Ramsay ... . Wit: None. Ackn 21 May 1770 & recorded. Attest: John Lee clerk. (Pg 354)

21 May 1770. Deed. John Richards of King George Co, VA merchant & Susanna his wife for 235 pd 7 sl sold to Robt Ferguson of Ayr in North Britain a 2 a. messuage & tr of land in St. Anns Parish on Rappahannock River & purch by the sd John Richards of Griffing Boughan & wife ... . Wit: None. Ackn 21 May 1770 by John Richards & recorded. Attest: John Lee clerk. (Pg 356)

21 Apr 1770. Deed. Augustine Compton (Cumpton) of Essex Co planter for 65 pd sold to Henry Kidd of same co a 125 a. tr of land in South Farnham Parish being the land devised by the will of William Compton decd to the afsd Augustine Compton his son & by him possessed & enjoyed ever since that time

which is bounded by Dix's land, Latane's land (formerly Haile's), Allen's line & Roane's line (formerly Gatewood's) ... . Wit: None. Ackn 21 May 1770 & recorded. Attest: John Lee clerk. (Pg 358)

24 Apr 1770. Deed. Archd McCall & Reuben Shelton the first of Essex Co & the other of Middlesex Co for 29 pd 5 sl 9 pn sold to Henry Street of Essex Co a 100 a. tr of land in Middlesex & Essex Cos bounded by Lattaney Montague, Dragon Swamp & Henry Street ... . Wit: Joseph Bohannan, E. Lawson Waring, Lauchr Mackentosh. Ackn 22 May 1770 by Archd McCall & proved as to Shelton & recorded. Attest: John Lee clerk. (Pg 359)

29 Mar 1770. Deed. Archibald McCall of South Farnham Parish, Essex Co for 3 pd 3 sl 9 pn sold to Charles Evans of same place a 12 a. parcel of land in South Farnham Parish bounded by the lands of William Young Junr, Phillimon Gatewood, John Webb & the land whereon the sd Charles Evans now lives ... . Wit: James Campbell, Abraham Campbell, Charles Mortimer. Ackn 22 May 1770 & recorded. Attest: John Lee clerk. (Pg 361)

8 Mar 1770. Bill of Sale. John Fogg of Essex Co for 28 pd 14 sl 11 pn sold unto Archibald McCall of Essex Co my Negro fellow Sam ... . Wit: Lauchr Mackintosh, Epaplroditus Lawson Waring. Proved 22 May 1770 & recorded. Attest: John Lee clerk. (Pg 362)

14 May 1770. Bill of Sale. James Oneal of Essex Co for 10 pd sold to Archibald McCall of sd co all my light bay mare & her increase branded on the near buttock "F", my two sows marked with a crop in each ear & a hole in the right ear, my seven shoats the same mark & their increase, my two iron potts & my blue painted chest ... . Wit: E. Lawson Waring, Lauchr Mackintosh. Proved 22 May 1770 & recorded. Attest: John Lee clerk. (Pg 362)

30 Oct 1769. Deed. Robert Sale & Hannah his wife of St. Anns Parish, Essex Co for 80 pd sold to Augustine Garrett of same parish a tr of land in the sd parish containing by a survey made by Larkin Garnett 188 a. ... . Wit: Benja Edmondson, Caleb Noell, Taylar Noell. Ackn 18 Jun 1770 by Robert Sale & recorded. Attest: John Lee clerk. (Pg 363)

-- Jun 1770. Deed. George Newbill & Mary his wife of South Farnham Parish, Essex Co for 115 pd sold to Thomas Wood of same parish a 163 a. parcel of land in the sd parish bounded by Thomas Roane, a br formerly called Jones's Storing Br, Thomas St. John, the Honourable John Robison esqr decd, the main run of Piscataway Cr, John Boughan, the mill pond now in possession of Wood it being a corner of another parcel of land belonging to the afsd Boughan & Spring Br formerly called Sarah Boughan's ... . Wit: Thomas Bourne, Josiah

Minter, Henry Allen. Ackn 18 Jun 1770 by George Newbill & Mary his wife (she being first privily examined & assenting thereto) & recorded. Attest: John Lee clerk. (Pg 364)

29 Nov 1769. Bill of Sale. John Curtis of Gloucester Co for 62 pd 8 sl 8 pn 3 farthings sold to Archibald Ritchie of Essex Co the schooner boat called the Sally now here at the sd Archd Ritchie's wharf of the following dimentions 27' keel 11' beam & 4'8" deep in the hould with her saills anchor cables masts & rigging ... . Wit: John Whitlock, John Hipkins. Proved 18 Jun 1770 & recorded. Attest: John Lee clerk. (Pg 366)

18 Jun 1770. Deed. James ONeale & Frankcay his wife of Essex Co for 25 pd sold to Francis Brizendine of same co a 90 a. parcel of land in South Farnham Parish being the tr of land that firmly (sic) belonged to his father John ONeal bounded by the swamp that divides the sd land from the land of Thomas Bush, Francis Brizendine & John Man ... . Wit: Thomas Bush, John Broocke Junr, John Hanes. Ackn 18 Jun 1770 by James Oneale & Frances his wife (she being first privily examined & assenting thereto) & admitted to record. Attest: John Lee clerk. (Pg 367)

28 Jun 1770. Deed. Humphrey Davis of South Farnham Parish, Essex Co for 120 pd sold to Joshua Boughton of same parish a 150 a. parcel of land in South Farnham Parish adj the lands of Francis Smith decd, William Broocke, Peter Broocke decd, Isaac Williams & the sd Joshua Boughton, it being the tr of land which the sd Humphrey Davis purch of George Newbill & Mary his wife ... . Wit: Henry Vass, John Blatt, John Simco, Thomas Boughton. Ackn 16 Jul 1770 & recorded. Attest: John Lee clerk. (Pg 369)

22 Feb 1770. Deed. William Porter & Elizabeth his wife of Essex Co for 85 pd sold to Elizabeth Allen of same co two trs of land (viz) the one of which contains 140 a. in South Farnham Parish near to Piscataway Church being 1/2 of the land devised by Henry Reeves father of the afsd Eliza Porter to his son Brewer in fee simple as by his will the sd Brewer dying an infant the same descended to his brother John who also dying in his infancy the whole of the sd two parcels of land descended to Mary his sister (now w/o Thomas Haddon) & Eliza party hereto as coheirs & is bounded by the road that leads from Piscataway Old Mill & Burnet's land, the other tr of which is the full 1/2 of 150 a. in the same parish & is the land purch by the same Henry Reeves of Wm Meador by deed dated 18 May 1728 & by him devised to his son John in fee simple who dying an infant the same also descended to his two sisters Mary (now w/o Thomas Haddon) & Eliza party hereto as coheirs which is bounded by Old Plantation Br, Eliza Allen & land sold to Ebenezer Stanfield by John

Meador ... . Wit: John Hipkins, Epaphros Lawson Waring, Henry Allen, Chs Mortimer, John Corrie. (Pg 370)

23 Feb ----. To Charles Mortimer & John Corrie of Essex Co gent greeting, whereas William Porter & Eliza his wife have by their deed [see above] conveyed unto Eliza Allen a tr of land, & whereas the sd Eliza is unable to travel to our sd co court to make acknowledgment thereof, therefore we command you to repair to the sd Eliza & that privily & apart from her sd husband you take such acknowledgment as she shall be willing to make ... . 23 Feb 1770 in obedience to the within commission to us directed we Charles Mortimer & John Corrie did examined the sd Elizabeth Porter privily & apart from her husband who answered that the annexed deed was her act & deed & that she was willing the same be recorded. Truly recorded. The deed was proved 16 Jul 1770 together with the commission for the privy examination of Eliza w/o the sd William Porter & the cert of her acknowledgment thereon are ordered to be recorded. Attest: John Lee clerk. (Pg 372)

10 Jul 1770. Bill of Sale. John Amos Samford of Essex Co do bargain sell & deliver unto John S. Chilton of sd co four Negroes Liddy, Winney, Siller & her last child for 80 pd with their increase ... . Wit: Smith Young, John Demerild. Proved 16 Jul 1770 & recorded. Attest: John Lee clerk. (Pg 373)

11 Aug 1770. Deed. William Murray & Sarah his wife & Martha Murry widow of Edward Murray decd of Caroline Co for 13 pd sold to Thomas Coghill of Essex Co a 56 a. tr of land on the s side of Rappahannock River in St. Ann's Parish adj the lands of the Honbl Secretary Carter decd, Wm Scott decd & John Hord decd which land having been purch by Edward Murray decd father of the afsd William Murray of Peter Rucker, John Rucker & Thomas Rucker by deed dated 1730 ... . Wit: Paul Micou, Simon Miller, John Melear, Robt Rennolds, Amb Hord, Richard Melear. Fully proved 20 Aug 1770 & recorded. Attest: John Lee clerk. (Pg 374)

13 Apr 1769. Deed. Jeremiah Bizwell & Frances his wife of St. Ann's Parish, Essex Co for 30 pd sold to Thomas Thorp of same parish a parcel of land being pt/o the land on which Sarah Thorp now lives, & which she is seised & possessed as her dower of & in the lands of her late husband Thomas Thorp the elder ... . Wit: Richard Rowzee, John Taliaferro, Thomas Boulware, John Lee. Proved 19 Mar 1770 & certified. Fully proved 20 Aug following & recorded. Attest: John Lee clerk. (Pg 375)

13 Mar 1770. Deed. William Parr of Amelia Co for 20 pd sold to John Hains of Essex Co a 50 a. tr of land in South Farnham Parish bounded by the sd Hains, Wm Covington, John Cheyney & William Cole ... . Wit: Wm Shepherd, Isaac

Webb, Ann Hudson, James Johnson. Proved 21 May 1770 & certified. Fully proved 20 Aug following & recorded. Attest: John Lee clerk. (Pg 376)

17 Jan 1770. Bond. John & Anne (Ann) Goode of South Farnham Parish, Essex Co are firmly bound unto Samuel Sale of Drysdale Co, Caroline Co in the penal sum of 500 pd ... the condition of this obligation is such that whereas there had been dispute in the title of a Negro wench Sarah Bunch & her six children Abel, Cate, Isaac, Will, Jude & Esther between the afsd John Goode & Ann Goode jointly & Samuel Sale & each desirous of settling amicably have agreed to divide the sd Negroes as follows, that is to say Samuel Sale to have Sarah Bunch, Isaac & Esther & all their increase, & John & Ann Goode to have Abell, Cate, Will & Jude & their increase ... if the afsd John Goode & Ann Goode do well & truly content themselves with their dividend that they nor their heirs do never molest the sd Samuel Sale or his heirs in the peaceable possession of the sd Sarah Bunch, Isaac & Esther together with their increase then this obligation to be void ... . Wit: Francis Taylor, Francis Coleman, William Johnston. Ackn 21 Aug 1770 by John Goode & Ann his wife & recorded. Attest: John Lee clerk. (Pg 378)

17 Jan 1770. Bill of Sale. John & Ann Goode of South Farnham Parish, Essex Co for 5 sl & for natural love sold unto Samuel Sale of Drysdale Parish, Caroline Co three Negroes, Sarah Bunch, Isaac & Esther ... . Wit: Francis Coleman, Francis Taylor, William Johnston. Ackn 21 Aug 1770 & recorded. Attest: John Lee clerk. (Pg 378)

17 Jan 1770. Bond. I Samuel Sale of Drysdale Parish, Caroline Co am firmly bound unto John Goode of South Farnham Parish, Essex Co in the penal sum of 500 pd ... the condition of this obligation is such that whereas there has been a dispute in the title of a certain Negro wench Sarah Bunch & her six children Abel, Cate, Isaac, Will, Jude & Esther between the afsd Samuel Sale & John Goode & each desirous of settling amicably have agreed to divide the sd Negroes as follows, that is to say, John Goode to have Abel, Cate, Will & Jude & their increase in full of his right claime & interest in the sd Sarah Bunch & her six children & Samuel Sale to have Sarah Bunch, Isaac & Esther in full of all his claime agt the sd Sarah Bunch her children afsd, if the afsd Samuel Sale do well & truly content himself so as he & his heirs never do molest the sd John Goode or his heirs in the peaceable possession of sd Abel, Cate, Will & Jude & their increase then this obligation to be void ... . Wit; Francis Coleman, Francis Taylor, William Johnston. Ackn 21 Aug 1770 & recorded. Attest: John Lee clerk. (Pg 379)

17 Jan 1770. Bill of Sale. Samuel Sale of Drysdale Parish, Caroline Co hath for 5 sl sold unto John Goode & Ann Goode four Negroes, viz, Abel, Cate, Will &

Jude, & for the love I bear the sd John & Ann Goode & for their just claime of right & title to Sarah Bunch & her children ... . Wit: Francis Coleman, Francis Taylor, William Johnston. Ackn 21 Aug 1770 & recorded. Attest: John Lee clerk. (Pg 380)

21 Aug 1770. Indenture. John Edmondson guardian to Wm Curtis orphan of Charles Curtis decd of St. Ann's Parish, Essex Co of the first part & James Wignell mariner of the Town of Liverpool in the Kingdom of Great Britain of the second part & the sd William Curtis of the third part, whereas the afsd Wm Curtis orphan being desirous of going to sea in order to learn the art of Navagation, therefore the sd John Edmondson as guardian by & with the consent of the sd William Curtis do hereby put him apprentice to the sd James Wignell to learn the art of Navagation till he shall attain to the age of 20 ... . Wit: None. Ackn by the parties, approved of by the court & ordered to be recorded 21 Aug 1770. Attest: John Lee clerk. (Pg 380)

3 Aug 1770. Deed. Augustine Garnett & Elizabeth his wife of St. Anns Parish, Essex Co for 200 pd sold to James Noell Junr of same parish a 156 a. tr of land in the parish afsd bounded by Joseph Fogg, John Cassel, Leonard Garnett, Francis Graves & John Latane & was purch by the sd Augustine Garnett of John Garnett Junr by deed dated 17 Aug 1765 & also a 92 a. tr of land in the sd parish adj the afsd tr & the lands of John Latane & Joseph Fogg purch by the sd Augustine Garnett of Archibald McCall & Leonard Garnett by deed dated 30 Mar 1767 ... . Wit: John Taylar, Taylar Noell. Ackn 17 Sep 1770 by Augustine Garnett & recorded. Attest: John Lee clerk. (Pg 381)

28 Jul 1770. Deed. Elizabeth Evans widow & relict of Micajah Evans decd for 20 pd sold to Charles Evans son & heir at law of Charles Evans decd all her estate right in right of her dower of in & to a 100 a. parcel of land devised to the afsd Micajah Evans decd her late husband by the will of Greensby Evans decd recorded in Essex Co Court bearing date 3 Dec 1765 adj the lands of Leonard Hill decd, John Webb, Charles Evans the elder decd, Philemon Gatewood & Wm Young Junr ... . Wit: Smith Young, Isaac Webb, Williamson Young. Proved 17 Sep 1770 & recorded. Attest: John Lee clerk. (Pg 384)

A poll taken for the electing a burgess for Essex Co 30 May 1770 per Leroy Hipkins clerk for Wm Montague sheriff of sd co.

Candidate Capt Wm Roane: James Upshaw, Thos Allen, John Upshaw, Phil Dunn, Thresibulus Minor, Henry Woolbanks, Isaac Jordan, Henry Cox, Thos Gordon, Richd Thos Haile, Thos Dix, Henry Allen, Vinct Coleman, Thos Greenstone, Nicho Atkinson, Humphry Davis, Paul Micou, Thos Croxton, Thos Dennet, Reuben Meador, Thos Sthreshly, Thos Faver, John Latane esqr,

Josiah Minter, Thos Brooks, Thomas Coleman, Richd Holt Junr, Henry Purkins, James Shaddock, Oliver Howard, Henry Kidd, Alexr Middleton, Thomas Meador, Danl Stodghill, Saml Davis, Joseph Warrick, Jos Gatewood, Benja Fisher, Jacob Shearwood, Richard Jones, John Boughan, John Burnett, Jas Banks, Jos Burnett, John Ball, Samuel Allen, Thos St. John, Joseph Farguson, Richd Meador, Robt P. Waring, Stephen Munday, James Munday, Abner Ball, Nathl Dunn, John Coleman, Benja Dunn, James Croxton, James Boughan, John Edmondson Senr, Thos Wood.

Candidate Capt Mer Smith: John Wmson, Wm Wmson, Richd Wmson, John Rodden Senr, Ezekiel Bizam, John Brooks, Phil Chaney, Ephraim Shepherd, Nathan Breedlove, Samuel Piles, Robt Mann, John Brizendine, Wm Bomar, Robt Beverley esqr, Robt Brooke, Saml Peachey, John Wmson Senr, John Byrom, Francis Brizendine, John Haynes, Evan Davis, Vinct Cauthorn, John Blatt, Thos Cauthorn, Thos Gaymes, Henry Young, Wm Young Junr, Chs Saunders, Henry Cauthorn, Thos Brooks Senr.

17 Sep 1770. These are to certify that Wm Montague sheriff of Essex Co made oath before me Jas Webb Junr that the above poll is a true copy. Recorded Sep Court 1770. Attest: John Lee clerk. (Pg 385)

24 May 1770. Deed. Constantine Smith of Essex Co for securing the payment of a debt & for indemnifying George Brooke from the engagement as security for the sd Constantine Smith & for 5 sl sold to the sd George Brooke of King & Queen Co two Negroes named Plato & Rachel & their future increase ... whereas the sd Constantine Smith is justly indebted to the sd George Brooke for 34 pd 3 sl 6 pn & the sd George Brooke is also engaged as security for the sd Constantine Smith to Boswell Richards deputy sheriff of King & Queen Co for an execution the sd Richards served on the sd Constantine Smith's estate ... the sd George Brooke shall within 12 months sell & dispose of the sd Negroes or as many of them as shall be sufficient to raise the debt afsd (with interest thereon) & also the sum of money for which the sd George Brooke is engaged as security & apply the money arising by such sale to such payment & indemnity & if any surplus shall remain such surplus shall be paid to the sd Constantine Smith ... . Wit: Robt Price, Thos Frazer. Proved 15 Oct 1770 & recorded. Attest: John Lee clerk. (Pg 386)

28 Feb 1770. Deed of Mortgage. Thomas Wyld of Essex Co for 63 pd 1 sl 1 penny 1/2 penny sold to Archibald Ritchie of the Town of Tappahannock, Essex Co merchant 7 feather beds & furniture, 1 black walnut desk, 6 black walnut chairs, 1 large black walnut table, 1 mahogony tea table, 1 small ditto, 1 pine table, 1 doz. flag chairs, 1 case, 2 horses viz 1 dark bay called China 1 bright

ditto bought of Thomas Ley, 1 cow & calf, 1 pair hand irons, 3 iron potts, a pot rack, 1 tea chest, 1 doz. pewter plates, 4 dishes, 1 doz shallow & 1 doz. deep earthen plates, 1 doz. knives & forks, 1 sett china & 1 sett of earthen tea ware ... provided that if the sd Thos Wyld shall well & truly pay unto the sd Archibald Ritchie the sd sum with interest on or before 1 Apr next ensuing then this instrument of writing & the sale hereby made to be void ... . Wit: John Hipkins, Wm Barton. Proved 16 Oct 1770 & recorded. Attest: John Lee clerk. (Pg 387)

Note: John Upshaw's commission to be sheriff is recorded in Folio 403. (Pg 388)

15 Oct 1770. Bond. John Upshaw, Archibald Ritchie & Muscoe Garnett gent are firmly bound unto our Sovereign Lord King George the third for 1,000 pd ... the condition of this obligation is such that whereas the afsd John Upshaw is constituted & appointed sheriff of Essex Co during pleasure by commission from the Governor dated 12 Oct instant, if the sd John Upshaw shall well & truly collect & receive all officers fees & dues put into his hands to collect & duly account for & pay the same to the officers to whom such fees are due at such times as are prescribed & limited by law & shall well & truly execute & due return make of all process & precepts to him directed & pay & satisfy all sums of money & tobacco by him received by virtue of any such process to the persons to whom the same are due & in all other things shall truly & faithfully execute & perform the sd office of sheriff during the time of his continuance therein then this obligation to be void ... . Sealed & delivered in the presence of Essex Court. Ackn 15 Oct 1770 & recorded. Attest: John Lee clerk. (Pg 388)

15 Oct 1770. Bond. John Upshaw, Archibald Ritchie & Muscoe Garnett gent are firmly bound unto our Sovereign Lord King George the third for 500 pd ... the condition of this obligation is such that whereas the afsd John Upshaw is constituted & appointed sheriff of Essex Co during pleasure by commission from the Governor dated 12 Oct instant, if the sd John Upshaw shall well & truly collect all quitrents fines forfeitures & Americiaments accruing or becoming due & shall account for & pay the same to the officers of his Majesty's revenue on or before the second Tuesday in June annually & in all things truly & faithfully execute the sd office of sheriff during his continuance therein then this obligation to be void ... . Sealed & delivered in presence of Essex Court. Ackn 15 Oct 1770 & recorded. Attest: John Lee clerk. (Pg 389)

12 Jul 1770. Deed of Mortgage. I Constantine Smith of South Farnham Parish, Essex co being justly indebted unto Edward Hill of St. Stephens Parish, King & Queen Co for 28 pd 10 sl 6 pn for my use paid & recd & to John Norton of London merchant for 2 pd 11 sl 2 pn do by this indenture sell & set over unto the sd Edward Hill & John Norton the following Negro slaves, to wit, Joe, Ben &

Lott & the future increase of the sd slaves with the following household goods, 1 black walnut 1 oak desk, 1 large 1 small walnut table, 6 feather beds & furniture, 2 doz. pewter plates, 4 dishes, also 1 light grey horse branded on the near shoulder with a stirrup iron & 1 bay mare branded on the near buttock with a "X" ... provided that if the sd Constantine Smith shall well & truly pay unto the sd Edward Hill & John Norton the afsd sums with interest then this present indenture to cease & become void ... . Wit: Humphrey Hill, Wm Hill. Ackn 19 Nov 1770 & recorded. Attest: John Lee clerk. (Pg 390)

6 Nov 1770. Deed of Gift. I Henry Motley of NC am seised for my life as tenant by the curtisy of England of & in a 120 1/2 a. tr of land in Essex Co which was convey'd by Nathaniel Fogg to my late wife Catharine Motley & her heirs, by the death of the sd Catharine the reversion & inheritance in fee tail is descended to Edwin Motley her eldest son & heir to whom I have delivered up the possession of the sd land, now know ye for love & affection I bear to my sd son Edwin Motley I the sd Henry Motley have give, granted & released unto the sd Edwin Motley all the estate right I ever had, now have or at any time hereafter may have in or to the sd tr of land ... . Wit: Robert Leeman, Shildrick Broaddus, Thos Motley, Joseph Leeman. Proved 19 Nov 1770 & recorded. Attest: John Lee clerk. (Pg 391)

10 Nov 1770. Deed. Cornelius Noell & Sally his wife of St. Anns Parish, Essex Co for 200 pd 10 sl sold to Joshua Garnett of same place a 232 a. parcel of land whereon I now live adj the lands of John Rowzee, James Noell, John Samuel, Winefred Gouldman & Francis Ramsay ... . Wit: Robt Rennolds, James Pattice, Reuben Garnett, Thos Andrews. Ackn 19 Nov 1770 by Joshua Garnett & recorded. Ackn 20 May 1771 by Sally w/o the sd Cornelius being first privately examined & consenting & is recorded. Attest: John Lee clerk. (Pg 392)

19 Nov 1770. Deed. Thomas Allen of Essex Co planter for 66 pd sold to Thomas Dix of same co planter a 192 a. tr of land & plantation which John Allen grandfather of the sd Thomas purch of James Gatewood & Penelope his wife by deed dated 24 Feb 1747 & upon the death of the sd John Allen intestate the same descended to the afsd Thomas Allen his heir at law, being in South Farnham Parish & bounded by Piscattaway Swamp & the land purch by the sd Thomas Dix of James Norwell ... . Wit: None. Ackn 19 Nov 1770 & recorded. Attest: John Lee clerk. (Pg 394)

11 May 1769. Deed. Thomas Grosham of Amherst Co & Susanna his wife for 80 pd sold to William Roane of Essex Co a 120 a. tr of land whereon John Morris now lives in South Farnham Parish bounded by house where Henry Crittendon formerly lived, Rennolds's corner, Tomlins Run & Tandy's line ... . Wit: Jos Magann, Thos Merritt, John Merritt, Jo Ryland, Wm Webb, H.

Campbell, Geo Randen, Archibald Ritchie. Proved 19 Nov 1770 & certified. Fully proved 20 Nov 1770 & together with a commission for the privy examination of the sd Susanna Grosham & the certificate of her acknowledgment thereon was admitted to record. Attest: John Lee clerk. (Pg 395)

24 Apr 1769. To Daniel Burford, Henry Rose & Ambrose Rucker of Amherst Co gent greeting, whereas Thomas Grosham & Susannah his wife have by their deed [see above] conveyed unto William Roane a 120 a. tr of land, & whereas the sd Susannah is unable to travel to our court to make acknowledgment thereof, therefore we command you to repair to the sd Susanna Grosham & that privily & apart from her husband you take such acknowledgment as she shall be willing to make ... . Wit John Lee clerk. 13 May 1769 at Amherst Co, by virtue of this commission we Henry Rose & Ambrose Rucker did personally go to the sd Susanna & having examined her privily & apart from the sd Thomas do certify that she declared that she freely ackn the conveyance & that she was willing the same should be recorded. Truly recorded. Attest: John Lee clerk. (Pg 398)

29 Aug 1770. Deed. Sarah Tharpe of St. Anns Parish, Essex Co widow for 150 pd sold to Muscoe Garnett of same parish gent the land & plantation whereon she now lives for & during the life of the sd Sarah Tharpe & untill the youngest child of the testator shall arrive to lawful age or marriage as directed in the will ... whereas Thomas Tharpe late of sd co did by his will dated 1 Apr 1767 devise as follows "I lease unto my loving wife Sarah Tharpe all my estate during her life or widowhood for the support & schooling of what children I have living with me unmarried at my decease. If she my sd wife should marry or depart this life before my youngest dau Frances Tharpe comes of age or married my will is my exors keep the estate together till she my sd dau do come of age or marry." In which devise & bequest is included the land & plantation whereon the testator then lived & whereas the sd Sarah Tharpe is the only acting executrix (the executors therein named having declined the burthen thereof) & being minded to sell & dispose of the sd land & plantation to enable her to support & educate the children afsd agreeable to the meaning & intention of the testator, hath agreed to sell the same to the sd Muscoe Garnett for 150 pd being the sum of 20 pd more than the annual rent of the sd land in the opinion of three disinterested gent by them the sd Sarah Tharpe & Muscoe Garnett for that purpose chosen would amount to by time the youngest dau afsd comes of age as appears by their determination in writing dated 21 Jul 1770 hereto annexed to be appropriated to the support & education of the sd children ... . Wit: Ann Garnett, Sarah Garnett, Milly Garnett. Ackn 17 Dec 1770 & recorded. Attest: John Lee clerk. (Pg 399)

21 Jul 1770. At the instance & request of Sarah Tharpe widow & Muscoe Garnett both of Essex Co we have viewed the land & improvements whereon the sd Sarah Tharpe now dwells & are of opinion that the sum of 10 pd is the real annual rent or value of the same & no more. Mrs. Bizwell who was w/o Thomas Tharpe the elder is now in possession of 1/3 of the sd tr of land at her death. We are of opinion that the whole of the sd land & improvements will be worth per annum 15 pd & to this opinion we are willing to make oath if required. Given under our hands Thos Boulware, John Henshaw, Ralph Rowzee. Proved 17 Dec 1770 & admitted to record. Attest: John Lee clerk. (Pg 401)

17 Dec 1770. Deed. Thomas Miller & Dorothy his wife of St. Stephens Parish, King & Queen Co for 160 pd sold to Benjamin Jones of South Farnham Parish, Essex Co a 200 a. tr of land in South Farnham Parish it being pt/o that tr of land that the sd Thomas Miller purch of John Farish bounded by Joseph Bohannun, Richard Hodges, James Booker, John Edmondson, Thomas Allen & Middle Br ... . Wit: Alexr Smith, Jas Edmondson, Ann Courtney. Ackn 17 Dec 1770 by Thomas Miller & Dorothy his wife (she being first privately examined & thereto consenting) & admitted to record. Attest: John Lee clerk. (Pg 401)

12 Oct ---- at Williamsburg. Appointment. To John Upshaw esqr, by virtue of the power & authority to me given I do hereby appoint you to be sheriff of Essex Co during pleasure ... . Norborne Baron de Botetourt his Majesty's Lieut & Governor General of VA & Vice Admiral of the same. At Oct Court 1770 the above commission was sworn to & ordered to be recorded. Attest: John Lee clerk. (Pg 403)

24 Sep 1769. Power of Attorney. Muscoe Livingston of London mariner have constituted John Livingston of Essex Co, VA planter my atty to cause or procure the entail to be lawfully cut off on a certain plantation situated in Essex Co afsd with the Negroes thereupon appertaining & which did formerly belong to my late grandfather Salvator Muscoe who bequeathed the same to my mother Frances Livingston who was dau of the sd Salvator Muscoe during her natural life & after her decease to her eldest son & his heirs male in tail & for that purpose for me & in my name to consent to do & perform all that shall be required & necessary for effecting the cutting off of the sd intail & on such intail being so cut off to accept & take with the consent of my sd mother the surrender of the sd plantation Negroes & premises to me & for my use & also for me & in my name to sell assign & convey the sd plantation Negroes & premises ... . Wit: Matt Maury, Thomas Woodford, Thos Adams, James Walker, John Anderson. Proved 21 May 1770 at Tappa & certified. Attest: John Lee clerk. Proved 13 Aug 1770 at James City Co & recorded. Attest: Ben Waller clerk. Further proved 19 Mar 1771 & ordered to be recorded. On 21 Jan 1771 on the motion of John Livingston admitted to record. Attest: John Lee clerk. (Pg 404)

15 Jan 1771. Deed. Ann Carter of Saint Stephens Parish, King & Queen Co for 7 pn sold to John Dobbyns of South Farnham Parish, Essex Co a 25 a. parcel of land in South Farnham Parish bounded by the lands of Thomas Williamson, Elizabeth Cooper, William Rosser, James Webb & the sd John Dobbyns ... . Wit: Thos Cox, Thomas Williamson, Isaac Bresindine. Proved 21 Jan 1771 & recorded. Attest: John Lee clerk. (Pg 406)

28 Nov 1770. Deed. James Bates & Ann his wife of Essex Co for 65 pd sold to John Sale of same co a tr of land in St. Anns Parish being 1/2 the tr of land on which the sd James Bates now lives bounded by John Sale's Spring Br, Meridy Brown, Thomas Sale's old line, Sale's Church & line formerly between John Sale & James Bates, containing as by survey thereof made by Caleb Lindsey 25 Oct 1770 87 a. (except 1/2 a. where the sd Bates's father is buried) ... . Wit: Reuben Garnett, Caleb Noell, Edwin Garnett, Jno Rowzee, Merriday Brown. Proved 21 Jan 1771 & recorded. Attest: John Lee clerk. (Pg 407)

28 Nov 1770. Deed. James Bates & Ann his wife of Essex Co for 55 pd sold to Merriday Brown of same co a 96 a. tr of land in St. Anns Parish the 1/2 pt/o land on which the sd James Bates now lives bounded by John Sale's Spring Br, Caleb Noell, Thomas Sale's old line & John Sale, being 9 a. more than the 1/2 pt/o the land on which the sd James Bates now lives ... . Wit: John Sale, Reuben Garnett, Jno Rouzee, Caleb Noell, Edwin Garnett. Proved 21 Jan 1771 & recorded. Attest: John Lee clerk. (Pg 409)

-- Oct 1770. Power of Attorney. Robert Ferguson late of Essex Co now of Ayr in North Britain merchant & Martha Ferguson spouses have appointed John Lee esqr clerk of Essex Co & David Cochrane of New Castle in Hanover Co, VA merchant our attys to ask demand sue for levy & recover from all & every person that are due us or our factors any sum of money & all & every debt goods merchandizes & every other subject matter & thing due adebted & owing to us or our factors by any person in VA, MD or ay other of his Majesties dominions in America ... . Wit: John Bowie, Archibald Pickan, Robert Watson, Alexr Toulis, Ishml Marychinok, Moore Fauntleroy. 6 Oct 1770 I David Ferguson esqr provost of the Burg of Ayr do hereby certify that personally appeared before me John Bowie shipmaster in Ayr & Archibald Picken his mate persons well known & worthy of good credit & by solemn oath did declare that they were present & did see Robert Ferguson & Martha Ferguson sign seal & execute the power of atty above written ... . Proved 18 Feb 1771 & certified. Further proved 18 Mar 1771 & recorded. Attest: John Lee clerk. (Pg 411)

19 Jan 1771. Deed. Francis Smith & Lucy his wife of Bedford Co & Richard Adams of Henrico Co gent for 550 pd sold to Newman Brockenbrough of Richmond Co a 662 a. parcel of land in South Farnham Parish bounded by the

main road which leads by Essex Lower Church over Cheyney's Bridge, lands of
Thomas Newbil, Henry Cruncher, William Broocke, the sd Francis Smith
formerly Hipkins's & John Broocke, it being pt/o the land devised to the sd
Francis Smith by the will of Francis Smith the elder decd dated 5 Mar 1760 .... .
Wit: Samuel Peachey, James Webb Junr, W. Smith, Ann Smith. Proved 18 Mar
1771 & recorded. Attest: John Lee clerk. (Pg 413)

19 Jan 1771. To Samuel Peachey, James Webb Junr & Mere Smith of Essex Co
gent greeting, whereas Frs Smith & Lucy his wife & Richard Adams of Bedford
& Henrico Cos by their indenture [see above] conveyed unto Newman
Brokenbrough of Richmond Co a 662 a. parcel of land, & whereas the sd Lucy
is unable to travel to our co court to make acknowledgment thereof, therefore we
command you to repair to the sd Lucy & that privily & apart from her husband
you take such acknowledgment as she shall be willing to make .... . Wit: John
Lee clerk. Pursuant to the above commission we Sam Peachey & James Webb
Junr have privily & apart from her husband examined the sd Lucy Smith
concerning the premises who freely acknowledges the deed & is desirous that
the same may be admitted to record. Truly recorded. Attest: John Lee clerk.
(Pg 415)

5 Sep 1770. Deed of Mortgage. John Taylar of St. Anns Parish, Essex Co for
45 pd 4 sl 9 pn sold to Muscoe Garnett of same parish the following slaves,
goods & chattels, viz: one old Negro man Jack, three Negro girls Cruse, Cate &
Lucy, 2 mares, 15 head of cattle, 10 sheep, 10 head of hoggs, 4 feather beds &
furniture, 3 iron potts, 1 chest, 1 trunk, 1 gun, 1 frying pan, 6 leather chairs, 6
flag chairs, 4 pewter dishes, 18 pewter plates & 1 table ... provided that if the sd
John Taylar shall well & truly satisfy & pay unto the sd Muscoe Garnett the afsd
sum with interest then this indenture to be void .... . Wit: John Lee, James
Davis. Proved 18 Mar 1771 & recorded. Attest: John Lee clerk. (Pg 416)

7 Aug 1770. This shall oblige me Richard Fuller not to be consarned with aney
of Mary Johnson's estate that she has before I am married to her but leavs all she
has to her one desposel. Wit: Wm Fuller, John Bush. Ackn 19 Mar 1771 &
recorded. Attest: John Lee clerk. (Pg 418)

15 Apr 1771. Deed. Nathan Waggener of South Farnham Parish, Essex Co for
12 pd 19 sl 6 pn sold to Alexander Smith of same place a 12 3/4 a. 36 square
poles tr of land in the sd parish on the road that leads to Hobs Hole adj the sd
Alexander Smith & the land of the orphan of Fauntleroy .... . Wit: None. Ackn
15 Apr 1771 & recorded. Attest: John Lee clerk. (Pg 418)

29 Dec 1770. Deed. Christian Baker of Essex Co for 70 pd sold to John Crow
of same co a tr of land devised by Henry Baker Senr's will to his dau Jane Baker

& her heirs & if she should die without such heir then in fee simple to the afsd Christian Baker which sd land by virtue of the devise afsd upon the death of the sd Jane without issue, came into the possession & seisin of her the sd Christian Baker & is bounded by the Dragon Swamp, lands of Allen, Crow & Jeffries, in South Farnham Parish containing 100 a. ... . Wit: Richd Tunstall, Isom Crow, William Tureman, Benjamin Dunn Junr. Ackn 15 Apr 1771 & recorded. Attest: John Lee clerk. (Pg 420)

16 Apr 1771. Deed. Whereas Thomas Waring formerly of Essex Co was in his lifetime seised & possessed of a 60 a. tr of land it being the land that the sd Waring purch of John Pagett & Mary his wife for 100 a. by deed dated 4 Dec 1740 but by a survey made by Richd Brown the land was found to contain 60 a., the sd Thomas Waring died leaving several legacys of land to his sons Robert Pane Waring, Epaphroditus Lawson Waring, & Wm Waring & left the remainder of his estate to be divided amongst all his children, the sd persal of land fell to the several children as pt/o the remainder of the sd Thomas Waring decd's estate it not being mentioned in the sd Waring's will ... now this indenture Robt Pane Waring & Catharine his wife of South Farnham Parish, Essex Co planter of the first part, William Todd & Catharine his wife of St. Stephens Parish, King & Queen Co, VA of the second part, Epaphroditus Lawson Waring of South Farnham Parish, Essex Co of the third part, William Waring of South Farnham Parish, Essex Co of the fourth part, Thomas Fauntleroy the heir of John Fauntleroy & Elizabeth his wife decd of South Farnham Parish, Essex Co of the fifth part, & John Rennolds of South Farnham Parish, Essex Co planter of the other part, wit that the sd Robert Pane Waring & Catharine his wife, Wm Todd & Catharine his wife, Epaphroditus Lawson Waring, William Waring & Thomas Fauntleroy have for 30 pd sold to the sd John Rennolds a messuage & 60 a. tr of land afsd in South Farnham Parish adj the Tobaccohouse Br into which Henry Paget's Spring Br falls & Lason's line ... . Wit: John Upshaw, John Latane, James Upshaw. Proved 16 Apr 1771 & admitted to record. Attest: John Lee clerk. (Pg 422)

20 May 1771. Deed. Nathan Waggener of South Farnham Parish, Essex Co for 92 pd 10 sl sold to Benjamin Waggener of same place a 92 1/2 a. tr of land in the parrish afsd bounded by Byrom's corner, Robert Pain Waring, a br formerly called Meckenys Br, the heir of William Waggener decd & the heir of John Fauntleroy ... . Wit: None. Ackn 20 May 1771 & admitted to record. Attest: John Lee clerk. (Pg 426)

6 Mar 1771. Power of Attorney. William Millar of the Island of Antigua esqr one of the executors of the will of Andrew Millar late of Saint James Parish, Westminster in Middlesex Co esqr decd ... whereas John Randolph barrister of the Middlesex Temple late from VA London (sic) & Philip Ludwell Lee esqr of

the Inner Temple late from VA but then residing in Cecil Street London did by a
bond dated 13 Apr 1750 become bound jointly & severally to the sd Andrew
Millar in the penal sum of 440 pd conditioned for the payment of 220 pd on 12
Apr 1751, now know ye that the sd William Millar hath in his sd capacity of
executor afsd made & constituted Archibald Ritchie & James Mills of
Rappahannock River in VA merchants his attys to ask demand sue for recover &
receive of & from the sd John Randolph & Philip Ludwell Lee all sums of
money now due or hereafter to grow due upon the sd bond & all other sums of
money whatever due from them & upon payment thereof to give proper releases
& discharges .... Wit: Daniel Ford, John Robinson. Proved 20 May 1771 &
recorded. Attest: John Lee clerk. (Pg 428)

15 Apr 1771. Deed. John Edmondson & Catherine (Caty) his wife of South
Farnham Parish, Essex Co for 36 pd 10 sl sold to Thos Wood of same place a 73
a. parcel of land in the sd parish bounded by the sd Edmondson & Wood &
James Booker .... Wit: William Edmondson Junr, James Edmondson. Ackn 20
May 1771 by John Edmondson & Catherine his wife (she being first privily
examined & thereto consenting) & recorded. Attest: John Lee clerk. (Pg 430)

19 Jan 1771. Deed. Francis Smith & Lucy his wife of Bedford Co & Richard
Adams of Henrico Co gent for 404 pd sold to William Smith of Essex Co a 571
a. parcel of land bounded by the Main Road which leeds by Essex Lower
Church over Cheyneys Bridge, Wm Young Junr, Alexr Bomer, William Bomer,
Henry Crutcher, John Blatt, Ralph Neale & Henry Gardner, immediately after
the death of Ann Smith mother to the sd Francis Smith who now lives thereon &
is intitled thereto during her natural life it being pt/o the tr of land devised to the
sd Francis Smith by the will of Francis Smith the elder decd dated 5 Mar 1760 ...
. Wit to Smith's: James Webb Junr, Samuel Peachey, Newman Brockenbro
(Brockenbrough), Ann Smith. Wit to R. Adams: Archibald Ritchie, Meriwether
Smith, Will Woddrop, Arch McCall. Proved 20 May 1771 & recorded. Attest:
John Lee clerk. (Pg 433)

20 Feb 1771. To Samuel Peachey, Meriwether Smith & James Webb Junr of
Essex Co gent greeting, whereas Francis Smith & Lucy his wife & Richard
Adams of Bedford & Henrico Cos have by their deed [see above] conveyed a
571 a. tr of land unto Wm Smith of Essex Co, & whereas the sd Lucy Smith is
unable to travel to our co court to make acknowledgment thereof, therefore we
command you to repair to the sd Lucy Smith & that privily & apart from her
husband you take such acknowledgment as she shall be willing to make .... Wit
John Lee clerk. 20 Jan 1771 Pursuant to the above commission we Samuel
Peachy & James Webb Junr did repair to the sd Lucy Smith & examined her
touching the premises she ackn that she does it freely & that she is willing the sd
deed be recorded. Truly recorded. Attest: John Lee clerk. (Pg 435)

10 Nov 1770. Quit Claim. Lidia Cole widow of John Cole decd of Essex Co for love & affection she doth bear to her son William & in order to impower him to make sale of a 60 a. tr of land, she forever quit claims unto the sd William Cole son & heir of the sd John Cole decd of NC all her estate right, title & interest of dower in of & to the sd tr of land ... whereas the sd William Cole is seized in fee tail of a 60 a. piece of land in Essex Co being minded to sell the same he has sued out his Majesties writ in the nature of an adqued damnum to dock the intail thereof & to make sale of the same ... . Wit: John Hanes, Joseph Durham. Proved 21 May 1771 & admitted to record. Attest: John Lee clerk. (Pg 436)

5 Apr 1771. Deed. James Mills of Urbanna, Middlesex Co gent for 89 pd 14 sl paid by Moore Fauntleroy gent in behalf of William Gray hath sold unto the sd William Gray eldest son & heir at law of James & Sarah Gray of Essex Co an indenture as all that tr of land therein mentioned to be convey'd by Richard Coleman to the sd James Gray in his life time ... whereas the sd James Gray in his life time by his deed dated 23 Apr 1763 reciting that the sd James Mills of the proper debt of the sd James Gray as his security & at his request had become bound with him in a bond to Richard Coleman of Spotsylvania Co with condition for the payment of 280 pd & the sd James Gray was otherwise considerably indebted to the sd James Mills by accompt did thereby as well for the counter security & indemnity of the sd James Mills on account of his said securityship as for securing the payment of the other debt afsd & for 5 sl to the sd Gray paid by the sd James Mills sell unto the sd James Mills a tr of land whereon Richard Covington formerly liv'd lately convey'd by Richard Coleman & Ann his wife to the sd James Gray provided that if the sd James Gray should well & truly pay to the sd Richard Coleman the sd 280 pd with interest or by any other ways or means save harmless & indemnified the sd James Mills from all losses & damages which he might sustain or suffer by means of that securityship & should moreover pay to the sd James Mills all such sums of money as were justly due & owing to him from the sd James Gray then those presents to be void, & whereas the sd James Gray did not pay unto the sd Richard Coleman the sd sum & the sd James Mills has been oblig'd to pay the sum to the sd Richard Coleman & did also as security for the sd James Gray at his request & for the proper debt of the sd James Gray pay unto Francis Brown & Richard Brown of Bristol merchants 89 pd 14 sl upon which interest is due from 13 Aug 1764 & the sd James Gray at the time of executing the above recited indenture & at the time of his decease was & his estate is now very considerably indebted to the sd James Mills by accompt to more than the value of the sd lands whereby not only the right convey'd by the sd indenture but an absolute title in equity to the sd lands is become vested in the sd James Mills ... . Wit: Archibald Ritchie, Chs Mortimer, John Fauntleroy, Hugh Campbell. Proved 21 May 1771 & certified & fully proved 15 Jul 1771 & admitted to record. Attest: John Lee clerk. (Pg 437)

14 May 1771. To Robt Beverley, Griffin Boughan & Henry Garnett gent of Essex Co greeting, whereas Robert Sale & Hannah his wife have by their deed dated 13 Oct 1769 convey'd unto Augustine Garnett gent a 188 a. tr of land in St. Anns Parish, & whereas the sd Hannah is unable to travel to our co court to make acknowledgment thereof, therefore we command you that you repair to the sd Hannah & her privily & apart from the sd Robert her husband examine touching the premises & receive her acknowledgment ... . Wit John Lee clerk. 14 May 1771 Pursuant to the within commission we Henry Garnett & Griffing Boughan have exam'd the within Hannah Sale privily & apart from her husband who says she does relinquish her dower to the lands & she is willing the sd deed be recorded. Attest: John Lee clerk. (Pg 440)

27 Apr 1771. Bill of Sale. Godwin Swift of Frederick Co, VA for 48 pd sold to John Lee of Essex Co one Negro woman named Rachel & her increase, whom I had of James Mills gent ... . Wit: Thomas Douglas, Meriwether Smith. Proved 17 Jun 1771 & recorded. Attest: John Lee clerk. (Pg 441)

17 Jun 1771. Deed. James Webb Junr of Essex Co gent & Mary his wife for 400 pd sold to Archibald Ritchie of same co gent the 1/2 of the water grist mill & several parcels of land thereto belonging which is called Webbs Lower Mill on one of the brs of Piscataway Cr near the sd Webb's dwelling house together with the 1/2 of the bakehouse & oven which the sd Webb has erected for carrying on the baking business on Piscataway Cr called Webbs Old House ... . Wit: None. Ackn 17 Jun 1771 by James Webb & Mary his wife (she being first privily examined & thereto consenting) & recorded. Attest: John Lee clerk. (Pg 442)

6 Apr 1770. To Robert Beverly, Griffin Boughan & Henry Garnett of Essex Co gent, whereas Rice Noell & Tabitha his wife have by their deed convey'd unto Caleb Noell of sd co a tr of land in St. Anns Parish, & whereas the sd Tabitha is unable to travel to our sd co court to make acknowledgment thereof, therefore we command you to repair to the sd Tabitha & her privily & apart from her sd husband examine touching the premises & receive her acknowledgment ... . Wit John Lee clerk. 15 --- 1771 By virtue of this commission to us directed we G. Boughan & Henry Garnett have examined the within mentioned Tabitha Noell privily & apart from her husband who declares she relinquishes her dower in the land & she is willing the deed be recorded. Truly recorded. Attest: John Lee clerk. (Pg 444)

--- 1771. Deed. John Gatewood & Ann his wife of [blank] Parish, Caroline Co overseer for 32 pd 10 sl sold to Cheney Gatewood of South Farnham Parish, Essex Co planter a messuage & tr of land on the s side of Hoskins's Swamp & is all that pt/o the tr of land devis'd to the sd John Gatewood by his father's will except the part sold & convey'd to his brother Philip, the residue undivided to contain 80 a. .... Wit: John Corrie, John Hipkins, Thomas Roane, Thomas Upshaw, James Upshaw. Proved 17 Jun 1771 & recorded. Attest: John Lee clerk. (Pg 445)

11 Mar 1771. To Thomas Lowry & James Upshaw of Caroline Co gent greeting, whereas John Gatewood & Ann his wife of Caroline Co have by their deed [see above] conveyed a tr of land unto Cheney Gatewood, & whereas the sd Ann Gatewood is unable to travel to our co court to make acknowledgment thereof, therefore we command you to repair to the sd Ann Gatewood & that privily & apart from her husband you take such acknowledgment as she shall be willing to make .... Wit John Lee clerk. 11 Apr 1771 By virtue of the above commission we Thomas Lowry & James Upshaw personally went to the afsd Ann & received her acknowledgment. Truly recorded. Attest: John Lee clerk. (Pg 447)

20 Feb 1771. Bill of Sale. Williamson Young of Essex Co for 99 pd 15 sl 5 pn paid by Archd McCall & also 77 pd 14 sl paid by McCall & Shedden have sold unto the sd Archd McCall & unto the sd McCall & Shedden both of Essex Co merchants my six Negroes, viz, Moll & her two children Stephen & Sam & Bett (or Bell?) & her two children Will & Little Sam & their future increase .... Wit: Lauchr Mackintosh, E. Lawson Waring, Geo McCall. Proved 17 Jun 1771 & recorded. Attest: John Lee clerk. (Pg 447)

17 Jun 1771. Deed of Gift. Sarah Scandrett widow of Essex Co for natural love & affection & 5 sl have given to her son Thomas Ley of same co gent all my right & title & interest in that pt/o the land formerly belonging to my first husband Thomas Ley decd in the town of Beaufort .... Wit: Theophilus Faver, Philip Richards, Leonard Chamberlain. Proved 17 Jun 1771 & recorded. Attest: John Lee clerk. (Pg 448)

11 Feb 1771. Deed. Richard Bush of Granville Co, NC & Jane his wife for 25 pd sold to Reubin Bush of Essex Co all their estate right in & to a tr of land devised him by his father John Bush by his will made 21 Dec 1765 .... Wit: Archibald Ritchie, William Fletcher, Sarah Fletcher, Richard Goode, Samuel Smith, Wm Webb, John Young. Proved 17 Jun 1771 & recorded. Attest: John Lee clerk. (Pg 449)

17 Jun 1771. Deed. Whereas at a General Assembly held at Williamsburg 7 Nov 1769 an act was made for establishing a town on the land of Thomas Ley at Leytons Warehouse & whereas the sd Thomas Ley in pursuance thereof hath survey'd & laid off pt/o his sd land into lotts & streets for a town which is call'd Beaufort & made sale of the sd lotts to sundry persons who after having built

thereon & improved them agreeable to the conditions of their deeds of conveyance will be entitled to & enjoy all the privileges & immunities that the freeholders & inhabitants of other towns in this colony have & enjoy, now this indenture wit that the sd Thomas Ley for 22 pd 2 sl 6 pn sold to Thos Garnett Noell one lott or 1/2 a. of land in the burgh of Beaufort being numbered 23 in the platt of sd town ... provided that the sd Thos Garnett do begin & without delay proceed to build & finish on the sd lott within 12 months one good house ... . Wit: W. Gatewood, Samuel Gresham, John Seayres. Ackn 17 Jun 1771 & admitted to record. Attest: John Lee clerk. (Pg 451)

4 Feb 1771. Deed. Richard Parker of Cople Parish, Westmoreland Co atty at law & Elizabeth his wife for 300 pd sold to John Brockenbrough of the Town of Tappahannock, Essex Co gent two lotts or 1/2 acres of land in the Town of Tappahannock numbered [blank] they being lotts which Alexander Parker late of the sd town gent decd lived on & possess'd in his life time ... . Wit: Archd McCall, Archibald Ritchie, William Shedden, Newman Brockenbro, Will Beale Junr. Wm Brockenbrough & Robert Wormley Carter as to Mr. Parker. Proved as to Richard Parker with the commission for the privy examination of Elizabeth & the cert of her acknowledgment thereon are ordered to be recorded. Attest: John Lee clerk. (Pg 452)

15 Jun 1771. To William Brockenbrough, Robert Wormley Carter & Williamson Ball of Richmond Co gent greeting, whereas Richard Parker & Elizabeth his wife of Westmoreland have by their deed [see above] conveyed unto John Brockenbrough of Essex Co two lotts in the Town of Tappa, & whereas the sd Elizabeth is unable to travel to our co court to make acknowledgment thereof, therefore we command you to repair to the sd Eliza & that privily & apart from her husband you take such acknowledgment as she shall be willing to make ... . 15 Jun 1771 Pursuant to the above commission we W. Brockenbrough & Robert Wormley Carter have privately & apart from her husband examined the sd Elizabeth Parker concerning the premises who voluntarily & freely acknowledges the deed & is desirous that the same be admitted to record. Truly recorded. Attest: John Lee clerk. (Pg 454)

29 Apr 1771. Deed of Gift. Cornelius Sale of St. Anns Parish, Essex Co fog good effection have sometime past given to Thomas Sthreshley a Negro child Betty the dau of Alce, therefore I the sd Cornelias Sale do by these presents give unto the sd Thomas Sthreshly the afsd Negro child as a confirmation of the former gift ... . Wit: Richard Lawry, Wm Sthreshly. Proved 15 Jul 1771 & admitted to record. Attest: John Lee clerk. (Pg 455)

11 Apr 1771. Deed. William Young Junr & Elizabeth his wife of South Farnham Parish, Essex Co for 68 pd sold to Williamson Young of same parish a

68 a. parcel of land in the sd parish bounded by Griffing Johnson, Evans's ordinary & John Mitchell, it being pt/o the tr of land which Mary Young mother to the afsd William Young gave him by deed of gift dated 18 Aug 1766 ... . Wit: Henry Young, Smith Young, Thomas Evans, John Evans. Proved 15 Jul 1771 & recorded. Attest: John Lee clerk. (Pg 456)

11 Apr 1771. Deed. William Young Junr of South Farnham Parish, Essex Co for 182 pd sold to Williamson Young of same parish a 168 a. parcel of land in the sd parish adj the lands of Charles Evans decd, John Mitchell, the land lately purch by the sd Williamson of the afsd William, Griffing Johnson, William Gatewood & Philemon Gatewood, it being the land which the sd Wm Young purch of Henry Young 24 Oct 1765 & whereon Mary Young now lives who enjoys the same for life ... . Wit: Henry Young, Smith Young, Thomas Evans, John Evans. proved 15 Jul 1771 & admitted to record. Attest: John Lee clerk. (Pg 457)

22 Nov 1770. Bill of Sale. I John Vass of Essex Co for 70 pd 15 sl 5 pn 1 farthing which sum I stand justly indebted to James Johnson of Lunenburg Co the balance of a judgment of Essex Co have sold to the sd James Johnson the following articles, to wit, 1 gray mare, 1 cow & yearling, 2 beds & furniture, a large chest, a table & 5 flag chairs, 1 iron pott & hooks ... . Wit: James Webb Junr, John Webb Junr. Proved 16 Jul 1771 & admitted to record. Attest: John Lee clerk. (Pg 459)

31 Aug 1765. Deed. John Harper Junr & Prudence his wife of South Farnham Parish, Essex Co for 75 pd sold to Thomas Roane of same place a messuage & 120 a. tr of land in the afsd parish which sd tr is pt/o that dividend or parcel of land which formerly belonged to Daniel Roberts & was sold by Jos Reeves (who was atty for the sd Roberts) at publick auction to the sd John Harper, bounded by Roanes Mill, South Swamp & the main run of Hoskins's Cr ... . Wit: James Upshaw, Thos Sthreshly, John Harper Senr. Ackn by John Harper Junr 21 Oct 1765 & admitted to record. Attest: John Lee clerk. (Pg 459)

19 Aug 1771. Deed. Archer West & Anne his wife of Chesterfield Co for 6 pd 5 sl sold to John Byrom of Essex Co a 10 a. parcel of land adj the lands of the sd Byrom, William Fletcher, Thomas Williamson decd & the main road which leads from Webb's & Ritchie's mill to the ordinary formerly keeped by James Webb decd, it being pt/o the land which descended to the sd Anne from her father James Byrom decd ... . Wit: None. Ackn 19 Aug 1771 by Archer West & Anne his wife (she being first privately examined & thereto consenting) & admitted to record. Attest: John Lee clerk. (Pg 461)

19 Aug 1771. Deed. Archer West & Anne his wife of Chesterfield Co for 8 pd sold to Ezekiel Byrom of Essex Co a 20 a. parcel of land adj the land of the sd Ezekiel Byrom & Webb's & Ritchie's mill creek & pond, it being pt/o the land which descended to the sd Anne from her father James Byrom decd ... . Wit: None. Ackn 19 Aug 1771 by Archer West & Anne his wife (she being first privately examined & thereto consenting) & admitted to record. Attest: John Lee clerk. (Pg 462)

11 May 1771. Deed. Ann (Anna) Cross widow of Samuel Cross decd of Essex Co for 15 pd sold to Cornelius Sale of same co all her dower or right of dower & all her right title & interest of & in the lands sold by her decd husband to the sd Cornelius Sale by deed dated 14 Jul 1764 ... . Wit: Wm Smether, James Hamelton, John Sale. Ackn 19 Aug 1771 & admitted to record. Attest: John Lee clerk. (Pg 464)

19 Aug 1771. Deed. Whereas at a General Assembly held at Williamsburg 7 Nov 1769 an act was made for establishing a town on the land of Thomas Ley at Leytons Warehouse & whereas the sd Thomas Ley in pursuance thereof hath survey'd & laid off pt/o his sd land into lotts & streets for a town which is call'd Beaufort & made sale of the sd lotts to sundry persons who after having built thereon & improved them agreeable to the conditions of their deeds of conveyance will be entitled to & enjoy all the privileges & immunities that the freeholders & inhabitants of other towns in this colony have & enjoy, now this indenture the sd Thomas Ley for 100 pd sold to Edward Voss five lotts or 1/2 acres of land in the burgh of Beaufort being pt/o the sd town land numbered 25, 26, 27, 29 & 30 in the platt of the sd town ... . Wit: Geo Stone, John Seayres. Ackn 19 Aug 1771 & admitted to record. Attest: John Lee clerk. (Pg 464)

19 Aug 1771. Deed. Sarah Farguson & Joseph Farguson & Patience his wife of South Farnham Parish, Essex Co for 75 pd sold to Thomas Roane of same place a messuage & 150 a. tr of land on some of the brs of Piscataway Cr in the parish afsd being the land & plantation whereon John Farguson decd lately lived & died & by him bequeathed to the sd Sarah Farguson his widow during her life & after his (sic) decease to the sd Joseph Farguson, bounded by Thomas Roane's land he purch of Saml Croxton, land of Thomas & John Croxton purch of John Meadors, Middle Br, Stodghill's Spring Br, spring formerly called Sillses, land Thomas Roane bought of John Smith & Barker's land ... . Wit: None. Ackn 19 Aug 1771 by Sarah Farguson & Joseph Farguson & Patience his wife (she being first privately examined & consenting) & admitted to record. Attest: John Lee clerk. (Pg 465)

4 Jul 1771. Deed of Gift. Ann Smith of South Farnham Parish for natural love & affection & 5 sl have given to her son William Smith of same parish for &

during the term of the life of the sd Ann Smith a 571 a. parcel of land in the sd parish whereon the sd Ann Smith now lives (which sd land Francis Smith gent decd late the husband of the sd Ann Smith devised to her by his will during her natural life) & two Negroes Aaron & Chloe & their future increase ... . Wit: Tho Newbill, Henry Crutcher, Thomas Hammond. Proved 19 Aug 1771 & recorded. Attest: John Lee clerk. (Pg 467)

19 Aug 1771. Deed. Whereas at a General Assembly held at Williamsburg 7 Nov 1769 an act was made for establishing a town on the land of Thomas Ley at Leytons Warehouse & whereas the sd Thomas Ley in pursuance thereof hath survey'd & laid off pt/o his sd land into lotts & streets for a town which is call'd Beaufort & made sale of the sd lotts to sundry persons who after having built thereon & improved them agreeable to the conditions of their deeds of conveyance will be entitled to & enjoy all the privileges & immunities that the freeholders & inhabitants of other towns in this colony have & enjoy, now this indenture the sd Thomas Ley for 19 pd sold to William Livingston one lott or 1/2 a. of land in the Burg of Beaufort being pt/o the sd town land & numbered 32 in the platt of the sd town ... . Wit: Geo Stone, John Edmondson Junr,. Ackn 20 Aug 1771 & admitted to record. Attest: John Lee clerk. (Pg 468)

16 Sep 1771. Deed. Elizabeth Wright of South Farnham Parish, Essex Co for 11 pd 17 sl 6 pn sold to James Webb & Archibald Ritchie of same parish a 23 3/4 a. tr of land bounded by Ezekiel Byrom, West's line, Ozwell Byrom & John Byrom ... . Wit: None. Ackn 16 Sep 1771 & admitted to record. Attest: John Lee clerk. (Pg 470)

13 Apr 1771. Deed. David Pitts Junr & Mary his wife of Essex Co for 26 pd 10 sl sold to Thomas Pitts of same co a 98 a. parcel of land that the sd David Pitts had of his father John Pitts bounded by Cornwald's patent, Page's patent, Elias Harrison, David Pitts, Landram's line, Martain Willard & Beasley's land ... . Wit: Edward Vawter, Reuben Pitts, James Vawter. Ackn 16 Sep 1771 by David Pitts Junr together with the privy examination of Mary his wife & the cert of her acknowledgment thereon ordered to be recorded. Attest: John Lee clerk. (Pg 471)

16 Sep 1771. Deed. Isaac Williamson & Francis his wife, Jno Roddin Junr & Pheby his wife of South Farnham Parish, Essex Co for 12 pd 10 sl sold to William Davis of same parish a 25 a. tr of land in the sd parish it being pt/o a dividend of land purch by the sd Isaac Williamson & John Roddin of LeRoy Hipkins bounded by Fishers Bridge, John Goode, sd John Roddin Junr, Wm Davis & Fishers Swamp ... . Wit: None. Wit to receipt: Edmund Pendleton Junr. Ackn 16 Sep 1771 by Isaac Williamson & Frances his wife & John

Roddin & Phebe his wife (the sd Frances & Phebe being first privately examined & consenting) & recorded. Attest: John Lee clerk. (Pg 473)

15 Aug 1771. To Simon Miller & Paul Micou of Essex Co gent greeting, whereas David Pitts Junr of sd co & Mary his wife have by their deed dated 13 Apr 1771 conveyed unto Thomas Pitts of same co a 98 a. parcel of land, & whereas the sd Mary is unable to travel to our co court to make acknowledgment thereof, therefore we command you to repair to the sd Mary & her privily & apart from the sd David examine whether she relinquishes her dower in the lands ... . Wit John Lee clerk. 13 Sep 1771 Pursuant to the within order we Simon Miller & Paul Micou have examined Mary Pitts separate & apart form her husband who hath relinquished her dower & is willing the deed may be admitted to record. Truly recorded. Attest: John Lee clerk. (Pg 475)

15 Mar 1771. Receipt. Received of my son John Davis full satisfaction of all mortgages bonds bills & sales & demands &c &c &c for a considerable sum paid me, Mary Davis. Wit: James ONeall, Francis ONeall. Proved 17 Sep 1771 & recorded. Attest: John Lee clerk. (Pg 476)

21 Oct 1771. Deed. Philemon Young of Talbot Co, MD for 75 pd sold to Henry Young of Essex Co, VA a 75 a. parcel of land which Henry Young gent decd father to the sd Philemon Young by his will devised to him adj the sd Henry Young's land & William Gatewood ... . Wit: Jno Brockenbrough, William Gatewood Junr, John S. Chilton, John Richards, W. Young. Ackn 21 Oct 1771 & admitted to record. Attest: John Lee clerk. (Pg 477)

XXI Oct 1771. Deed of Gift. Robert Payne Waring of Essex Co gent & Katherine his wife for natural love & affection & also for his better support maintenance & preferment have given to our brother William Waring of same co a parcel of land lately surveyed for him & divided from his brother Epaphroditus Lawson Waring's bounded by the sd Epa Lawson Waring, Occupatia Cr, Rappa River & Lawson's Neck, containing 314 1/2 a. being 1/2 of the land called Lawson's Neck in Saint Ann's Parish ... . Wit: None. Ackn 21 Oct 1771 & Robert Payne Waring & admitted to record. Attest: John Lee clerk. (Pg 478)

XXI Oct 1771. Deed of Gift. Robert Payne Waring of Essex Co gent & Katharine his wife for natural love & affection & also for better maintenance & preferment of him have given unto our brother Epaphroditus Lawson Waring of same co a tr of land bounded by Charles Weeks, Henry Garnett, Occupatia Cr, the spring formerly Edmondson's, the dividing line lately made between the afsd Epahro Lawson Waring & his brother William Waring & Rappahannock River, being in Leytons Neck in Saint Anns Parish ... . Wit: None. Ackn 21 Oct 1771 by Robert Payne Waring & admitted to record. Attest: John Lee clerk. (Pg 480)

16 Oct 1771. Deed. Thomas Ley of Essex Co for 81 pd 10 sl sold to James Ritchie & Company of Glasgow in North Britain two lotts in the town of Beaufort numbers 1 & 2 as likewise a slipe of land betwixt lott No. 1 & the land of Thomas Bridgeforth together with the slipes of land now betwixt the River Rappa & the present boundary of sd lotts No. 1 & 2 & sd slip of land adj Lott No. 1 & the afsd Thomas Bridgeforth's land ... . Wit: None. Ackn 21 Oct 1771 & admitted to record. Attest: John Lee clerk. (Pg 481)

18 Nov 1771. Deed. John Daley & Anne his wife of South Farnham Parish, Essex Co for 100 pd sold to Christn Barby of same place a 183 a. parcel of land in the sd parish adj the lands of John Fauntleroy decd, Thomas Gresham, Erasmus Jones & Haroway Owen, it being pt/o the tr of land purch by the sd John Daley, Francis Jones & Erasmus Jones of Meriwether Smith gent 12 Oct 1764 ... . Wit: Thomas Haile Junr, John Kesee, John Evans Junr. Ackn 18 Nov 1771 by John Daley & Anne his wife (she being first privately examined & consenting) & admitted to record. Attest: John Lee clerk. (Pg 483)

11 Nov 1771. Deed. Ralph Neale of South Farnham Parish, Essex Co & Elizabeth his wife for 40 pd sold to Meriwether Smith of same place gent a 50 a. parcel of land in the parish afsd bounded by William Smith, John Dunn, Smith's formerly Webb's mill pond, Mill Swamp, land of Philip Cheney formerly Johnson's & Eliza Cheney ... . Wit: Andrew Allen, Alexr Saunders, Wm Bond, W. Young. Wit to receipt: James Jones Junr, Griffin Fauntleroy. Proved 18 Nov 1771 as to Ralph Neale which together with a commission for the privily examination of the within named Eliza Neale & the cert of her acknowledgment thereupon are ordered to be recorded. Attest: John Lee clerk. (Pg 485)

12 Nov 1771. To Chas Mortimer, Saml Peachey & James Webb of Essex Co gent greeting, whereas Ralph Neale & Elizabeth his wife of Essex Co by their deed [see above] conveyed unto Meriwether Smith gent a 50 a. parcel of land, & whereas the sd Elizabeth is unable to travel to our co court to make acknowledgment thereof, therefore we command you to repair to the sd Elizabeth & that privily & apart from her husband you take such acknowledgment as shell shall be willing to make ... . Wit John Lee clerk. 12 Nov 1771 By virtue of the within commission to us directed we Samuel Peachey & James Webb have privily examined Eliza separate & apart from her husband who declared that she freely acknowledged the land & that she is willing the conveyance be recorded. Truly recorded. Attest: John Lee clerk. (Pg 486)

2 Nov 1771. Deed. Thomas Newbill & Ann his wife of South Farnham Parish, Essex Co & George Newbill & Mary his wife of St. Stephens Parish, King & Queen Co for 43 pd 16 sl 4 pn sold to William Coughland of St. Stephens Parish, King & Queen Co a tr of land in South Farnham Parish bounded by

William Howerton, Roger Shackelford, Samuel Coats, Richard Phillips & Redd's land ... . Wit: None. Ackn 18 Nov 1771 by Thomas Newbill & Anne his wife & George Newbill & Mary his wife (the sd Anne & Mary being first privately examined & consenting) & admitted to record. Attest: John Lee clerk. (Pg 487)

19 Mar 1771. Deed of Mortgage. Richard Brown of Richmond Co for 25 pd sold to Thomas Glascock of same co one Negro girl named Joanna, 2 feather beds, 1 chest, 9 chairs & 2 horses ... provided that if the sd Richard shall well & truly pay unto the sd Thomas Glascock the full sum of 25 pd with interest on or before 1 May next then these presents to be void ... . Wit: James Booth, James Muse, Thomas Howard. Proved 18 Nov 1771 & admitted to record. Attest: John Lee clerk. (Pg 490)

18 Nov 1771. Deed. John Waggener & Rachel his wife of Culpepper Co for 90 pd sold to James Gatewood & William Gatewood of Essex Co a messuage & 200 a. tr of land in South Farnham Parish adj Thomas Meador, Elizabeth Allen & Thomas Allen ... . Wit: None. Ackn 19 Nov 1771 by John Waggoner & Rachel his wife (she being first privately examined & consenting) & admitted to record. Attest: John Lee clerk. (Pg 491)

18 Nov 1771. Deed. Thomas Haddon of South Farnham Parish, Essex Co & Mary his wife for 50 pd sold to William Edmondson of same parish a 98 1/2 a. parcel of land in the sd parish bounded by Elizabeth Allen, Waters Dunn, William Gatewood & Daingerfield's Mill Pond ... . Wit: Thos Wood, Jno Rennolds, J. Edmondson. Ackn 18 Nov 1771 by Thomas Haddon & Mary his wife (she being first privately examined & consenting) & admitted to record. Attest: John Lee clerk. (Pg 492)

15 Nov 1771. Deed. Robert Cole of South Farnham Parish, Essex Co planter & Frances (Frankey) his wife for 140 pd sold to Heritage Howerton of same place planter a 200 a. tr of land in South Farnham Parish bounded by John Howerton's swamp formerly called Covington's swamp, Richard St. John & Dragon Swamp ... . Wit: William Bird, John St. John, Richard St. John, Charles Howerton, Wm Young Junr, Ann Mitchel. Ackn 18 Nov 1771 by Robt Cole & Frances his wife (she being first privately examined & consenting) & admitted to record. Attest: John Lee clerk. (Pg 494)

A true copy of the original poll of an election held for Essex Co at the Court House on Friday, 22 Nov 1771.

Candidate William Roane: Richard Street, Henry Street, James Gatewood, Rhodes Greenwood, Leonard Hill, Joshua Garnett, William

Greenwood, Mace Pickett, James Webb, John Smith S.C., Henry Woolbanks, William Prosser, James Clark, Isaac Hawes, Henry Cox, Oliver Howard, Richard Fuller, Thomas Faver, Nicholas Faulkener Junr, Richard Meador, Thomas Coleman, Richard Holt Senr, John Hill, Joseph Fogg, James Colquet, James Shaddock, Elias Harison, James Adkinson, Thomas Greenstreet, John Shenault, James Davis Junr, Thomas Andrews, James St. John, Edward Gouldman, Nicholas Atkinson, Martin Willard, John Mitchell, Edward Rouzee, Thomas Gouldman, John Conelly, Benjamin Fisher, Ephraim Shepard, Thomas Games, Daniel Stodghill, John Townley, Richard Holt Junr, Samuel Piles, Memaduke Thorp, Thomas Wood, James Booker, John Ball, Thomas Dix, Francis Ramsey, Samuel Gresham, Thomas Meador, Reuben Meador, Thomas Fogg, Samuel Davis, Thomas St. John, James Allen, Andrew Gatewood, James Munday, Thomas Allen, John Dobbins, Ambrose Pilkinton, John Taylor, James Sullivan, Richard Hill, Isaac Jordan, Ellison Noel, Jonathan Sheerwood, John Smither, Caleb Elliot, John Fogg, Mark Davis, Samuel Shaw Junr, John Spindle Junr, Thomas Gordon, Williamson Young, John Coleman, Thomas Croxton, Josiah Minter, John Hodges, Richard Noell, David Pitts (younger), Thomas Newman, Charles Weeks, Thomas Wise, Thomas Hawkins, Stephen Munday, Thomas Brookes, Henry Kidd, Richard Thos Haile, Isaiah Cole, Thomas Pitts, Thomas Bradburn, Thomas Sullivan, Thomas Cox Junr, Benj Bowler, Nathan Waggener, James Stokes, Thos Henry Brookes, Wm Hayes, James Clark Junr, Thomas Dunn, James Croxton, John Flitcher, Philip Kidd, Nathaniel Dunn, John Gray, John Sale, Bernard Noell, Thomas Dennett, Haraway Owen, Richd Brown, John Burnett, Jacob Sheerwood, John Burk, Joseph Gatewood, John Cassell, Thomas Ayres, John Crow, Chaney Gatewood, Theophilus Faver, Ezekiel Byrom, John Byrom, William Dobson, Timothy Longest, Francis Graves, John Gatewood, Vincent Coleman, Isaac Williamson, William Davis, Samuel Hawes, Leonard Clark, Henry Vass, Alexander Saunders, Richard Burk, John Boughan, John Sadler, William Cole, Caleb Noell, Cornelius Sale, Augustin Gatewood, Robert Shackelford, Richard St. John, Nicholas Faulkner, Abner Ball, William Webb, Robert Rennolds, Thomas Sale, Thomas Loyd, Achillis Garnett, William Clark, Alexr Middleton, Joseph Warrick, John Dickerson, Francis Brizendine, Rice Noell, Thomas Newbill, Henry Purkins, Wm Cheaney, Thomas Ley, Abraham Montague, James Banks, Thomas Sthreshly, James Upshaw, Thomas Roane, Meriday Brown, Wm Howerton.

Candidate James Edmondson: Richard Street, Richard Hodges, James Gatewood, Henry Street, Leonard Hill, John Owen, John Brizendine, Thomas Williamson, Joshua Garnett, Mace Pickett, John Vass, Smith Young, Robert Clark, James Webb, John Smith S.C., Henry Woolbanks, Wm Prosser, James Clark, Isaac Hawes, Henry Cox, Oliver Howard, Richard Fuller, Alexander Bowmen, John Roddain, John Williamson Junr, John Roddain Junr, Richard Williamson, Nicholas Faulkoner Junr, Richard Meador, Thomas Coleman, John

Boughton, Richard Holt, John Hill, Joseph Fogg, James Colquet, James
Shadock, Elias Harrison, James Atkinson, Thomas Greenstreet, John Chenault,
James Davis Junr, Thomas Andrews, James St. John, Edward Gouldman, John
Williamson, Evan Davis, Nicholas Atkinson, Martin Willard, John Mitchel,
Edward Rowzee, Thomas Gouldman, John Canelly, Benjamin Fisher, Daniel
Stodghill, John Townsley, Richard Holt Junr, Samuel Piles, Marmaduke Thorp,
Thomas Cox, John Harper, John Cooper, Wm Young Junr, Wm Brooks Junr,
Andrew Allen, John Blatt, John Ball, Thomas Dix, Francis Ramsey, Samuel
Gresham, Thomas Meador, Reuben Meador, Peter Trible, Hugh Marshal,
Thomas Fogg, Samuel Davis, John Brooks, Thomas St. John, James Allen,
Philip Cheney, William Bowmer, Andrew Gatewood, James Munday, Thomas
Allen, John Dobbyns, Ambrose Pilkinton, John Taylor, James Sullivan, Richard
Hill, Isaac Jordan, Thomas Bush, Ellison Noell, Jonathan Sheerwood, John
Smither, Caleb Elliot, John Fogg, Mark Davis, Nathan Breedlove, Allaman
Breedlove, Samuel Peachey, John Webb, Samuel Shaw Junr, John Spindle Junr,
Thomas Gordon, Williamson Young, John Coleman, Thomas Croxton, Josiah
Minter, Wm Mountague, Henry Young, John Hodges, John Haynes, Thomas
Dean, Joseph Minter, Thomas Newman, Charles Weeks, Thomas Wise, Thomas
Hawkins, Stephen Munday, Thomas Brookes (H?), William Brooke, Philip
Dunn, Henry Kidd, Richard Thos Haile, James Townley, Benjamin Bowler,
Nathan Waggener, James Stokes, Thos Henry Brooke, Wm Hayes, Joseph
Reeves, James Clark Junr, Thomas Cauthorn, Thomas Dunn, Robt Mann, John
Gordon, Jas Croxton, John Flitcher, Philip Kidd, Nathaniel Dunn, John Gray,
John Sale, Bernard Noel, Thomas Dennett, Haraway Owen, Richard Brown,
John Burnett, Jacob Sheerwood, Henry Cauthorn, John Burk, Vincent Cauthorn,
Joseph Gatewood, John Casel, Thomas Ayres, Benjamin Dunn, Chaney
Gatewood, Ezekiel Byrum, John Byrum, Gilbert Stureman, William Dobson,
Timothy Longest, John Gatewood, Vincent Coleman, Samuel Montague,
Charles Saunders, Isaac Williamson, William Davis, Titus Farguson, Samuel
Hawes, Leonard Clark, Richard Burk, John Boughan, John Sadler, William
Cole, Caleb Noel, Oz Byrum, Aug Gatewood, Roger Shackleford, John
Howerton, Nicholas Faulkoner, Abner Ball, William Webb, Henry Gardner,
Thomas Loyde, Henry Dunn, Wm Bonds, Achillis Garnett, Wm Clark, Joseph
Warrick, John Dickerson, John Richards, Henry Purkins, John Cheney, John
Brookes, John Goode, Thomas Ley, James Banks, Thomas Sthreshly, James
Upshaw, Thomas Roane, John Evans, Wm Tureman.

Candidate Meriwether Smith: Smith Young, Richard Hodges (obj),
Rhodes Greenwood, John Owen, John Brizendine, Thomas Williamson B,
William Greenwood, John Vass (Voss?), Robert Clark, Alexander Bowmen,
John Tayloe esqr, John Roddain, John Williamson Junr, John Roddain Junr,
Richard Williamson, John Boughan, John Williamson, Evan Davis, Ephraim
Shepard, Thomas Games, Thomas Cox, John Harper, John Cooper, William

Young Junr, Wm Brooks Junr, Andrew Allen, John Blatt, Thomas Wood, James Booker, Peter Treble, Hugh Marshall, John Brooks, Philip Cheney, Wm Bowman, Thomas Bush, Nathan Breedlove, Allamon Breedlove, Samuel Peachey, John Webb, James Halbert, Wm Montague, Robt Beverley, Charles Mortimer, Henry Young, John Beale, John Haynes, Richard Noell, David Pitts y(ounger), Thomas Deane, Joseph Minter, Wm Brooks, Philip Dunn, James Townley, Isaiah Cole, Thomas Pitts, Thomas Bradburn, Thomas Sullivan, Thomas Cox Junr, William Smith, Moore Fauntleroy, Joseph Reeves, Thomas Cauthorn, Robert Mann, John Gordon, Henry Cauthorn, John Crow, Vincent Cauthorn, Benja Dunn, Theophilus Faver, Gilbert Stureman, Francis Graves, William Young, Wm Gatewood, Sam Montague, Charles Saunders, Titus Farguson, Henry Vass, Alex Saunders, Cornelius Sale, Oz Byrum, Richard St. John, John Howerton, Henry Gardner, Robt Rennolds, Thomas Sale, Henry Dunn, William Bonds, Alexr Middleton, Francis Brizendine, John Richards, Rice Noell, Thomas Newbill, John Cheney, John Brookes, John Goode, Wm Cheney, Abra Montague, Meriday Brown, John Evans Senr, Wm Howerton, Wm Tureman.

Candidate John Lee: Robert Beverley.

Candidate Robert Beverley: John Tayloe esqr, Thomas Faver, James Halbert, Charles Mortimer, John Beale, William Smith, Moore Fauntleroy, Wm Young, Wm Gatewood, Wm Thomas.

A true copy of the original poll of an election held for Essex Co at the Court House on Friday, 22 Nov 1771. Attest: John Upshaw sheriff. Sworn to this 9 Dec 1771 before Thomas Roane. Truly recorded. Attest: John Lee clerk. (Pg 496-502)

16 Dec 1771. Deed. Thomas Haddon & Mary his wife of Essex Co for 70 pd sold to Henry Allen of same co a tr of land & plantation lately allotted to the sd Thos Haddon & Mary his wife by a division with Wm Porter & Elizabeth his wife the sd lands by the will of Henry Reeves decd father of the sd Mary & Elizabeth was devised to his son Brewer in fee simple who dying in his infancy the same descended to John his brother who also dying in his infancy the same descended to the afsd Mary & Elizabeth who entered & is thereof possessed containing 140 a. near Piscataway Church in South Farnham Parish bounded by the road that leads from Piscataway Old Mill to the Church ... . Wit: None. Ackn 16 Dec 1771 by Thomas Haddon & Mary his wife (she being first privately examined & consenting) & admitted to record. Attest: John Lee clerk. (Pg 503)

3 May 1771. Bond. Thomas Thorp Junr of Essex Co am firmly bound unto George Gaines of co afsd for 33 pd 9 sl ... the condition of this obligation is such that whereas the afsd George Gains has this day by his note to Richard Hipkins made himself liable to pay the sd Hipkins 33 pd 9 sl by or upon 25 Dec next & for the security of the payment of the afsd sum the sd Thomas Thorp hath & doth sett over unto the sd George Gains all the estate that shall fall unto him by the death of Francis Bizwell as also the estate the sd George Gains has made himself liable for to the sd Hipkins which was then property of the sd Mrs. Bizwell with the rent that shall be due to him from Edward Gouldman 1 Jan next also the crop that shall fall to him from the sd Goldman with all the rest of his estate & if should happen that the afsd sum of 33 pd 9 sl should not be paid by the sd Thomas Thorp unto the sd Richard Hipkins that then it shall & may be lawfull to & for the sd George Gaines to advertise & sell the sd estate or so much thereof as shall be of value sufficient to satisfy the sd debt ... then this obligation to be null & void ... . Wit: Ann Thorp, Mary Thorp. Proved 16 Dec 1771 & admitted to record. Attest: John Lee clerk. (Pg 505)

19 Apr 1771. Bill of Sale. David Powell of Essex Co for 5 pd 9 sl 2 pn sold to Robert Ferguson the following goods & chattles, viz, 1 black colt, 1 paisd cow & calf with a crop & slitt in the left ear with a single slitt in the right ear, 1 loom, 1 chest, 2 spinning wheels, 1 feather bed, 6 pewter plates, 1 dish, 1 bason ditto, 4 pair cotton cards, 1 frying pan & 1 table ... . Wit: John Lee, Wm Ferguson. Proved 16 Dec 1771 & admitted to record. Attest: John Lee clerk. (Pg 506)

Observations & dimentions of 294 a. of land in South Farnham Parish, Essex Co on the brs of Piscataway Cr it being pt/o the estate of James Munday & Lucy his wife (decd) to which the sd James & Lucy leaving five daus they being coheirs the sd land is equally divided among them this 30 Jan 1771 by Richard Brown. (Pg 506)

The explanation [drawing not included here]: A is James Banks & Wm Dunn's corner; B is corner of Thos Shelton's & James Croxton's on sd Dunn's line; C is a corner on Dunn's line of James Croxton's & Lucy Munday; D is a corner of the afsd Dunn's & Nathaniel Dunn's; E is corner of Lucy Munday & John Boughan on sd Nathl Dunn's line; F is Nathl Dunn & John Edmondson's corner; G is a corner of John Boughan's & Betsey Munday's on John Edmondson's line; H is a corner of John Edmondson's & James Boughan's; I is corner of Betsey Munday's & Lucy Munday's on James Boughan's line; K is a corner on James Boughan's line of Lucy Munday's & Jas Croxton; L is corner of James Croxton's & Thomas Shelton's on the line of Capt Thos Roane; M is Roane's & Banks's corner; N is John Boughan & Betsey Munday's on Lucy Munday's line. (Pg 507)

In obedience to an order of Essex Co Court we the subscribers have met & examined sundry vouchers & papers produced by Lucy Munday adminr & widow of James Munday decd relative to her administration of the sd decd's estate & by the consent & approbation of the parties [?] his personal estate we find that the disbursement & expences in raising & maintaining the children & Negroes after deducting the several demands agt this decedent amount to the full value of the personal estate & therefore we made no division thereof. We also have divided the Negroes among the several children as well the money arising from the sale of the Negroes, Cork & Milley, as follows, viz, To John Boughan who married Ursula, Negro Nan valued to 35 pd & to receive of the Negro money 14 pd 4 3/4 pn; to Thos Shelton who married Katharine 1/2 of Negro Harry valued to 30 pd & to receive of the Negro money 19 pd 4 3/4 pn; to Jas Croxton who married Mary the 1/2 of Negro Harry valued to 30 pd & to receive of the Negro money 19 pd 4 3/4 pn; to Lucy Munday the 1/2 of Negro General valued to 30 pd & to receive of the Negro money 19 pd 4 3/4 pn; To Betty Munday 1/2 of Negro General valued to 30 pd & to receive of the Negro money 19 pd 4 3/4 pn which several Negroes & money we have allotted accordingly. We also have with the assistance of Richard Brown surveyor divided the lands between the sd five daus, viz, the Lot No. 1 containing 50 3/4 a. to Thos Shelton & Katharine his wife, to James Croxton & Mary his wife the Lot No. 2 containing 58 3/4 a., to Lucy Munday the Lot No. 3 containing 58 3/4 a., to Betsy Munday the Lot No. 4 containing 53 3/4 a. & to John Boughan & Ursula his wife the Lot No. 5 containing 55 3/4 a. which several lotts of land we assigned to the several children accordingly. Given under our hands 14 Dec 1771 James Booker, Thomas Wood, James Banks. At a court held 16 Dec 1771 this division of the lands & slaves of James Munday decd was returned by the gent appointed to perform the same & ordered to be recorded. Attest: John Lee clerk. (Pg 508)

16 Dec 1771. Deed. Thomas Allen & Henry Allen of Essex Co for 75 pd sold to Thomas Dix of same co a 190 a. tr of land whereon John Allen father of the sd Henry formerly lived in South Farnham Parish bounded by lands of the sd Thomas Dix, Benjamin Cofland & William Roane, & is the tr of land sold by James Dicks & Judy his wife to Erasmus Allen who dying thereof seised & possessed the same descended to his brother John grandfather to the afsd Thos Allen who also dying seised & possessed thereof descended to the sd Thos Allen his grandson & heir at law ... . Wit: Joseph Gatewood, Richd Thos Haile, William Gatewood, Richard Ryland, Leonard Burnett. Proved 17 Feb 1772 & admitted to record. Attest: John Lee clerk. (Pg 509)

26 Dec 1771. Deed. Archibald Ritchie & Charles Mortimer feoffees of the Town of Tappahannock by virtue of several Acts of Assembly & for 450 lbs of tobacco sold to Martha Jones & Mary Jones of Essex Co one lott or 1/2 a. of

land in the sd town numbered in the plan 64 the sd lott now being in the possession of the sd Martha Jones & Mary Jones ... . Wit: None. Ackn 17 Feb 1772 & admitted to record. Attest: John Lee clerk. (Pg 510)

21 Dec 1771. Assignment. I Muscoe Garnett of Essex Co for 47 pd 1 sl 10 pn 1/2 penny do sell & make over unto Muscoe Garnett & Company of sd co the deed of mortgage passed from John Taylar of sd co to me dated 5 Sep 1770 & all & singular the goods chattels & effects therein contained & expressed & all my right title & interest in the same ... . Wit: Charles Weeks, Wm Livingston, Reuben Garnett. Proved 16 Mar 1772 & recorded. Attest: John Lee clerk. (Pg 511)

20 Aug 1771. Deed of Mortgage. Williamson Young of South Farnham Parish, Essex Co for securing several sums, their interest & the costs of four suits brought by McCall & McCall & Shedden agt sd Young & for 5 sl sold to Archibald McCall & McCall & Shedden of the Town of Tappahannock merchants a tr of land in South Farnham Parish bounded lands of John Mitchell, Charles Evans decd, Philemon Gatewood, William Gatewood, Griffin Johnson, Samuel Johnson decd & John Evans decd, being the land he purch of his brother William Young conveyed to him by two separate deeds ... whereas the afsd Williamson Young passed his bond to Archibald McCall dated 20 Feb 1771 for 199 pd 10 sl 11 pn 1/2 penny conditioned for the payment of 99 pd 15 sl 5 pn 3 farthings with interest on 85 pd 18 sl 5 pn 3 farthings from 1 Jan 1771 till paid & interest on the balance of 13 pd 17 sl from 26 Aug 1770 till paid, as also one other bond to McCall & Shedden dated the day & year last mentioned for 155 pd 8 sl conditioned for the payment of 77 pd 14 sl on or before 23rd day of month last mentioned which bond is not to bear interest till 1 Oct next ensuing as also one other bond to James Emmerson dated 29 Nov 1770 for 28 pd 15 sl 8 pn conditioned for the payment of 14 pd 7 sl 8 pn on demand which sd bond was assigned by the sd James Emmerson to the sd Archibald McCall & whereas the sd Williamson Young is further indebted to the sd McCall & Shedden by open account in a large sum of money which is to be liquidated by Meriwether Smith gent ... provided that if the sd Williamson Young shall well & truly pay to the sd McCall & McCall & Shedden the afsd sums with interest then this indenture to cease & become utterly void ... . Wit: W. Smith, John Lee, Meriwether Smith, William Ferguson, Richard Parker. Proved 16 Mar 1772 & recorded. Attest: John Lee clerk. (Pg 512)

20 Aug 1771. Bill of Sale. I Williamson Young of South Farnham Parish, Essex Co to secure to Archd McCall & McCall & Shedden the payment of several sums of money mentioned in an indenture of mortgage [see above] & for 5 sl have sold unto the sd Archibald McCall & McCall & Shedden & their heirs five Negro slaves, viz, Rachel & her children Tom & Mintas, the children of

Sally who was sold to Tobias Allen & all the future increase of the female ... .
Wit: W. Smith, John Lee, Richd Parker, Meriwether Smith, Wm Ferguson.
Proved 16 Mar 1772 & admitted to record. Attest: John Lee clerk. (Pg 514)

16 Mar 1772. Deed. James Townley & Ann his wife of South Farnham Parish,
Essex Co for 125 pd sold to William Harwood of Gloucester Co a parcel of land
on the n side of Smarts Swamp & the Bestland Swamp in South Farnham Parish
it being pt/o that tr of land that John Townley decd by his will left to his son
James Townley bounded by John Crow, Joseph Man, John Townley & George
Newbel, containing 200 a. ... . Wit: Henry Vass, Thos Miller, Benja Wright.
Ackn 16 Mar 1772 by James Townley & Anne his wife (she being first privately
examined & consenting) & admitted to record. Attest: John Lee clerk. (Pg 515)

15 Nov 1771. Deed. John Richards of Essex Co gent only acting & surviving
executor of the will of Richard Gatewood late of sd co gent decd pursuant to the
will of the sd Richard Gatewood & for 150 pd sold to Robert Cole of same co a
parcel of land ... whereas the sd Richd Gatewood was in his lifetime & at the
time of his death seised in fee simple of & in a 200 a. tr of land whereon he then
lived bounded by John Howerton's Swamp (formerly Covington's Swamp),
Richard St. John & Dragon Swamp, & being so seized the sd Richard Gatewood
by his will dated 1 Apr 1760 did desire & direct that all his just debts should be
discharged & in order thereto that his two Negroes Harrison & Tulip be sold at
public auction & if the money arising by the sd sale with the profits of his estate
be not sufficient for that purpose with what money is due to him, then he desired
that the land & plantation whereon he then lived should be sold & appointed his
good friends Richard Tyler, Thomas Roane, John Richards & his son William
Gatewood executors & soon after died seised as afsd, & the sd John Richards
together with the sd Richard Tyler who is since dead under took the execution of
the will & it being found that the money arising from the sale of the sd two
Negroes together with the profits of the testator's estate & what was due to him
were not near sufficient to pay his debts, the sd John Richards pursuant to the
will did set up & expose to sale by way of public auction the sd tr of land & the
afsd Robert Cole was the best bidder & purchaser thereof for 151 pd ... . Wit:
Wm Young Junr, T. Gardner, H. Young, John Webb, G. Boughan. Proved 18
Nov 1771 & certified. Ackn 20 Apr 1772 & admitted to record. Attest: John
Lee clerk. (Pg 517)

4 Oct 1771. Deed of Lease. James Mills of Middlesex Co merchant for 5 sl
sold to James Hunter of King George Co pt/o a lot of land in the Town of
Tappahannock (that Archibald Ritchie & Mary his wife sold by their deeds of
lease & release dated 18 & 19 Oct 1756) distinguished by the number 77, that is
to say that pt/o the sd lot of land whereon a warehouse 60' in length & 24' in
breadth is erected & free passage to & from all the doors of the same, & also all

the land from the sd warehouse to the river ... for the term of 1 year paying one pepper corn on Lady (Day) next if demanded .... Wit: James Campbell, Archd McCall, Geo Larimer, Thomas Webb. Proved 20 Apr 1772 & admitted to record. Attest: John Lee clerk. (Pg 520)

5 Oct 1771. Deed of Release. James Mills of Middlesex Co for 150 pd release unto James Hunter of King George Co pt/o a lot of land ... [same as above] .... Wit: James Campbell, Archd McCall, Geo Larimer, Thomas Webb. Proved 20 Apr 1772 & admitted to record. Attest: John Lee clerk. (Pg 521)

XX Jan 1772. Deed. Henry Dunn & Mary his wife of Essex Co for 39 pd sold to John Brooks of same co planter an 80 a. tr of land whereon the sd Henry Dunn lately lived & is the same tr by him purch of John Williamson on the South Br of Piscataway Cr called Dunns Mill Swamp in South Farnham Parish bounded by the lands of John Edmondson, Thos Henry, Broocks Allen & Mary Marlow .... Wit: James Booker, Josiah Minter, Vinct Godfrey Cauthorn, W. Roane. Ackn 20 Apr 1772 by Henry Dunn & Mary his wife (she being first privately examined & consenting) & admitted to record. Attest: John Lee clerk. (Pg 524)

1 Jan 1772. Deed. John Bagot mariner for 25 pd sold to James Johnson (Johnsone) (Johnstone) of Essex Co a 36 a. tr of land in South Farnham Parish bounded by the lands of Thomas Allen, Capt Wm Roane, Sophia Waggener & Greensbe Waggener .... Wit: Samuel Allen Junr, John Whitlock, John Kerchevall. Ackn 20 Apr 1772 & admitted to record. Attest: John Lee clerk. (Pg 525)

25 Mar 1772. Deed of Gift. Mary Garnett of Essex Co widow for natural love & affection & 5 sl have given to my son Reuben Garnett of sd co all my estate right title interest reversion & remainder which I have may have or claim to the slaves & other estate in the possession of my mother Elizabeth Fogg under the will of my late father Nathaniel Fogg decd .... Wit; Thos Gartt Noell, Edwin Garnett. Proved 20 Apr 1772 & recorded. (Pg 527)

17 Feb 1772. Deed of Release. William Woddrop factor for James & Henry Ritchie & James Campbell atty in fact for Robert Gordon & Robert Reid for the consideration below mentioned & 5 sl released & forever discharged Andrew Crawford from the payment of any further or other sum of money ... whereas Andrew Crawford did by indenture dated 11 Oct 1770 mortgage to the sd James & Henry Ritchie two trs of land which the sd Andrew Crawford purch of William Porter & Elizabeth his wife & Thomas Haddon & Mary his wife to secure the payment of two several sums of money due from the sd Andrew Crawford to the sd James & Henry Ritchie & by indenture dated [blank] did also

mortgage to the sd Robert Gordon & Robert Reid the same two trs of land to secure to the sd Robert Gordon & Robert Reid the payment of a sum of money due from the sd Andrew Crawford to them, & whereas the sd Andrew Crawford hath since paid & satisfied unto the sd William Woddrop factor as afsd for the sd James & Henry Ritchie & to the sd James Campbell atty in fact as afsd for the sd Gordon Reid the full value of the lands mentioned above .... Wit: Chs Mortimer, Jack Power. Ackn 20 Apr 1772 & admitted to record. Attest: John Lee clerk. (Pg 528)

3 Apr 1772. Deed of Mortgage. William Bray of South Farnham Parish, Essex Co to secure to Charles Mortimer the payment of 82 pd 5 sl 3 pn due from the sd William Bray to the sd Charles Mortimer & for 5 sl sold to the sd Charles Mortimer of same parish a tr of land on Piscataway Old Mill Run which land was devised to the sd William Bray by the will of his father Charles Bray, also a Negro man slave named Moric (or Morie?) & a Negro man slave named Duke, 17 head of cattle, 8 sheep, 19 hoggs, 1 bed & furniture, 2 mares & 1 horse ... provided that if the sd William Bray shall well & truly pay unto the sd Charles Mortimer the afsd sum on or before 1 Oct next then this present sale shall cease .... Wit: Jack Power, James Lang, Alexr Smith. Proved 20 Apr 1772 & admitted to record. Attest: John Lee clerk. (Pg 530)

17 Feb 1772. Deed. Andrew Crawford of Essex Co for 1300 pd sold to William Daingerfield of Spotsylvania Co two trs of land on Rappahannock River adj the land whereon the late Col William Daingerfield lived containing according to a survey dated 29 Jan 1764 made by Edward Vawter persuant to an order of co court of Essex 372 a., 186 a. of which the sd Andrew Crawford purch of William Porter & Elizabeth his wife & 186 a. the remainder the sd Andrew Crawford purch of Thomas Haddon & Mary his wife .... Wit: Chs Mortimer, Will Woddrop, Chs Mortimer Junr, John Beale. Proved 20 Apr 1772 & admitted to record. Attest: John Lee clerk. (Pg 531)

11 Jan 1772. Power of Attorney. John Hopkins, Thos Jackson & Christopher Taddy of the City of London druggist & partners appoint Charles Mortimer of VA esqr our atty to ask demand sue for levy recover & receive of & from all & every person whatsoever who now are or stand indebted unto us on any account whatsoever all such sums of money as such person or persons now owe or stand indebted to us .... Wit: Wm Fox, Jacob Fox. Proved 20 Apr 1772 & admitted to record. Attest: John Lee clerk. (Pg 533)

13 Apr 1772. Deed. James Greenwood & Caty his wife of Essex Co sold to William Greenwood of same co a 100 a. tr of land in his actual possession now being by virtue of a bargain & sail to him made by the sd James Greenwood & Caty his wife bounded by Cole's land, upon the Dragon Run, Rhodes

Greenwood, William Howerton, Newbill's land, Thomas Parron & Covington's land ... . Wit: Rhodes Greenwood, John Mullens, Samuel Greenwood. Ackn 20 Apr 1772 by James Greenwood & Caty his wife (she being first privately exam'd & consenting) & admitted to record. Attest: John Lee clerk. (Pg 534)

10 Apr 1772. Deed of Mortgage. William Daingerfield (Dangerfield) Senr of St. Georges Parish, Spotsylvania Co for the purpose recited below & 5 sl sold to Chs Mortimer of Tappa in Essex Co a 376 a. tr of land the sd Wm Daingerfield purch of Andrew Crawford, & the following slaves (viz) Daniel, Charles, Antony, Moll, Sarah & Marmoh ... whereas the sd Wm Daingerfield did some time ago pass his bond to the sd Chs Mortimer for 1366 pd payable at the expiration of 3 years with interest & the sd Wm Daingerfield is desirous of securing to the sd Chs Mortimer the payment of the sd sum without changing the nature of the debt ... provided that if the sd Wm Daingerfield shall well & truly pay unto the sd Charles Mortimer the afsd sum with interest then this present sale shall cease & become utterly void ... . Wit: James Campbell, J. Power, William Shedden. Proved 20 Apr 1772 & admitted to record. Attest: John Lee clerk. (Pg 536)

18 May 1772. Deed. Ezekiel Byrom & Elizabeth his wife of South Farnham Parish, Essex Co for 2 pd sold to James Webb & Archibald Ritchie of same place a 2 a. parcel of land in the sd parish bounded by Mill Cr, Byrom's Landing, sd Webb & Ritchie belonging to their mill called Piscataway Mills & sd Ezekiel Byrom ... . Wit: Edward Wiatt, John Williamson, James Edmondson Junr, Elizabeth Webb. Ackn 18 May 1772 by Ezekiel Byrom & Elizabeth his wife (she being first privately examined & consenting) & admitted to record. Attest: John Lee clerk. (Pg 538)

10 Dec 1771. Indenture Tripartite between Thomas Gouldman & Sally his wife of the first part, Achilles Garnett & Jean his wife of the second part & Jas Noell Senr (all of St. Anns Parish, Essex Co) of the third part, whereas the sd Thomas Gouldman & Sally his wife by deed dated sometime in 1770 but which was never ackn did convey to the sd Achilles Garnett & Jeane his wife a 78 a. tr of land bounded by Occupatia Run, sd James Noell & Achillis Garnett, John Garnett & John Lee gent, now this indenture wit that the sd Thomas Gouldman & Sally his wife for 65 pd doth hereby ackn & acquit, release & discharge unto the sd Achilles Garnett the afsd 78 a. tr of land, & this indenture further wit that the sd Achilles Garnett & Jean his wife for 115 pd 14 sl hath sold unto the sd James Noell Senr a 178 a. tr of land whereon the sd Achilles Garnett now lives conveyed by Gouldman to Garnett part which sd tr of land was purch by the sd Achilles Garnett of his father John Garnett bounded by Occupatia Run, John Lee & Daniel Walner's Spring Br ... . Wit: Austine Garnett, John Greensteed, Samuel Shaw, Leonard Noell, Saley Noell. Ackn 16 Dec 1771 by Thomas

Gouldman & Sally his wife (she being first privately examined & consenting) & certified. Ackn 20 Jan 1772 by Jane w/o Achilles Garnett (being first privately examined & consenting) & certified. Proved 18 May 1772 as to Achilles Garnett & admitted to record. Attest: John Lee clerk. (Pg 539)

18 May 1772. Deed. Peter Montague of South Farnham Parish, Essex Co for 86 pd 15 sl sold to Joseph Gatewood of same place a 173 1/2 a. parcel of land part in the sd parish & co & part in Drisdale Parish, King & Queen Co bounded by the land of Capt John Richards, Capt Thomas Roane, Richard Lowry, Capt William Mountague, Col John Latane, John Gatewood & Mountagues Spring Br ... . Wit: None. Ackn 18 May 1772 & admitted to record. Attest: John Lee clerk. (Pg 543)

26 Jan 1769. To Archibald Ritchie & John Upshaw of Essex Co gent greeting, whereas John Smith & Mary his wife of sd co have by their deed dated 3 May 1767 conveyed unto Thomas Roane gent a messuage & 268 a. tr of land in South Farnham Parish, & whereas the sd Mary is unable to travel to our sd co court to make acknowledgment thereof, therefore we command you to repair to the sd Mary & that privily & apart from her husband you take such acknowledgment as she shall be willing to make ... . By virtue of the within commission to us directed we Archibald Ritchie & John Upshaw did on 28 Jan 1769 go to the sd Mary & receive her acknowledgment ... . Truly recorded. Attest: John Lee clerk. (Pg 545)

INDEX

COLE, Frances, 175; Frankey, 14, 33, 175; Isaak, 34; Isaiah, 33, 112, 126, 128, 143, 144, 176, 178; Isiah, 102; John, 33, 166; Josiah, 121, 123; LeeRoy, 113; Lidia, 166; Robert, 14, 33, 121, 123, 131, 143, 144, 175, 182; Thomas, 122, 123; William, 28, 33, 34, 78, 112, 113, 121, 123, 124, 126, 128, 143, 144, 154, 166, 176, 177

COLEMAN, Ann, 5, 24, 166; Elizabeth, 5; Francis, 155, 156; George, 3, 49, 106; James, 151; John, 88, 125, 127, 128, 143, 145, 157, 176, 177; Mille, 3, 4; Richard, 5, 8, 15, 24, 26, 166; Robert, 3, 4; Robert Spilesby, 15; Robert Spilsby, 5, 8, 20, 151; Sarah, 3, 4; Thomas, 3, 4, 93, 106, 125, 127, 143, 145, 157, 176; Vincent, 143, 145, 156, 176, 177; Whitehead, 97

COLEMAN'S LAND, 98

COLES, William, 45

COLE'S LAND, 184

COLLINS, William, 55

COLQUET, James, 121, 123, 143, 145, 176, 177

COLQUIT, James, 1, 2, 75, 106, 107; John, 1, 2, 52; Sarah, 106

COMPTON, Augustine, 125, 128, 143, 145, 151; William, 151

COMPTON'S LINE, 49

CONDUIT, John, 1, 82, 125, 127; Nathaniel, 81

CONDUITT, Nathaniel, 62, 63

CONELLY, John, 176

CONNELL, William, 5, 9

CONNER, Edward, 69; Margaret, 69; Margrat, 69; Martin, 57; Mary, 69

CONNERLEY, John, 121, 123

CONNERS, Margaret, 69; Margrat, 69; Mary, 69

CONNILEY, John, 125, 127, 128

CONOLEY, John, 143

CONOLY, John, 145

CONQUEST, Richard, 83, 91

COOK, Robert, 20

COOKE, John, 8; Stephen, 112

COOK'S CORNER, 134

COOL SPRING BRANCH, 11

COOPER, Elizabeth, 162; John, 20, 71, 121, 122, 126, 127, 144, 145, 177; Richard, 71; Sarah, 3; Thomas, 3

COOPER'S CORNER, 71

COPELAND, Nicholas, 21

COPLE PARISH, 169

CORBIN, Richard, 121, 124

CORDELL, George, 37

CORNELIUS, John, 19

CORNWALD'S PATENT, 172

CORRIE, Catherine, 5; John, 44, 48, 53, 54, 56, 66, 67, 98, 99, 103, 107, 121, 124, 127, 128, 133, 138, 139, 143, 144, 154, 168

COTTON PATCH BRANCH, 89

COTTON PATH BRANCH, 88

COUGHLAND, William, 174

COUNTY ROAD, 22, 34, 48, 55

COURT HOUSE, 142, 147, 175, 178

COURTNEY, Ann, 161

COVINGSTONS SWAMP, 23

COVINGTON, Ann, 24; Captain, 34; Edmund, 16; Elizabeth, 111; John, 32, 41; L., 20, 21, 28; Luke, 5, 10, 20, 22, 25, 33, 40, 41, 42, 43, 60, 63, 83, 110, 112, 117, 121, 124, 127, 128, 136, 143, 144; Richard, 1, 2, 16, 24, 111, 166; Sarah, 111, 117, 136; Thomas, 111; William, 1, 2, 10,

KERCHEVALL, John, 183
KERCHIVALLE, John, 145
KERCHWALL, John, 76
KERRIGAN, John, 125
KESEE, John, 174
KEY, James, 121, 123
KIDD, Henry, 1, 4, 8, 40, 62, 65, 101,
    122, 123, 126, 128, 144, 145,
    151, 157, 164, 176, 177; Isaac,
    12, 13, 119, 122, 123, 133, 139,
    143, 144; James, 115; Lucy, 12;
    Mary, 8; Philip, 126, 127, 144,
    145, 176, 177; Phillip, 1, 2, 49,
    119, 122, 123; William, 8
KING & QUEEN County, 3, 4, 5, 15,
    22, 24, 33, 37, 43, 46, 47, 49, 50,
    53, 55, 56, 59, 70, 71, 76, 83,
    108, 118, 151, 157, 158, 161,
    162, 174, 186
KING GEORGE County, 14, 20, 95,
    120, 130, 132, 151, 182, 183
KINGSTON PARISH, 57
KINSALE, 73
KIRKTOWN, 138
LACEY, John, 86
LAINE, Harry, 59
LANCASTER, 56
LANCASTER County, 20, 66, 96,
    146
LANDRAM, Esther, 36; James, 65
LANDRAM'S LINE, 172
LANDRUM, Benjamin, 9, 90; James,
    121, 123, 125, 127, 128; John,
    112; Martha, 90; Thomas, 108
LANDRUMS CREEK, 53
LANDRUM'S LAND, 76
LANE, Harry, 102
LANG, James, 33, 39, 54, 66, 72, 73,
    79, 80, 107, 150, 184; John, 67
LANTANE, John, 23, 82
LARIMER, George, 183
LASEN, Nicholas, 119

LASON, Betty, 135; Elizabeth, 11,
    119, 135; Hannah, 135; Majer,
    143, 145; Major, 94, 101, 122,
    123; Mary, 11, 12, 135;
    Nicholas, 11, 119, 135; Richard,
    11, 135
LASON'S LINE, 164
LATANE, John, 72, 101, 126, 128,
    144, 145, 156, 164, 186
LATANEE, John, 1, 2
LATANE'S LAND, 152
LATANY, John, 96
LATANY'S LAND, 44
LATAONE, John, 30
LATENEY, John, 123
LATNEY'S LINE, 29
LATTAINEY, John, 95
LATTENEY, John, 124
LAWRY, Richard, 169
LAWSON'S NECK, 173
LAYTONS FERRY, 17
LAYTONS WAREHOUSE, 24
LEE, Hancock, 82, 110, 111; John, 2,
    3, 4, 5, 6, 7, 8, 9, 10, 11, 12, 13,
    14, 15, 16, 17, 18, 19, 20, 21, 22,
    23, 24, 25, 26, 27, 28, 29, 30, 31,
    32, 33, 34, 35, 36, 37, 38, 39, 40,
    41, 42, 43, 44, 45, 46, 47, 48, 49,
    50, 51, 52, 53, 54, 55, 56, 57, 58,
    59, 60, 61, 62, 63, 64, 65, 66, 67,
    68, 69, 70, 71, 72, 73, 74, 75, 76,
    77, 78, 79, 80, 81, 82, 83, 84, 85,
    86, 87, 88, 89, 90, 91, 92, 93, 94,
    95, 96, 97, 98, 99, 100, 101, 102,
    103, 104, 105, 106, 107, 108,
    109, 110, 111, 112, 113, 114,
    115, 116, 117, 118, 119, 120,
    121, 124, 125, 127, 129, 130,
    131, 132, 133, 134, 135, 136,
    137, 138, 139, 140, 141, 142,
    144, 146, 147, 148, 149, 150,
    151, 152, 153, 155, 156, 157,

Heritage Books by Mary Marshall Brewer:

Abstracts of Administrations of Montgomery County, Pennsylvania, 1822–1850

Abstracts of Land Records of King George County, Virginia, 1752–1783

Abstracts of Land Records of Richmond County, Virginia, 1692–1704

Abstracts of the Wills of Montgomery County, Pennsylvania, 1824–1850

Early Union County, New Jersey Church Records, 1750–1800

Essex County, Virginia Land Records, 1752–1761

Essex County, Virginia Land Records 1761–1772

Essex County, Virginia Land Records 1772–1786

Kent County, Delaware Guardian Accounts: Aaron to Carty, 1752–1849

Kent County, Delaware Guardian Accounts: Caton to Edinfield, 1753–1849

Kent County, Delaware Guardian Accounts: Edmondson to Hopkins, 1744–1855

Kent County, Delaware Guardian Accounts: Houston to McBride, 1739–1856

Kent County, Delaware Guardian Accounts: McBride to Savin, 1739–1851

Kent County, Delaware Guardian Accounts: Savin to Truax, 1754–1852

Kent County, Delaware Guardian Accounts: Truitt to Young, 1755–1849

Kent County, Delaware Land Records, 1776–1783

Kent County, Delaware Land Records, 1782–1785

Kent County, Delaware Land Records, 1785–1789

Kent County, Delaware Land Records, 1788–1792

King George County, Virginia Court Orders, 1746–1751

King George County, Virginia Court Orders, 1751–1754

Land Records of Sussex County, Delaware, 1681–1725

Land Records of Sussex County, Delaware, 1753–1763

Land Records of Sussex County, Delaware, 1763–1769

*Land Records of Sussex County, Delaware: Various Dates:
1693–1698, 1715–1717, 1782–1792, 1802–1805*

Land Records of York County, Pennsylvania, Libers A and B, 1746–1764

Land Records of York County, Pennsylvania, Libers C and D, 1764–1771

Land Records of York County, Pennsylvania, Libers E and F, 1771–1775

Land Records of York County, Pennsylvania, Libers G and H, 1775–1793

New Castle County, Delaware Wills, 1800–1813

Northumberland County, Virginia: Deeds, Wills, Inventories, etc., 1737–1743

Northumberland County, Virginia: Deeds, Wills, Inventories, etc., 1743–1749

Probate Records of Kent County, Delaware, Volume 1: 1801–1812

Probate Records of Kent County, Delaware, Volume 2: 1812–1822

Probate Records of Kent County, Delaware, Volume 3: 1822–1833

Quaker Records of Cedar Creek Monthly Meeting: Virginia, 1739–1793

www.ingramcontent.com/pod-product-compliance
Lightning Source LLC
Chambersburg PA
CBHW071049280326
41928CB00050B/2148